Graduate Leadership
Third Edition, Volume 1

4900 LaCross Road
North Charleston, SC 29406, USA

www.DrMarkGreen.com

Release 1.0, June 1, 2015

Library of Congress
Cataloging-in-Publication
Data is available

Leadership Press
ISBN-13: 978-0692416532
ISBN-10: 0692416536

Dedicated to the Sisters of Divine Providence

Who Model How to Serve People Whose Needs are Being Neglected
Who Educate Within a Broad Vision of Ministry
Who Not Only Teach but Renew People's Faith and
Who Serve Them Constantly Through Works of Mercy

Graduate Leadership
Preface

One of the differences people often cite between their undergraduate and graduate experiences is the volume of reading required at the graduate level.

Often, at the undergraduate level, students learn elements of theories.

At the graduate level, students gain a deeper appreciation for who developed those theories and why the theories are considered important.

In the field of organizational leadership, undergraduate programs are a relatively new phenomenon. Consequently, many adults who pursue graduate work in organizational leadership didn't major in leadership for their undergraduate degrees.

As a result, many first semester graduate students in the area of organizational leadership, are exposed to a large number of theories and authors that are completely new to them.

To aid graduate students, this book summarizes 51 of the most popular theories of organizational leadership and management. Each theory is summarized in about one page and provides the essence of what you "should have remembered" if you had been exposed to the theory at the undergraduate level, years ago.

Graduate Leadership
Acknowledgements

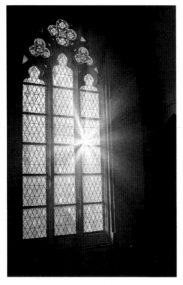

For the past 21 years, I have been supported by the students, staff, faculty and administration at Our Lady of the Lake University. The university only exists because thousands of Sisters of Divine Providence dedicated their lives to the institution.

In my small window of time at Our Lady of the Lake University, I have been fortunate to observe this dedication from Sisters Ann, Elizabeth Anne, Isabel, Jane Ann, Janet, Madlyn, Margit, Maria and Rose Annelle.

For the past 17 years, my work at Our Lady of the Lake University has been in the Department of Leadership Studies. Dr. Jacquelyn Alexander started the department and its associated doctoral program in leadership studies. Dr. Robert Bisking led the expansion of the program to three campuses. More importantly, Dr. Bisking's leadership helped my colleagues to continue to be graduate faculty primarily focused on collaborative teaching rather than competitive research.

Dr. Dwayne Banks is continuing this tradition of being a servant leader, and helping the leadership studies faculty to serve our students in the heritage of the Sisters of Divine Providence.

Within my department, four colleagues have enabled me to make the transition from a department chair to a teacher/ researcher by performing a great deal of administration in addition to their own teaching and research. Dr. Meghan Carmody-Bubb has handled everything related to our San Antonio masters program in leadership. Dr. Phyllis Duncan has handled all of the administration for our doctoral program in San Antonio. Dr. Jared Montoya has handled all of the administration for our masters and doctoral programs in the Rio Grande Valley.

Dr. Esther Gergen has handled all of the administration for our doctoral program in Houston and all of the departmental level administration.

The dedication of these colleagues to our students has provided me the time to create this book and the opportunity to migrate from the role of a department chair to that of slightly eccentric but loveable professor who can explain meta-analyses to students but can't tell them how to register for the next semester.

Graduate Leadership
Acknowledgements

Staff members Norma Anderson, Anne Gomez, Gloria Urrabazo and Dan Yoxall have each been instrumental in supporting the leadership programs in which I have honed my teaching analogies and metaphors. Ms. Valerie Hernandez provided a significant amount of administrative support for this book.

Contributing Students

Since 1998, I have taught a first-year leadership sequence to over 400 doctoral students. As part of this teaching, I have explained multiple aspects of leadership ideas in multiple ways. Some of these methods have resulted in happy expressions and small epiphanies from a variety of adult learners. Many of those methods have been used in this book.

Collectively, the dissertation literature reviews that I have directed and read from many of these students add up to over 6,000 pages.

My work with hundreds of doctoral student practitioner-scholars to synthesize the literature related to each student's leadership interest has also given me a range of teaching tools that were used in this book.

There are simply too many alumnae and current doctoral students to mention in this acknowledgement. Their work on each of their individual journeys has assisted me in compiling this book. My hope is that this textbook makes the journey toward understanding organizational leadership a bit easier and much more enjoyable for those students just beginning their journeys.

Final Acknowledgement

My wife of 17 years, Justina, continues to support my academic career in countless ways.

She has grown accustomed to my absences on Saturdays when classes meet, and my recurrent answer of "working on a book" to most of her questions about my day.

I couldn't have compiled this textbook without her love and support.

Graduate Leadership
Table of Contents

Acknowledgements i

Chapter 1 Introduction 1

Chapter 2 A Brief History of Organizational Leadership Theories............................23

Chapter 3 The Era of Leadership Traits 49

Chapter 4 The Era of Leadership Behaviors 69

Chapter 5 The Era of Transforming Followers 101

Chapter 6 The Search for the Successor to Transformational Leadership 133

Summary 163

Subject Index.. 176

Author Index 184

Credits 190

References 196

Chapter 1
Introduction

Introduction
The Empirical Study of Leadership

Over the past three decades, there has been a dramatic rise in the number of books written on the subject of leadership. The chart to the right illustrates this growth.[1]

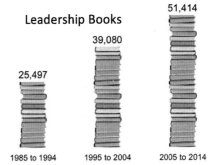

Leadership Books

51,414

39,080

25,497

1985 to 1994   1995 to 2004   2005 to 2014

Beyond leadership books, in 2015, entering the phrase "leadership program" into a search engine would return over 126 million results.

In addition to the explosion of leadership programs, popular press books and web sites, there has been a concomitant increase in for-credit undergraduate and graduate leadership programs at universities.

This book is designed to assist graduate students who want to become acquainted with the results of the body of research in the field of organizational leadership. Most people who want to learn more about leadership, however, likely start with a popular book rather than dive into research articles. As a start, then, we'll need to differentiate between leadership books with and without a significant empirical foundation.

Mass Appeal Books versus Scholarly Research

There are undoubtedly some valuable mass appeal books on leadership. The vast majority, however, lack a rigorous research foundation. There are several types of non-textbook leadership books.[2]

One type of leadership book is the case study or autobiographical book – the "How I did it at Acme Corporation," type of book. These are interesting, but there were so many variables at Acme Corporation that your organization doesn't have, that generalizing those lessons learned is sometimes a challenge.

A second type of popular leadership book usually involves the numbers 7, 10 or 21. These books usually provide lists of seven because we have seven days in a week, 10 because we have 10 fingers and 21 because it's a great number for blackjack.

While packaged nicely, these types of leadership books are often based on someone's observations rather than a body of research.

A third type of mass appeal leadership book often chronicles how a great figure was a leader. These books range from religious and political figures to Santa Claus.

They are interesting biographies, but, like the autobiographical books, there is often a challenge generalizing those lessons.

A fourth type of mass appeal leadership book chronicles "the way." A quick on-line seller search will result in leadership books on the women's way, Marine Corps way, Jesus' way, Toyota way, West Point way, business way and so forth. Like the other mass appeal types of books, these almost certainly have value, but typically lack a deep empirical base.

Introduction
The Empirical Study of Leadership

Qualitative versus Quantitative Research

While many mass appeal books lack an empirical foundation, books or articles with an empirical foundation, can be based on different research philosophies. Quantitative research is typically designed to test questions, called hypotheses in as unbiased a manner as possible.

A simple quantitative leadership example might be to analyze the relationship between a particular leadership style and follower satisfaction. A somewhat large number of followers – say 500 out of 5,000 who work in an organization – might be randomly selected to complete a leadership assessment of their leader and a job satisfaction assessment on themselves. Statistical analyses would then be done to determine how much confidence we had that the leadership style and job satisfaction were related and what the direction and magnitude of that relationship was.

A qualitative approach might be to do a focus group with a limited number of followers and ask them open-ended questions about how their leaders lead and how satisfied they are with their jobs. The researchers would then analyze themes they heard.

Although the qualitative approach is richer, it is also much more amorphous. There will be a lot of noise provided in the answers. Because of this, one interviewer might interpret certain dialogue as an important theme while another might interpret it as irrelevant. Even with methodological safeguards such as triangulation, it is still quite reasonable that two qualitative researchers listening to the same focus groups might hear different themes.

With quantitative research, if two different researchers were given the same data set of 500 leadership and satisfaction scores and ran the same statistical tests, they would obtain the exact same results.

A second challenge with the qualitative approach is what is called generalizability. Because qualitative research is so time intensive, it would be very unusual to see a qualitative study of leadership and job satisfaction in which the researchers interviewed 500 workers – it could be done, but consider the following.

Imagine that 10 workers were interviewed in each focus group. Fifty focus groups would be required for a sample of 500 workers. If each focus group was 30 minutes long, the researcher would already be required to spend 25 hours just interviewing workers. From those 25 hours of interviews there would most likely be thousands of pages of verbatim transcripts to prepare – this would take weeks. Those pages would then need to be analyzed for important themes heard. Even with computer assisted content analysis software, that is still a long process. Because qualitative research is so time intensive, most qualitative studies are done on small rather than large samples.

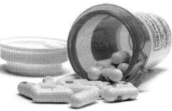

A third challenge with qualitative research is establishing how confident we are in our findings. For this example, pretend the Food and Drug Administration doesn't exist.

Imagine that you had to rush a loved one – perhaps a child, spouse or parent – to the emergency room. The attending physician tells you that the condition is grave, and unless your loved one receives the correct medicine, she/he will die within the hour.

The physician indicates that *Medication A* has been tested on 5,000 patients. In the clinical trials, 2,500 patients received the medication and 2,500 received a placebo. Statistical analysis indicated that the medication has a life-saving effect at a confidence level of 99.99%. *Medication B* has been tested with 50 patients. The researchers, however, conducted in-depth interviews with the patients about how they felt after taking the medication.

Which drug would you choose for your loved one?

A reasonable position is that qualitative research should be done before or after quantitative research, rather than in lieu of it.

Qualitative	**Quantitative**	**Qualitative**
Identify Follower Concerns	Large Sample Research	Based on Quantitative Findings,
Identify Areas to be Analyzed	Hypothesis Testing	Interview Small Groups to
	Multivariate Analyses	Garner Additional Insights
	Confidence Intervals	Related to Statistical Findings

In the illustration above, small group qualitative research might be used to identify potential areas for large sample research. Based on what the qualitative research indicated, appropriate instruments would be selected, a rigorous methodological design applied and appropriate statistical tests would then be run. Based on the statistical findings, additional qualitative research might be conducted to probe why the statistical results found what they did.

Because this book will provide you with synopses of the generalizable body of literature related to the most popular leadership theories, the studies referenced will almost exclusively be large sample studies for which hypothesis testing could occur.

Introduction
The Empirical Study of Leadership
Experimental and Non-Experimental Approaches

Within large sample, quantitative, empirical research, there are two broad approaches. These are generally called experimental and non-experimental research.

Experimental research is typically easier to conduct in the physical sciences than in the social sciences. To better understand this, lets consider a physical science example. Imagine that a researcher wanted to study whether a new coating that she or he had invented to protect dinner plates against scratches actually was an improvement over the current plates that don't have a coating.

Example of Performing an Experiment in the Physical Sciences

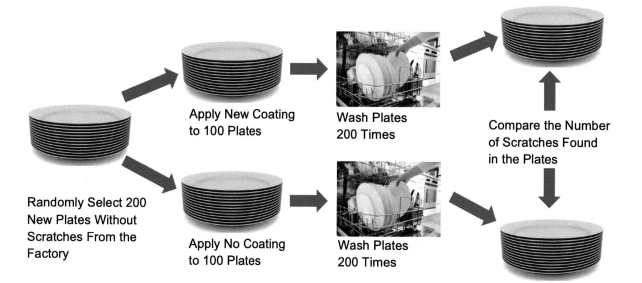

Randomly Select 200 New Plates Without Scratches From the Factory

Apply New Coating to 100 Plates

Wash Plates 200 Times

Compare the Number of Scratches Found in the Plates

Apply No Coating to 100 Plates

Wash Plates 200 Times

In the example above, the researcher would randomly select some number of plates – say 200 – from the factory production line. The researcher would then apply the new coating to half of the plates, and do nothing additional to the other half.

A next step might be to wash all of the plates 200 times in a dishwasher to simulate some of the wear and tear plates might undergo in customers' kitchens. After the 200 dish washes, the researcher would count the number of scratches on both the uncoated and the coated plates. The researcher would then run a statistical test to determine whether the coated plates had fewer scratches than the uncoated plates.

Example of the Difficulty Performing Experiments in the Study of Leadership

Now imagine trying to do a very similar experiment to determine whether paying attention to followers' feelings makes a difference in how satisfied the followers are with their leaders.

A similar experimental design for leader attention to feelings and follower satisfaction with the leader would require us to first, randomly select 200 leaders (plates). We would then need to convince 100 leaders (plates) to ignore their followers' feelings (no coating) for one month (200 washes) and convince the other 100 leaders (plates) to pay attention to their followers' feelings (coated) for one month (200 washes).

We'd then need to get those followers who worked for one month under the leaders who ignored their feelings to rate their leaders on how satisfied they were with their leader (number of scratches). We would do the same for the followers who worked for the leaders who paid attention to their feelings.

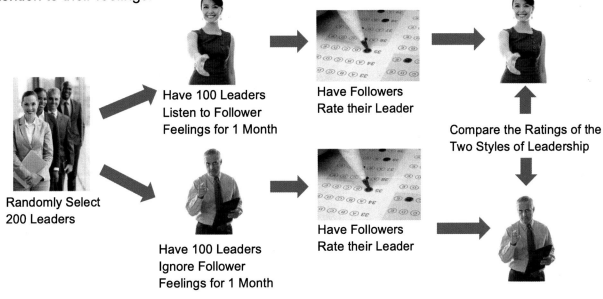

Randomly Select 200 Leaders

Have 100 Leaders Listen to Follower Feelings for 1 Month

Have 100 Leaders Ignore Follower Feelings for 1 Month

Have Followers Rate their Leader

Have Followers Rate their Leader

Compare the Ratings of the Two Styles of Leadership

What is quickly apparent is that it is relatively easy to experiment on plate coatings in a research lab, but very difficult to experiment with approaches to leadership in an actual workplace. Put simply – a typical follower will likely object very strongly to being "manipulated" as part of a leadership "experiment." Additionally, we can't just reassign leaders and tell them to lead differently for a period of time in an actual organization. Workplace issues such as productivity or human resources complaints make leadership experiments done with actual leaders and followers very unlikely.

Consequently, the vast majority of leadership research falls into what is called non-experimental research. At first, the prefix "non" sounds like a lesser form of research. The "non" part generally means we are not manipulating something (the coating on plates or attention to followers' feelings). So, if it makes you feel better, envision experimental research as manipulative and non-experimental research as non-manipulative (because real followers in real organizations are needed).

Introduction
The Empirical Study of Leadership
Experimental and Non-Experimental Approaches

Example of the Non-Experimental Study of Leadership

A very common approach in large sample, empirical leadership research is to do no manipulation whatsoever with the followers. Instead, we often ask followers to complete two different assessments.

In a non-experimental design, we might ask followers to rate their leaders on a survey of satisfaction and a different survey of how well followers believed their leaders listened to them. We would then run statistical tests to determine if there is a relationship between those two dimensions. It is much more feasible to perform this type of leadership research because we are simply surveying followers rather than "manipulating" something related to them as part of an experiment.

Obtain a Sample of Followers

Have Followers Rate How Well Their Leaders Listen

Have Followers Rate How Satisfied They are with Their Leaders

Analyze the Relationship Between How Well Leaders Listen and How Satisfied Followers are with Their Leaders

This book will review the development of leadership theory over the last century. It will also provide a comprehensive explanation of five popular theories of leadership.

Each chapter on a popular leadership theory will also provide you with a summary of what the peer-reviewed literature indicates as evidence of the degree to which those five theories seem to actually work.

Most of the research results summarized in this book will be from non-experimental research.

Introduction
The Empirical Study of Leadership
Sources of Leadership Research

In addition to 90,000 leadership books published in the last two decades and 126,000,000 web links, there are thousands of magazine and peer-reviewed articles about leadership.

So how do we decide which evidence from all of these sources to consider when analyzing leadership theories? While not exhaustive, the table below illustrates a progression of sources. Generally the last two sources of evidence, peer-reviewed conferences and journals, are used when discussing "what the literature says" about leadership.

Sample Sources of Leadership Research	Comments
Social Media Postings on Leadership	There are undoubtedly many valuable points made about leadership in blogs, tweets, social media sites and so forth. Very often, these exchanges are based on the personal experiences of those who post, rather than structured research.
Civic Group Talk about Views on Leadership	Talks about leadership at gatherings such as a chamber of commerce, religious or civic meetings are likely valuable to those in attendance. Often, however, these talks are also based on the personal experiences of the speaker, rather than structured research.
Leadership Article in a Magazine	It is common to see articles in magazines that offer tips about how to become a better leader. These may be absolutely correct or just the writer's opinion. Magazine articles often lack a list of references that support the ideas presented, a description of the participants, instruments used and so forth.
Mass-Appeal Leadership Book	As previously discussed, many of these types of books are based on someone's opinion.
Presentation of Leadership Research at a Peer-Reviewed Conference[3]	The term peer-reviewed generally indicates that several individuals with expertise and/or credentials in an area review each submission to the conference. Some conference proposals are accepted and some are rejected. The higher the rejection rate, the more "prestigious" the conference is often perceived to be. One wrinkle in research presented at peer-reviewed conferences is that the presenter typically must register (pay to attend) for the conference and then present her or his research paper. Consequently, there are many conferences with very high acceptance rates.
Presentation of Leadership Research in a Peer-Reviewed Journal	Just as there are rejection rates for peer-reviewed conferences, there are also rejection rates for peer-reviewed articles. It is not unusual to see several hundred presenters have papers accepted and then present those papers at a peer-reviewed conference. A prestigious journal that is published quarterly, however, might only have a handful of articles every three months. This form of research is generally valued as evidence more than conference presentations.[4]

Definitions of Leadership

Two fundamental questions typically underlay the study of leadership: a) how do we define leadership and b) how is leadership different from management.

Burns' often repeated observation is that "Leadership is one of the most observed and least understood phenomena on earth." (1978, p. 2). Many years later, we continue to study leadership, but have yet to agree on a definition.

As part of studying leadership at the graduate level, it is very helpful to develop your own personal definition of leadership.

One way to do this is to look for themes in the myriad definitions already available. Bass and Bass (2008) divide definitions of leadership into four categories:

Leader-Centric

Behavioral

The Effects of the Leader (Results)

The Interaction of the Leader and Follower

A slightly more parsimonious method might be to collapse the ideas of leader centricity and leader follower interaction into a single dimension called focus: the degree to which the definition focuses on the leader, the follower or an interaction of the leader and follower. This produces a model with three aspects.

Focus ➡ Behavior ➡ Results

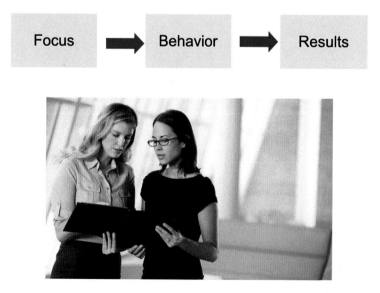

Introduction
Definitions of Leadership

Sample Definitions of Leadership

Here are a variety of definitions of leadership to ponder.

Leadership is "the behavior of an individual . . . directing the activities of a group toward a shared goal." (Hemphill and Coons, 1957, p. 7)

"Leadership over human beings is exercised when persons with certain motives and purposes mobilize, in competition or conflict with others, institutional, political, psychological, and other resources so as to arouse, engage, and satisfy the motives of followers." (Burns, 1978, p. 18)

Leadership is "the influential increment over and above mechanical compliance with the routine directives of the organization." (Katz and Kahn, 1978, p. 528)

"Leadership is realized in the process whereby one or more individuals succeed in attempting to frame and define the reality of others." (Smircich and Morgan, 1982, p. 258)

Leadership is "the process of influencing the activities of an organized group toward goal achievement." (Rauch and Behling, 1984, p. 46)

"Leadership is about articulating visions, embodying values, and creating the environment within which things can be accomplished." (Richards and Engle, 1986, p. 206)

"Leadership is a process of giving purpose (meaningful direction) to collective effort, and causing willing effort to be expended to achieve purpose." (Jacobs and Jaques, 1990, p. 281)

"Leadership is an influence relationship among leaders and followers who intend real changes that reflect their mutual purposes." (Rost, 1991, p. 4)

Leadership "is the ability to step outside the culture ... to start evolutionary change processes that are more adaptive." (Schein, 1992, p. 2)

"Leadership is a process whereby an individual influences a group of individuals to achieve a common goal." (Northouse, 1999, p. 3)

Leadership is "the art of mobilizing others to want to struggle for shared aspirations." (Kouzes and Posner, 2002, p. 6)

Leadership is "the ability of an individual to influence, motivate, and enable others to contribute toward the effectiveness and success of the organization." (House et al., 2004, p. 184)

Elements of Sample Leadership Theories

Using the table below as inspiration, take a few moments to write out your definition.

Year	Author	Focus	Behavior	Results
1957	Hemphill and Coons	Leader	Directing the Activities	Shared Goal
1978	Burns	Leader and Follower	Inducing Followers to Act	Goals That Represent Shared Values
1978	Katz and Kahn	Leader	Influential Increment	Over and Above Mechanical Compliance with the Routine Directives
1982	Smircich and Morgan	Leader	Attempting to Frame and Define	Reality of Others
1984	Rauch and Behling	Leader	Influencing the Activities of an Organized Group	Goal Achievement
1986	Richards and Engle	Leader	Articulating Visions, Embodying Values	Creating the Environment Within Which Things Can Be Accomplished
1990	Jacobs and Jaques	Leader and Follower	Giving Purpose (Meaningful Direction); Causing Willing Effort to Be Expended	Achieve a Purpose
1999	Northouse	Leader and Group	Influence	Achieve a Common Goal
1992	Schein	Leader	Step Outside the Culture	Evolutionary Change Processes That Are More Adaptive
2002	Kouzes and Posner	Leader and Follower	Mobilize Others	Struggle for Shared Aspirations
2004	House et al.	Leader	Influence, Motivate, and Enable	Effectiveness and Success of the Organization

To develop your own definition of leadership review the elements above and answer the questions on the following page.

Introduction
Definitions of Leadership

Leadership Reflections

Take a moment and answer the following questions.

 What do good leaders do, that poor leaders don't do?

 What do poor leaders do, that good leaders don't do?

 How do you determine how ethical a leader is?

 How do good leaders deal with uncertainty and change?

 Using the table on the opposite page, and your reflections above, write a one-sentence definition of leadership.

Introduction
Leadership versus Management

There are quite a few books and many more web sites that speculate on differences between the areas of management and leadership. Three popular authors' distinctions are provided below.

Leadership	Management
Bennis and Nanus (1985)	
Innovates	Administers
Develops	Maintains
People	Systems and Structure
Inspires Trust	Relies on Control
Long-Range Perspective	Short-Range View
Asks When and Why	Asks How and When
Eye is on the Horizon	Eye Always on the Bottom Line
Own Person	Classic Good Soldier
Kotter (1990)	
Coping with Change	**Coping With Complexity**

Setting The Direction
   Gathering a Broad Range of Data
   Looking for Patterns and Relationships
   Developing a Vision of the Future
   Developing Strategies for Producing the
      Changes Needed to Achieve That
      Vision
	Planning and Budgeting
	   Producing Orderly Results

Aligning People	**Developing the Capacity to Achieve the Plan**
Communicating the New Direction Creating Coalitions That Understand the Vision	Organizing and Staffing Creating Human Systems to Implement Plans
Achieving the Vision	**Ensuring Plan Accomplishment**
Motivating and Inspiring Satisfying Followers' Higher Order Needs	Controlling and Problem Solving
Bass and Bass (2008)	
Envisioning an Attractive Future	Planning
Enabling Followers to Improve Performance	Organizing and Structuring
Empowering Followers to Make Decisions	Controlling What Happens

A broad question exists, however, as to the degree to which we should envision these leadership and management activities as unique. Generally, there can be three ways to think about management and leadership.

View 1 – Leadership and Management Overlap Significantly

The first view is that finding clear distinctions between leadership and management is difficult to do. Yukl (2012), for example, points out that, while there is no shortage of articles proposing differences, there is also little research that supports that they are different.

View 2 - Leadership and Management are Quite Distinct

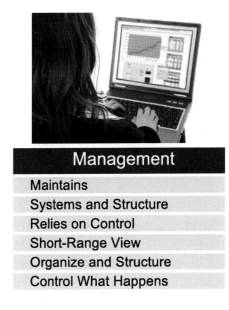

Leadership	Management
Develops	Maintains
People	Systems and Structure
Inspires Trust	Relies on Control
Long-Range Perspective	Short-Range View
Enable Followers	Organize and Structure
Empower Followers	Control What Happens

Hackman and Johnson (2009) qualify this perspective by noting that managers tend to focus their efforts on maximizing the physical resource limitations of the organization (financial and raw materials), while leaders tend to focus their attention on maximizing the impact of the human resources of the organization (including the emotional, intellectual, and psychological resources).

Other researchers such as Kouzes and Posner (2007), Kotter (1990), and Bennis and Nanus (1985) also advance models that provide distinctions between leadership and management.

View 3 – Leadership and Management are on a Continuum

Given the lack of a clearly defined set of research-based distinctions between leadership and management, a third perspective is that there is a murky middle area between the two in which individuals engage in both activities simultaneously.[5] This is vital since few individuals are strong in both leadership and management roles. The table below provides a few examples of areas that encompass leadership, leadership/management and management.

Leadership	Leadership/Management	Management
Developing a Vision of the Future	Planning and Resource Allocation for the Vision	Ensuring Resources Are Used Efficiently
Communicating a Long-Range Perspective	Developing a Series of Understandable, Intermittent Goals That Everyone Can Understand	Ensuring That Short-Range Goals Are Met
Developing Strategies for Producing Change	Analyzing What New Resources, Employees and Partnerships Are Needed for the Strategy	Monitoring Timelines and Plans for Implementing The Strategy
Aligning the Human Resources to Maximize the Impact of Work Teams on Goal Achievement	Ensuring that Qualified Persons Are Hired, Developed and Retained in Strategically Aligned Work Groups, Designed Around Organizational Objectives	Establishing a Staffing Plan to Ensure That All Jobs Are Filled with Qualified Individuals
Focusing on the Results of Overall Efforts and Instituting Needed Changes to Ensure Success	Maintaining Simultaneous Clear Lines of Vision on the Results of Goal Completion Efforts and Motivational Needs of Personnel in Meeting Those Goals	Focusing on Providing External Motivation to Overcome Human, Political, and Resource Barriers to Ensure Goal Accomplishment

Leadership and Management Reflections

Take a moment and answer the following questions.

How might the time horizon differ for leadership and management?

What makes someone a good leader?

What makes someone a good manager?

Take a moment and write down how you explain leadership versus management.

Leadership | Leadership/Management |  Management

Introduction
Key Points

We develop our philosophies and styles of leadership from a variety of influences.

For many of us, our leadership philosophies and styles tend to be a product of various interactions we have had with others or books and articles we have read.

Some of us may have been fortunate enough to have had a mentor who told us "the secret" to being a good leader.

Others of us may have read books in which someone told us "the secret."

This secret has likely influenced how we lead.

Most of us at one time or another have worked for someone we considered a poor leader.

Most likely, our vow not to be like that leader also influenced our leadership philosophy and style.

Some of us have also been fortunate enough to experience people who we believed were great leaders.

Almost assuredly, we have adopted some of their philosophies and behaviors into our own leadership philosophy and style.

There is, however, a body of empirical research on aspects of effective and ineffective leadership.

Becoming more fluent in these research findings can help us to refine our leadership philosophy and style in a more systemic manner, than our random life experiences of which great and poor leaders we've encountered.

This book will distill a portion of the empirical research on organizational leadership to assist you in widening the context against which you assess what constitutes effective and ineffective leadership.

Introduction
Summary

In addition to learning and applying concepts and theories, masters programs typically emphasize becoming familiar with the research foundations for those concepts and theories. Doctoral programs add conducting original research related to those concepts and theories.

Mass appeal leadership books have value, but often tend to be based on biographical information or a set of tips, principles or "the way." Although these books often lack an empirical foundation, they can still assist us in thinking about leadership.

Qualitative research is often able to garner richer information than quantitative research. However, different qualitative researchers can easily draw different conclusions from the same set of observations. Qualitative research also lacks the equivalence of a confidence interval that allows researchers to accept or reject null hypotheses. Finally, qualitative research is very time intensive and is typically conducted with small samples.

Bass and Bass (2008) divided definitions of leadership into four categories: leader-centric, behavioral, effects of the leader, and the interaction of the leader and follower. A slightly more parsimonious method is to collapse the ideas of leader centricity and leader follower interaction into a single dimension called focus: the degree to which the definition focuses on the leader, the follower or an interaction of the leader and follower. This model has three aspects: focus, behaviors and results.

It is common to think of leadership as being future and people oriented and management as being more focused on present work, rules and procedures. It is more likely that there is a continuum in which there is a middle ground that comprises a combination of both leadership and management activities.

Introduction
Notes

[1] The data for this chart are based on a search of the worldcat.com database with the phrase leader* in the title.

[2] This is simply my synopsis based on observation rather than empirical research.

[3] For page space reasons masters theses and doctoral dissertations were not included in the table. They likely fall somewhere around the peer-reviewed conference level. That research would have been "faculty-reviewed" but all reviewers are typically from the same institution as the student.

[4] Peer-reviewed journal articles are in flux. The advent of on-line peer-reviewed journals allows this type of journal to accept many more articles than traditional paper-based journals. There is no extra cost to have 10 articles in a particular issue online, but paper, printing and shipping costs of traditional journals affect the number of articles accepted.

Recently some peer-reviewed journals have begun charging authors to have their article presented. The distinction between a peer-reviewed conference at which an author pays to present her or his accepted work and a peer-reviewed journal in which an author pays to present her or his accepted work is blurring traditional lines.

[5] Kotter does not provide the table shown. He does, however, point to a less rigid distinction between leadership and management. His 1990 article, *What Leaders Really Do*, was the inspiration behind creating the leadership/management column. The contributing authors and I created this table.

Chapter 2
Overview of the History of Organizational Leadership Theories

A Brief History of Organizational Leadership Theories
Leadership versus Management

Chapter 1 introduced a model that provided a continuum between leadership and management. In this model, some organizational activities fall under management, some under leadership and others are a somewhat fluid mix of both leadership and management.

Leadership	Leadership/Management	Management
Developing a Vision of the Future	Planning and Resource Allocation for the Vision	Ensuring Resources Are Used Efficiently
Communicating a Long-Range Perspective	Developing a Series of Understandable, Intermittent Goals That Everyone Can Understand	Ensuring That Short-Range Goals Are Met
Developing Strategies for Producing Change	Analyzing What New Resources, Employees and Partnerships Are Needed for the Strategy	Monitoring Timelines and Plans for Implementing the Strategy
Aligning the Human Resources to Maximize the Impact of Work Teams on Goal Achievement	Ensuring that Qualified Persons Are Hired, Developed and Retained in Strategically Aligned Work Groups, Designed Around Organizational Objectives	Establishing a Staffing Plan to Ensure That All Jobs Are Filled with Qualified Individuals
Focusing on the Results of Overall Efforts and Instituting Needed Changes to Ensure Success	Maintaining Simultaneous Clear Lines of Vision on the Results of Goal Completion Efforts and Motivational Needs of Personnel in Meeting Those Goals	Focusing on Providing External Motivation to Overcome Human, Political, and Resource Barriers to Ensure Goal Accomplishment

Within the column we think of as leadership, however, there are many different ideas and models.

This chapter will discuss some of the ways in which authors classify aspects of leadership and identify some of the most enduring theories of leadership.

A Brief History of Organizational Leadership Theories
Where to Start?
Domains of Organizational Leadership

Because leadership occurs in so many situations, it can be studied from many different viewpoints.

Deciding just where to start the study is always a challenge.

There are a variety of different terms used to represent different areas of study. We often talk about concentrations, foci, emphases and so forth. One term that is commonly used to describe an area of study is *domain*.

Bass and Bass (2008) provided the following examples of domains of leadership.

a. Political Leadership

b. Military Leadership

c. Leadership of Crowds

d. Educational Leadership

e. Intellectual Leadership

f. Heroic Leadership

g. Executive Leadership

h. Group Leadership

i. Legislative Leadership

j. Governmental Leadership

k. World-Class Political Leadership

l. Reform Leadership

m. Revolutionary Leadership

Among all of the various domains of leadership for study, generally, ***organizational leadership*** tends to be an area of study with which most of us have both personal experience and interest.

A Brief History of Organizational Leadership Theories
Where to Start?
Domains of Organizational Leadership

A Sample of Various Domains of Leadership

Political	Military	Crowds	Education	Intellectual	Heroic

Executive	Groups	Organizational Leadership	Governing	Revolutionary

Organizational leadership theories, however, can be classified many ways.

Fleishman, Mumford, Zaccaro, Levin, Korotkin and Hein (1991), for example, reviewed 65 different taxonomies of leaders' behaviors published between 1944 and 1986. Fleishman et al. posited four commonalities among the 65 taxonomies.

Facilitating Group Social Interaction
Pursuing Task Accomplishment
The Occurrence of Management and Administrative Functions
Emphasis on Leader-Group Interactions

Bass and Bass (2008) offered that most leadership theories can be placed along an autocratic-democratic spectrum, and that four common themes appear among the body of leadership theories.

The leader energizes and directs others to pursue the organization's missions and goals.

The leader helps provide the structure, methods, tactics and instruments for achieving those goals.

The leader helps resolve conflicting views about means and ends related to those goals.

The leader evaluates the individual, group or organizational contribution toward those goals.

A Brief History of Organizational Leadership Theories
Where to Start?
Domains of Organizational Leadership

Yukl, Gordon and Taber (2002) analyzed questions from 10 frequently used measures of leadership. Based on that analysis, they proposed a hierarchical taxonomy of leadership behavior. The taxonomy contains three high-level classifications: *task, relations* and *change*. Yukl, Gordon and Taber believe that these three classifications can be broken down further using the 12 dimensions shown.[1]

Task

Clarifying Roles Assigning tasks and explaining job responsibilities and expectations.

Monitoring Operations Checking on the progress and quality of work.

Short-Term Planning Determining how to use personnel and resources to accomplish a task efficiently and determining how to schedule and coordinate unit activities efficiently.

Relations

Consulting Checking with people before making decisions that affect them, encouraging participation in decision making and using the ideas and suggestions of others.

Supporting Acting considerate, showing sympathy and support when someone is upset or anxious and providing encouragement and support when there is a difficult, stressful task.

Recognizing Providing praise and recognition for effective performance, significant achievements, special contributions and performance improvements.

Developing Providing coaching and advice, providing opportunities for skill development and helping people learn how to improve their skills.

Empowering Allowing substantial responsibility and discretion in work activities and trusting people to solve problems and make decisions without prior approval.

Change

Envisioning Change Presenting an appealing description of desirable outcomes that can be achieved by the unit. Describing a proposed change with great enthusiasm and conviction.

Taking Risks For Change Taking personal risks and making sacrifices to encourage and promote desirable change in the organization.

Encouraging Innovative Thinking Challenging people to question their assumptions about their work and consider better ways to do it.

External Monitoring Analyzing information about events, trends and changes in the external environment to identify threats and opportunities for the organizational unit.

A Brief History of Organizational Leadership Theories
Where to Start?
Domains of Organizational Leadership

Models such as those provided by Fleishman et al., Bass, and Yukl et al. can also be applied to organizational leadership. Within organizational leadership, for example, some researchers study how leaders communicate information. Other researchers analyze how various resources are allocated. Studying organizational strategy, how leaders handle conflict and how leaders clarify the high-level goals of an organization are also possible areas on which to focus.

While certainly not exhaustive, the image below helps us to envision that organizational leadership is just one of many viewpoints or domains from which to study leadership, and that, in turn, organizational leadership can have its own domains or areas of foci.

Examples of Domains of Organizational Leadership

Information	Resources	Group Interactions	Goal Clarification	Conflict Management	Strategy
Leader Focus	Tasks	Relationships	Research Base	Democratic	Follower Focus

From all of the various possible domains of organizational leadership, the six shown in beige will be used in chapters 3 to 6 for a review of the various theories that have influenced how we think about leadership in organizations.

Tasks and Relationships

While it is tempting to view tasks and relationships as a single construct on a continuum, the research base is less clear. These dimensions are often, positively correlated with each other.

Since most theories are unlikely to indicate "don't be task or relationship focused" it is more likely that some authors tended to leave task or relationship out of their theories in any explicit description. Getting things done and taking care of followers are likely implied, but one needs to work at actually recognizing those dimensions per se.

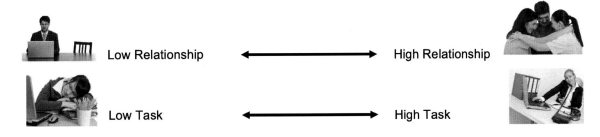

Leader and Follower Focus

The same distinction exists for the degree to which theories emphasize leaders or followers. It is tempting to see this as one construct, but it is quite possible to emphasize both in the same theory. Also, like task/relationship, most theories are unlikely to advocate ignoring leaders or followers; they just may not emphasize one of those aspects.

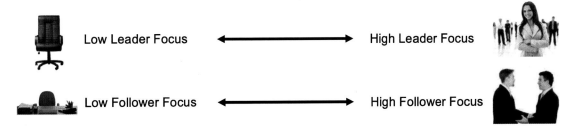

Autocratic versus Democratic and Theoretical versus Research Based

The last two dimensions can likely be thought of on a continuum. The first is the idea of the degree to which a theory emphasizes a somewhat autocratic or democratic view of leadership.

The second dimension is the degree to which the theory has been researched by large sample studies.

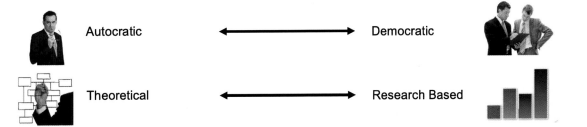

A Brief History of Organizational Leadership Theories
How to Select Which Theories to Review

Eras and Influences

The time dimension covered in chapters 3 to 6 is from the early 1900's into the twenty-first century – that's a lot of years.

An educational device used to manage such a large period of time is to break the overall topic into smaller topics – similar to bite sized chunks. In the review of the history of organizational leadership theories covered in chapters 3 to 6, this will be done using eras.

Eras

There are many different authors who categorize leadership theories into various eras. For this book, we will refer to four broad eras.

The 1900's through the 1940's: The Era of Leadership Traits
The 1950's through the 1960's: The Era of Leadership Behaviors
The 1970's through the 1980's: The Era of Transforming Followers
The 1990's through the Present: The Search for the Successor to Transformational
         Leadership

It is important to remember that these are broad eras created to help better conceptualize changes over a long time period, rather than precise starting and stopping points. It is also important to understand that the conclusion of an "era" doesn't mean that one or more theories developed in that era were no longer used. Rather, the focus of leadership researchers often shifted toward different lines of research.

Influences

Think of the study of leadership in organizations as a wonderful salad. There are many ingredients that contribute to the success of the overall dish.

Some ingredients, however, are more influential than others. In the Greek salad shown, if the lettuce, tomatoes, olives or cheese were omitted, the salad would suffer significantly.

Conversely, if some of the grains of salt, pepper or other seasonings were omitted, we'd still have a good salad. The seasonings add to the flavor, but less so than the lettuce, tomatoes, olives or cheese.

Chapters 3 to 6 provide summaries of 51 of the theories that have contributed to our understanding of leadership in organizations. Some theories are as important as lettuce, tomatoes, olives or cheese, while others add richness, but are similar to seasonings.

So how do we decide which theories are more influential than others? For this summary, three steps were taken.

Step 1 – Previous Sources

Leadership Sources

Several very valuable sources exist that already serve as references for leadership theories. These range from extraordinarily detailed and scholarly to those designed for an introductory exposure to leadership. Among those used were:

Herman's (1994) *The Jossey-Bass Handbook of Nonprofit Leadership and Management;* Hiebert and Klatt's (2001) *The Encyclopedia of Leadership;* Goethals, Sorenson and Burns' (2004) four-volume *Encyclopedia of Leadership;* Wren's (2008) *The Leader's Companion* and Nohria and Khurana's *Handbook of Leadership Theory And Practice* (2010).

Beyond these anthologies, four works provided the most benefit. Northouse's (2013) and Yukl's (2012) introductory textbooks provided an excellent sense of the most parsimonious list of important theories. Van Seters and Field's (1990) article *The Evolution of Leadership Theory* was also a valuable, concise summary.

Bass and Bass' (2008) *The Bass Handbook of Leadership* served as the most helpful exhaustive reference.

Management Sources

Chapter 1 briefly discussed inter-relationships between management and leadership. While not *leadership* theories in the strictest sense, multiple management theories were included in this review because of their widespread influence on leaders and followers in organizations. To determine which management theories to include, seven sources were used.

For trends in the evolution of management theory, Wren's (2005) *History of Management Thought;* Miner's (2006) *Organizational Behavior 3: Historical Origins, Theoretical Foundations, and the Future* and Witzel's (2011) *A History of Management Thought* were reviewed.

Two quantitatively compiled lists were also used. Miner (2003) surveyed past presidents of the Academy of Management, past editors of the *Academy of Management Journal,* past editors of the *Academy of Management Review,* and editorial board members from both of those publications who were serving as board members in 1999 and 2000. This survey produced rankings of the importance and estimates of the scientific validity for 73 management theories.

A Brief History of Organizational Leadership Theories
How to Select Which Theories to Review
Step 1 – Previous Sources

Bedian and Wren (2001) surveyed 137 members of the Fellows Group of the Academy of Management to create a list of the most influential management books of the 20th century. Influential was defined as having a major impact on management thinking at the time of publication.

Both the Miner and Bedian studies were conducted at the turn of the century. Because theories need time to slowly influence managers and leaders, no theories from the 1990's made it onto either the Miner or Bedian lists. Similar analyses for the period beyond 2000 were unavailable. As a next best thing, two lists of influential management books from more popular press sites were used: *Time Magazine's* list of the most influential business management books and *Forbes Magazine's* list of the most influential management books were reviewed.

Broadly speaking, management theories that were considered important by several of these six sources were considered for review in chapters 3 to 6.

History of Technology Sources

Many of our theories of how to manage and lead followers have been influenced by what is often called *disruptive technologies*. For example, technological impacts such as the industrial assembly line, personal computer and Internet have, during certain periods, fundamentally changed how we work.

For technology trends, Chandler's (2008) *Inventing the Electronic Century: The Epic Story of the Consumer Electronics and Computer Industries;* Nielson's (2011) *Computing: A Business History;* and Ceruzzi's (2012) *Computing: A Concise History* were used.

Decades

The leadership eras discussed in chapters 3 to 6 are organized around decades.

While there is no magical difference in describing changes between 1958 and 1967 versus 1960 and 1969, discussing "the sixties" versus the "58-67's" resonates better with most people. For these various eras/decades, societal trends will be provided to better appreciate the influences on how we conceived of effective leadership during those periods.

A Brief History of Organizational Leadership Theories
How to Select Which Theories to Review
Steps 2 and 3 – Popularity and Research Base

Step 2 – Popularity

As a second step, a sense of relevance or popularity was factored. I have been a classroom professor for over two decades. I've taught leadership and management to over 600 masters and 400 doctoral students. I've also either directed or assisted in directing over 100 doctoral dissertations in leadership.

From these experiences I have garnered a sense of which theories seem to be of interest to graduate students and which ones tend to result in those same students multi-tasking on their mobile devices and feigning participation in classroom discussions.

Step 3 – Empirical Research Base

Finally, because this book will provide readers with a sense of the quantitative empirical base for the widely referenced theories of management and leadership, a review of the degree to which these theories were influential based on their theoretical base versus a body of quantitative research was included. This resulted in 51 theories that will be reviewed in chapters 3 through 6.

Those theories shown in grey are management or leadership ideas that have had some influence on the development of organizational leadership theory. For conciseness, a review of each of these theories will typically be limited to one page or less.

Those theories shown in beige have had a bit more influence. These will typically be reviewed in about one page.

Those shown in blue have had a significant influence on the development of leadership theory. A much more thorough discussion of these theories can be found in volume 2 of *Graduate Leadership*.

A Brief History of Organizational Leadership Theories
A Chronology of Influential
Management and Leadership Theories

Year	Theory	Authors	Comments
The Era of Leadership Traits			
1880's to 1920's	Great Person	Carlyle, Goldberg, Brattin and Engel (1888)	This early leadership theory lacked an empirical base. The theory advanced that successful leaders were born to greatness.
1911	Scientific Management	Taylor (1911)	Taylor's principles describing specialization of work were related to the changes occurring as a result of the industrial revolution.
1933	Hawthorne Studies	Mayo (1933, 1945)	The Hawthorne studies were designed to measure the impact of workplace environment on productivity. A related finding was that whenever workers were studied, productivity increased.
1938	Executive Functions	Barnard (1938)	Barnard's book on the functions of an executive emphasized more of the relational aspects of management than did the scientific management approach.
1947	Theory of Administrative Behavior in Organizations	Simon (1947) March and Simon (1958)	Rather than allocate all of our time and energy to an optimal solution for a single problem, we search for a decision for most problems that is good enough, called satisficing. Organizations typically run on a collection of decisions that were good enough rather than optimal.
1948	Leader Traits	Stogdill (1948)	Stogdill analyzed 128 published trait studies, but was unable to develop a definitive list.
1949	Principles of Management	Fayol (1949)	Fayol's five functions and 14 principles of management were largely an extension of the scientific management approach. The impact of the labor movement, however, likely influenced a bit more emphasis on fair treatment of all workers.

A Brief History of Organizational Leadership Theories
A Chronology of Influential
Management and Leadership Theories

The Era of Leadership Behaviors			
1954	Maslow's Hierarchy	Maslow (1954, 1962, 1965)	Maslow's ideas on self-actualization influenced later writers such as Burns' (1978) and Bass' (1985) conceptualizations of transformational leadership.
1954	Management by Objectives	Drucker (1954)	Management by objectives was an important milestone in the history of management. It emphasized leader/follower participative goal setting.
1955	Ohio State Studies	Fleishman, Harris and Burtt (1955) Hemphill and Coons (1957) Stogdill (1963)	These studies were foundational to most subsequent leadership theories. Several meta-analyses have found both leader task and relationship behaviors to be important in organizational and follower outcomes.
1956	Five Bases of Social Power	French (1956) French and Raven (1959)	This model of leader power has been the subject of nearly 400 peer-reviewed studies.
1957	Personality and Organization	Argyris (1957, 1964, 1973, 1983)	Argyris argued that organizations typically structure followers' roles and direct their work in order to achieve organizational objectives. Followers, on the other hand, generally want to be self-directive and feel fulfilled through exercising initiative and responsibility.
1959	Motivation Hygiene Theory	Herzberg (1959, 1966, 1976)	Herzberg developed a theory on aspects of work that motivate followers versus hygiene factors or dissatisfiers. Dissatisfiers don't motivate followers, but their absence lessens motivation.
1960	Theory X and Theory Y	McGregor (1960, 1966)	A theory X view is that the average follower is lazy, dislikes work and will try to do as little as possible. A theory Y view is that followers want responsibility.
1960	University of Michigan Studies	Katz and Kahn (1952) Cartwright and Zander (1960) Likert (1961)	These studies were also foundational to most subsequent leadership theories.

A Brief History of Organizational Leadership Theories

A Chronology of Influential
Management and Leadership Theories

The Era of Leadership Behaviors

1961	Management Systems	Likert (1961, 1967) Likert and Likert (1976)	Likert described four types of leadership/management styles: exploitive, authoritative benevolent, authoritative consultative and participative.
1961	Mechanistic and Organic Systems	Burns and Stalker (1961)	Burns and Stalker used the terms mechanistic and organic to describe two different organizational forms and philosophies.
1963	Behavioral Theory of the Firm	Cyert and March (1963)	Cyert and March introduced the idea of problemistic searching in which problem solving is usually triggered by a specific problem and the goal is to solve that one problem.
1964	Managerial Grid	Blake and Mouton (1964, 1965, 1972, 1978)	The managerial (leadership) grid was a highly influential book/theory. The grid describes the leadership dimensions of concern for production and concern for people.
1964	Contingency Theory	Fiedler (1964, 1966, 1967, 1971), Fiedler and Mahar (1979) Fiedler and Chemers, (1974), Fiedler, Chemers and Mahar (1976) Fiedler and Garcia (1987)	Fiedler's contingency model provides eight scenarios, based on: the leader-follower relationship, the structure of the task at hand and how much position power the leader holds.
1965	Technological Determinism	Woodward (1965, 1970)	Woodward argued that the technology an organization used seemed to influence the type of structure the organization created. This idea came to be known as technological determinism, connoting that, to some degree, technology determines organizational structure.
1966	Four-Factor Theory	Bowers and Seashore (1966)	Bowers and Seashore proposed an integrative framework for understanding similarities of earlier leadership research. Their four leadership dimensions were support, goal emphasis, interaction facilitation and work facilitation.

A Brief History of Organizational Leadership Theories
A Chronology of Influential
Management and Leadership Theories

1966	Social Psychology of Organizations	Katz and Kahn (1966, 1978)	Katz and Kahn encouraged managers and leaders to envision workplace organizations as open rather than closed systems.
1969	Situational Theory	Hersey and Blanchard (1969, 1977)	Beyond the two leader behavior dimensions of supportive and directive behavior, Hersey and Blanchard theorized that leaders should adjust their styles of leading based on two dimensions related to followers: the follower's capability to do a particular task/job and the follower's commitment to do that task/job.

The Era of Transforming Followers

1970	Servant Leadership	Greenleaf (1970, 1972, 1974, 1977, 1979)	The idea of leaders being servants of their followers is popular. The theory, however, lacks a deep research base. Several promising instruments to measure servant leadership, however, have recently been developed.
1971	Path-Goal Theory	Evans (1970) House (1971, 1996)	Path-goal theory indicates that leaders should engage in combinations of directive path-goal clarifying, supportive, participative and achievement oriented behaviors in order to assist followers to reach their goals.
1973	Normative Theory	Vroom and Yetton (1973) Vroom and Jago (1978, 1988)	Vroom, Yetton and Jago are known for their work on decision-making. Their theory used seven questions that could lead to five types of leader decision-making approaches.
1974	Traits Continued	Stogdill (1974)	Stogdill analyzed 163 new studies related to leadership traits. He grouped the 26 most frequently referenced traits into three categories: leadership skills, relationship with the group and personal characteristics.

A Brief History of Organizational Leadership Theories
A Chronology of Influential
Management and Leadership Theories

The Era of Transforming Followers			
1975	Leader Member Exchange Theory	Dansereau, Graen and Haga (1975) Graen and Uhl-Bien (1991,1995)	Leader-member exchange theory points out that leaders form different relationships with different followers within the same work areas – often called out-groups and in-groups. Leaders and followers often go through three developmental stages: stranger, acquaintance and partner.
1977	Charismatic Theory	House (1977, 1992)	House and others developed explanations of the personal characteristics, behaviors and effects on followers that surround charismatic leadership.
1978	Theory Z	Ouchi and Jaeger (1978) Ouchi (1981, 1984)	In 1978, Ouchi contrasted what he described as a typical set of American leadership/work assumptions with those that might be typical Japanese assumptions. He then proposed a hybrid set that he labeled type Z assumptions. This slowly became known as theory Z.
1978	Substitutes for Leadership	Kerr and Jermier (1978)	Kerr and Jermier asked whether certain factors could lessen the need for leadership. They divided possible substitutes into three sources: followers, the tasks being done and the organization.
1978	Transformational Leadership	Burns (1978)	While there have been many contributions to the idea of transformational leadership, the theory was first fully described by Burns in 1978. In transformational leadership, pooled interests of the leaders and followers result in being united in the pursuit of "higher" leader and follower goals.
1981	Six Sigma	Motorola (1981) General Electric (1995)	Six sigma refers to a standard of quality that equates to 3.4 defects per one million opportunities (DPMO). This equates to 99.997% "quality."
1982	In Search of Excellence	Peters and Waterman (1982)	Peters and Waterman reported what they believed were best practices among excellent Fortune 500 companies.

A Brief History of Organizational Leadership Theories
A Chronology of Influential
Management and Leadership Theories

	The Era of Transforming Followers		
1985	Full Range Model of Leadership	Bass (1985, 1998, 1999) Bass and Avolio (1994, 1995, 1996, 1997, 2002) Bass, Avolio and Jung (1999)	More than 100 peer-reviewed studies have been published on this theory. Meta-analyses have found that the full range model of leadership is related to individual-level performance, group performance, task performance, leader effectiveness, follower satisfaction with leaders, follower job satisfaction, follower motivation and leader job performance.
1986	Total Quality Management	Deming (1986)	Total quality management is a phrase used to describe various quality initiatives suggested by Deming and others. The methods were highly influenced by Japanese manufacturing methods.
1986	Traits Continued	Lord, de Vader and Alliger (1986)	Lord, de Vader and Alliger conducted a meta-analysis of trait research. They found that intelligence, masculinity-femininity, adjustment, dominance, extraversion and conservatism were related to leadership.

A Brief History of Organizational Leadership Theories
A Chronology of Influential
Management and Leadership Theories

The Search for the Successor to Transformational Leadership			
1990	Big-Five Personality	McCrae and Costa (1987, 1990, 2010)	Generally, extraversion, agreeableness and openness are often associated with effective leadership, and neuroticism and lack of conscientiousness with ineffective leadership.
1990	Emotional Intelligence	Salovey and Mayer (1990) Goleman (1995) Bar-On (1997) Mayer, Salovey and Caruso (2004)	Mayer, Salovey and Caruso developed a four-dimension model of emotional intelligence that is measured by the MSCEIT. Their four dimensions are perception of emotions, facilitating thought, understanding emotions and managing emotions. Bar-On developed a six-dimension model of emotional intelligence that is measured by the EQ-i 2.0. His six dimensions are self-perceptions, self-expression, interpersonal, decision making, stress management and well-being.
1990	Learning Organizations	Senge (1990)	Senge argued that leaders of learning organizations engage in five disciplines: systems thinking, personal mastery, mental models, shared vision and team learning.
1993	Reengineering	Hammer and Champy (1993)	Hammer described reengineering as "the notion of discontinuous thinking - of recognizing and breaking away from outdated rules."
1994	Built to Last	Collins and Porras (1994, 1996)	Based on their analysis of 32 different companies in 16 industries, Collins and Porras developed what they called *Twelve Shattered Myths* related to being a lasting organization.
1996	Competing for the Future	Hamel and Prahalad (1994, 1996)	Hamel and Prahalad's article and subsequent best-selling book, was targeted toward senior executives. The book provided ideas about how to think strategically about a rapidly changing world.
2001	Good to Great	Collins (2001)	Collins compared companies that had made a leap from being good to great. As part of the study, Collins described what he called level 5 leaders.

A Brief History of Organizational Leadership Theories
A Chronology of Influential
Management and Leadership Theories

2004	The Global Leadership Project GLOBE	Den Hartog, House, Hanges, Ruiz-Quintanilla, Dorfman, Peter Ashkanasy and Falkus (1999) House and GLOBE Research Team (2004, 2012)	The GLOBE project surveyed 17,370 middle managers from 951 organizations in three industries in 62 societies. Charismatic/value-based, team-oriented and participative leadership were considered important worldwide. Conversely, self-protective leader behaviors were believed to inhibit being an outstanding leader.
2007	Authentic Leadership	Kernis and Goldman (2003-6) George (2003) George and Sims (2007) Avolio, Gardner and Walumbwa (2007) Walumbwa, Avolio, Gardner, Wernsing and Peterson (2008)	A leading instrument to measure authentic leadership is the *Authentic Leadership Questionnaire*, by Avolio, Gardner and Walumbwa. They describe authentic leadership as consisting of four components: self-awareness, relational transparency, balanced processing and internalized moral perspective.
2011	Traits Continued	Derue, Nahrgang, Wellman and Humphrey (2011)	Derue, Nahrgang, Wellman and Humphrey performed meta-analytic regressions, using 143 bivariate relationships, to predict leader effectiveness, follower job satisfaction and follower satisfaction with their leader. Their results found that leader behaviors, particularly consideration, transformational leadership, contingent reward and not being passive-avoidant, were more important in predicting leadership outcomes than leader personality, intelligence or gender.
2000's	Genetic Studies	Li, Arvey, Zhang and Song (2011) Chaturvedi, Arvey, Zhangmand and Christoforou (2011) Loehlin, McCrae, Costa and John (1998)	The results of twin studies have estimated that somewhere around 50% of the variance in both personality and transformational leadership can be explained by genetic factors.

A Brief History of Organizational Leadership Theories
Summary

There are a lot of domains of leadership one can study, including: political leadership, military leadership, leadership of crowds, educational leadership, intellectual leadership, heroic leadership, executive leadership, group leadership, legislative leadership, governmental leadership, world-class political leadership, reform leadership and revolutionary leadership.

Organizational leadership can also be studied from a variety of viewpoints, or domains, such as: information use, resource allocation, group interactions, goal setting and clarification, conflict management and strategy. For this book, organizational leadership theories will be reviewed from six perspectives: leader focus, follower focus, task orientation, relationship orientation, autocratic versus democratic leadership style and the degree to which a theory has an empirical research base.

There are many approaches to dating leadership theories. This book will refer to four, broad eras.

The 1900's through the 1940's: The Era of Leadership Traits
The 1950's through the 1960's: The Era of Leadership Behaviors
The 1970's through the 1980's: The Era of Transforming Followers
The 1990's through the Present: The Search for the Successor to
    Transformational Leadership

Various theories have contributed to the history of leadership research. Some theories add a great deal to our thoughts while others contribute fine points that add to our overall understanding.

The next four chapters will review 51 management and leadership theories that span the four broad eras from 1900 to the present.

A Brief History of Organizational Leadership Theories
Notes

Most Influential Management Books of the 20th Century
Bedian and Wren (2001)

1. Frederick W. Taylor, *The Principles of Scientific Management* (1911)
2. Chester I. Barnard, *The Functions of the Executive* (1938)
3. Peter F. Drucker, *The Practice of Management* (1954)
4. Douglas M. McGregor, *The Human Side of Enterprise* (1960)
5. Herbert A. Simon, *Administrative Behavior: A Study of Decision-Making Processes in Administrative Organizations* (1947)
6. Paul R. Lawrence and Jay W. Lorsch, *Organization and Environment: Managing Differentiation and Integration* (1967)
7. James G. March and Herbert A. Simon *Organizations* (1958)
8. Abraham H. Maslow, *Motivation and Personality* (1954)
9. Michael E. Porter, *Competitive Strategy: Techniques for Analyzing Industries and Competitors* (1980)
10. Fritz J. Roethlisberger and William J. Dickson (with the assistance of Harold A. Wright), *Management and the Worker* (1939)
11. Alfred D. Chandler, Jr., *Strategy and Structure: Chapters in the History of American Enterprise* (1962).
12. Richard M. Cyert and James G. March, *A Behavioral Theory of the Firm* (1963)
13. Max Weber, *The Theory of Social and Economic Organization* (1922)
14. Daniel Katz and Robert L. Kahn, *The Social Psychology of Organization* (1966)
15. Chris Argyris, *Personality and Organization: The Conflict Between System and Individual* (1957)
16. Henri Fayol, *General and Industrial Management* (1916)
17. Renesis Likert, *New Patterns of Management* (1961)
18. Joan Woodward, *Industrial Organization: Theory and Practice* (1965)
19. Elton Mayo, *The Human Problems of our Industrial Revolution* (1933)
20. Tom Burns and George M. Stalker, *The Management of Innovation* (1961)
21. W. Edwards Deming, *Quality Productivity and Competitive Position* (1982)
22. James D. Thompson, *Organizations in Action* (1967)
23. George C. Homans, *The Human Group* (1950)
24. David C. McClelland, *The Achieving Society* (1961)
25. Frederick Herzberg, Bernard Mausner and Barbara B. Synderman, *The Motivation to Work* (1959)

A Brief History of Organizational Leadership Theories
Notes

Time Magazine's Most Influential Business Management Books
http://www.time.com/time/specials/packages/completelist/0,29569,2086680,00.html
> *The Age of Unreason* (1989), by Charles Handy
> *Built to Last: Successful Habits of Visionary Companies* (1994), by Jim Collins and Jerry Porras
> *Competing for the Future* (1996), by Gary Hamel and C. K. Prahalad
> *Competitive Strategy: Techniques for Analyzing Industries and Competitors* (1980), by Michael E. Porter
> *Emotional Intelligence* (1995), by Daniel Goleman
> *The E-Myth Revisited: Why Most Small Business Don't Work and What to Do about It* (1985), by Michael E. Gerber
> *The Essential Drucker* (2001), by Peter Drucker
> *The Fifth Discipline: The Art and Practice of the Learning* Organization (1990), by Peter Senge
> *First, Break All the Rules* (1999), by Marcus Buckingham and Curt Coffman
> *The Goal* (1984), by Eliyahu Goldratt
> *Good to Great: Why Some Companies Make the Leap ... and Others Don't* (2001), by Jim Collins
> *Guerilla Marketing* (1984), by Jay Conrad Levinson
> *How to Win Friends and Influence People* (1936), by Dale Carnegie
> *The Human Side of Enterprise* (1960), by Douglas McGregor
> *The Innovator's Dilemma* (1997), by Clayton Christensen
> *Leading Change* (1996), by John P. Kotter
> *On Becoming a Leader* (1989), by Warren Bennis
> *Out of the Crisis* (1982), by W. Edwards Deming
> *My Years with General Motors* (1964), by Alfred P. Sloan Jr.
> *The One Minute Manager* (1982), by Kenneth Blanchard and Spencer Johnson
> *Reengineering the Corporation: A Manifesto for Business Revolution* (1993), by James Champy and Michael Hammer
> *The 7 Habits Of Highly Effective People* (1989), by Stephen R. Covey
> *The Six Sigma Way: How GE, Motorola and other Top Companies are Honing Their Performance* (2000), by Peter S. Pande, Robert P. Neuman and Roland R. Cavanagh
> *Toyota Production System* (1988), by Taiichi Ohno
> *Who Moved My Cheese?* (1998), by Spencer Johnson

Forbes 2002 List of Most Influential Management Books (1982 to 2002)
http://www.forbes.com/2002/09/30/0930booksintro_3.html
> *In Search of Excellence: Lessons from America's Best-Run Companies* (1982), by Thomas Peters, Robert H. Waterman
> *Built to Last: Successful Habits of Visionary Companies* (1994), by James C. Collins, Jerry I. Porras
> *Reengineering the Corporation: A Manifesto for Business Revolution* (1993), by Michael Hammer, James A. Champy
> *Competitive Advantage: Creating and Sustaining Superior* Performance (1998), by Michael E. Porter
> *Crossing the Chasm: Marketing and Selling Technology Products to Mainstream Customers* (1999), by Geoffrey A. Moore, Regis McKenna
> *Seven Habits of Highly Effective People: Powerful Lessons in Personal Change* (1990), by Stephen R. Covey
> *The Six Sigma Way* (2000), by Peter S. Pande et al, Robert P. Neuman, Roland R. Cavanagh
> *The Innovator's Dilemma: When New Technologies Cause Great Firms to Fail* (1997), by Clayton M. Christensen
> *The Essential Drucker* (2001), by Peter F. Drucker
> *Competing for the Future* (1994), by Gary Hamel, C. K. Prahalad
> *Good to Great: Why Some Companies Make the Leap...and Others Don't* (2001), by James C. Collins

A Brief History of Organizational Leadership Theories
Notes

Organizational Behavior Theories Considered Influential
Miner (2003)

Preorganizational Behavior (General)
1. Conceptualizations Derived from the Hawthorne Studies (Elton Mayo, Fritz Roethlisberger, William Dickson)
2. The Functions of the Executive Concepts (Chester Barnard)
3. Social Psychological Views of Leadership and Change (Kurt Lewin)
4. Social Philosophy and Prophetic Statements on Management (Mary Parker Follett)
5. Theory of Bureaucracy (Max Weber)
6. General and Industrial Management Formulations (Henri Fayol)
7. Scientific Management Formulations (Frederick Taylor)

First Generation Theories (Motivation)
8. Need Hierarchy Theory (Abraham Maslow)
9. Existence, Relatedness, and Growth Theory (Clayton Alderfer)
10. Achievement Motivation Theory (David McClelland)
11. Psychoanalytic Theory Applied to Organizations (Harry Levinson)
12. Motivation Hygiene Theory (Frederick Herzberg)
13. Job Characteristics Theory (Richard Hackman, Edward Lawler, Greg Oldham)
14. Expectancy Theory—Work and Motivation (Victor Vroom)
15. Expectancy Theory—Managerial Attitudes and Performance (Lyman Porter, Edward Lawler)
16. Cognitive Evaluation Theory (Edward Deci, Richard Ryan);
17. Operant Behavior and Reinforcement Theory (Clay Hamner)
18. Organizational Behavior Modification (Fred Luthans, Robert Kreitner)
19. Equity Theory (Stacy Adams)
20. Goal-Setting Theory (Edwin Locke, Gary Latham)
21. Role Motivation Theory (John Miner)

First Generation Theories (Leadership)
22. Theory X and Theory Y (Douglas McGregor)
23. Consideration and Initiating Structure (John Hemphill, Ralph Stogdill, Carroll Shartle)
24. Managerial Grid Theory of Leadership (Robert Blake, Jane Mouton)
25. Situational Leadership Theory (Paul Hersey, Kenneth Blanchard)
26. Path-Goal Relationship Theory (Martin Evans)
27. Path-Goal Theory of Leader Effectiveness (Robert House)
28. Leadership Pattern Choice Theory (Robert Tannenbaum, Warren Schmidt)
29. Normative Decision Process Theory (Victor Vroom, Philip Yetton, Arthur Jago)
30. Influence Power Continuum Theory (Frank Heller)
31. Contingency Theory of Leadership (Fred Fiedler)
32. Cognitive Resource Theory (Fred Fiedler, Joseph Garcia)
33. Vertical Dyad Linkage/Leader Member Exchange Theory (George Graen)

First Generation Theories (Systems Concepts of Organization)
34. Theory of Systems 1-4 and 4T (Rensis Likert)
35. Control Theory and the Control Graph (Arnold Tannenbaum)
36. Group-Focused Systems Theory (Ralph Stogdill)
37. Social Psychology of Organizations (Daniel Katz, Robert Kahn)
38. Sociotechnical Systems Theory (Eric Trist, Fred Emery)
39. Sociological Open Systems Theory—Organizations in Action (James Thompson)

40. Mechanistic and Organic Systems (Tom Burns, G. M. Stalker)
41. Technological Determinism (Joan Woodward)
42. Technology in a Comparative Framework (Charles Perrow)
43. Contingency Theory of Organizations—Differentiation and Integration (Paul Lawrence, Jay Lorsch)

First-Generation Theories (Bureaucracy-Related Concepts)
44. Theoretical Underpinnings of the Aston Studies (Derek Pugh, David Hickson, C. R. Hinings)
45. Structural Contingency Theory (Lex Donaldson)
46. Theory of Differentiation in Organizations (Peter Blau)
47. Dysfunction of Bureaucracy (Victor Thompson)
48. Compliance Theory (Amitai Etzioni)
49. Goal Congruence Theory—Personality and Organization (Chris Argyris)
50. Theory of Organizational Learning and Defensive Routines (Chris Argyris) A bridging theory
51. Theory of Bureaucratic Demise (Warren Bennis)
52. Grid Organization Development (Robert Blake, Jane Mouton)
53. Process Consultation Theory of Organization Development (Edgar Schein)
54. Theory of Organizational Culture and Leadership (Edgar Schein)

First-Generation Theories (Organizational Decision Making)
55. Theory of Administrative Behavior/Organizations (Herbert Simon, James March)
56. Behavioral Theory of the Firm (Richard Cyert, James March)
57. Garbage Can Model of Organizational Choice (Michael Cohen, James March, Johan Olsen)
58. Organizational Learning Concepts (James March)
59. Social Psychology of Organizing/Sense-making Theory (Karl Weick)

Second-Generation Theories (Motivation and Perception)
60. Theory of Behavior in Organizations (James Naylor, Robert Pritchard, Daniel Ilgen)
61. Attributional Model of Leadership and the Poor Performing Subordinate (Terence Mitchell, Stephen Green)

Second-Generation Theories (Leadership)
62. Implicit Leadership Theories—Leadership and Information Processing (Robert Lord, Karen Maher)
63. Substitutes for Leadership (Stephen Kerr)
64. Charismatic Leadership Theory (Robert House)
65. Transformational and Transactional Leadership Theory (Bernard Bass)
66. The Romance of Leadership (James Meindl)

Second-Generation Theories (Concepts of Organization)
67. Resource Dependence Theory—The External Control of Organizations (Jeffrey Pfeffer, Gerald Salancik)
68. Organizational Ecology (Michael Hannan, John Freeman, Glenn Carroll)
69. Neoinstitutional Theory—Institutional Environments and Organizations (John Meyer, Richard Scott)
70. Neoinstitutional Theory—Institutionalization and Cultural Persistence (Lynne Zucker)
71. Neoinstitutional Theory—Institutionalism in Organizational Analysis (Walter Powell, Paul DiMaggio)

Second-Generation Theories (Organizational Decision Making)
72. Image Theory (Lee Roy Beach, Terence Mitchell)

[1] From Yukl, G., Gordon, A. and Taber, T. (2002). A hierarchical taxonomy of leadership behavior: integrating a half century of behavior research. *Journal of Leadership & Organizational Studies, 9,* 1, 15-32.

Chapter 3
The Era of Leadership Traits
1900-1949

The Era of Leadership Traits
Predominant Management and Leadership Theories

Prior to the 1950's, the dominant line of leadership research was the search for traits that explained why some individuals seemed to excel at leadership and others did not. This began with what is often referred to as the great man (person) era, in which the belief was that some people were simply born to greatness.

This completely speculative theory eventually gave way to the search for traits in a more scientific manner.

The movement from the great person to the trait era is marked by the use of empirical methods to measure aspects of leadership. During the trait era, traits studied included aspects such as appearance, personality, intelligence and social background. Today, this line of inquiry is called leadership trait theory or trait research.

The Era of Leadership Traits		
1911	Scientific Management	Taylor (1911)
1933	Hawthorne Studies	Mayo (1933, 1945)
1938	Executive Functions	Barnard (1938)
1947	Theory of Administrative Behavior in Organizations	Simon (1947) March and Simon (1958)
1948	Leader Traits	Stogdill (1948)
1949	Principles of Management	Fayol (1949)

The five management theories shown in grey provided important foundations for proceeding leadership and management theories, but none are likely used in 21st century workplace discussions of leadership and management that occur around the office. Consequently, each will only be given a brief treatment in this chapter.

Additionally, because 1900 – 1949 is such an expansive period, it will be briefly reviewed in two sections: 1900 to 1939 and 1940 to 1949.

The Era of Leadership Traits
Societal Influences
1900 - 1939

1900 to 1939

Between 1900 and 1939, the industrial revolution was influencing how leaders and followers in the United States both worked and lived. The first graph highlights a decline in the percentage of the workforce who worked in primary occupations (those acquiring raw materials) and a related rise in secondary occupations (those converting, distributing and repairing things made from raw materials) and tertiary occupations (professionals, technical workers and service workers).[1]

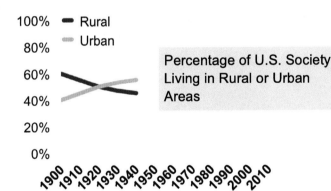

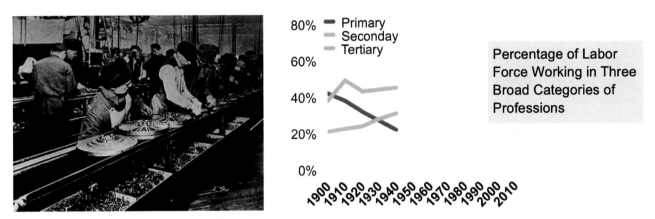

Percentage of Labor Force Working in Three Broad Categories of Professions

The second graph reflects a concomitant movement toward urban centers of industrialization.

Percentage of U.S. Society Living in Rural or Urban Areas

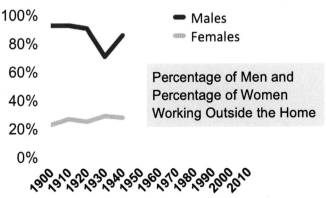

The third graph illustrates a trend of more women working outside the home.

Percentage of Men and Percentage of Women Working Outside the Home

The Era of Leadership Traits
Societal Influences
1900 - 1939

The unemployment graph reminds us of the impact that the Great Depression had on followers. Although how we calculate unemployment has changed a few times since 1900, in 1933, 24.9% of the civilian workforce ages 14 and over (those were different times) was unemployed.

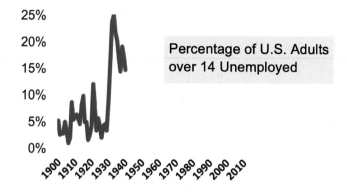

Percentage of U.S. Adults over 14 Unemployed

Between 1900 and 1939, most communication was in person or by post office mail. Even in 1939, less than 40% of United States households had a telephone. Because radio was wireless, its penetration into homes grew more rapidly than did the telephone.

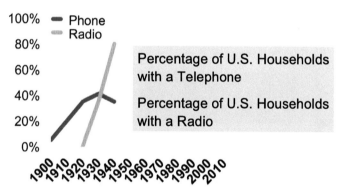

Percentage of U.S. Households with a Telephone

Percentage of U.S. Households with a Radio

Finally, society was less formally educated than today. In 1900, in the entire United States, 1,405 men and 339 women earned master's degrees. Only 334 men and 31 women earned doctorates that year. In 1939, there were approximately 27,000 adults over the age of 22 who held a master's degree and about 4,000 who held a doctorate. In 1939, if you held a bachelor's degree or higher, you were in the top 7% of educated adults over the age of 21.[2]

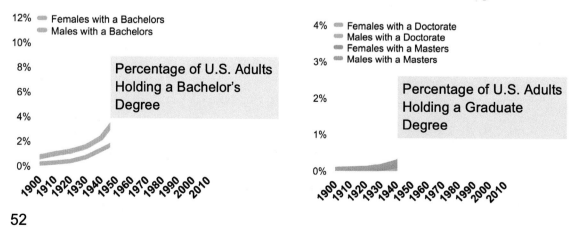

Percentage of U.S. Adults Holding a Bachelor's Degree

Percentage of U.S. Adults Holding a Graduate Degree

The Era of Leadership Traits
Technology Trends
1900 - 1939

At the turn of the century, limitations in aspects of life such as communication, transportation, production, energy and agriculture shaped the living and working environments of leaders and followers.

Today, we take for granted transportation options such as air, train, bus and car. In 1910, however, there were only five cars for every 1,000 people in the United States. Even in 1939, there were only 236 cars for every 1,000 people.

The most common form of local transportation was the horse. For longer distances, wealthy individuals used the train. Because of geographic limitations, communities were formed based on access to resources. These communities typically lived and worked within narrow geographic and transportation limitations.

At the turn of the century, the primary technological method was what is often referred to as a craft focus. A single worker often performed multiple steps involved in creating a product. A frequently used example is that of a shoemaker. In this example, the shoemaker took sheets of leather, thread, nails and glue and created a shoe, performing all of the activities from start to finish.

A technological revolution however was occurring. Henry Ford's improved application of the assembly line and other mass production techniques fundamentally changed the nature of work for millions of followers. Before the assembly line, workers performed a series of semi-skilled activities as a process of creating a product. The assembly line moved the product across physical space. Rather than perform a range of activities, workers now performed the same activity repetitively throughout the day.

The impact that the assembly line had on models and theories of work and leadership was profound. The efficiencies it created lowered the prices for products, which, in turn, increased the demand for those products. This in turn, created more jobs working on assembly lines.

Decades of study, however, eventually began to point to the human costs of asking workers to perform repetitive functions with machine-like dispassion and precision. For this time period though, the assembly line mentality was the dominant image of work.

Management Trends

One common way to describe organizations is by using Burns and Stalker's (1961) distinctions of mechanistic versus organic.

Mechanistic structures strive for efficiency by emphasizing a highly centralized hierarchy in which both roles and job tasks are clearly delineated and in which followers are closely supervised. Mechanistic structures tend to evolve when the environment in which the organization operates is relatively predictable or stable. A common analogy for a mechanistic view of organizations is envisioning workers as interchangeable parts in a well-oiled machine.

Organic structures tend to evolve in environments in which the organization must be nimble enough to react to change quickly. Consequently, it is much more difficult to have tightly conscripting rules. In organic structures, authority is much more decentralized and there is much greater lateral, cross-department communication. More reliance is placed on the individuals in the organization to make decentralized decisions than in mechanistic organizations.

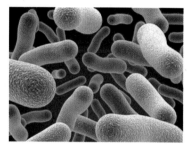

In the period between 1900 and 1939, the dominant management model was likely that of a highly structured, mechanistic view of organizations.

1911, Scientific Management, Taylor (1911)

Because of the increase in mass production techniques, managers were interested in how to increase industrial productivity. Taylor (1911) and other researchers like him began to study better methods for moving from a craft process, to specialization in which each worker performed a limited number of tasks repetitively. Taylor developed his ideas on increasing mass production efficiency in the four principles below.[3]

1. Study the way workers perform their tasks, gather all the informal job knowledge that workers possess and experiment with ways of improving the way tasks are performed.

2. Codify the new methods of performing tasks into written rules and standard operating procedures.

3. Carefully select workers so that they possess skills and abilities that match the needs of the task, and train them to perform the task according to the established rules and procedures.

4. Establish a fair or acceptable level of performance for a task and then develop a pay system that provides a reward for performance above the acceptable level.

The Era of Leadership Traits
Management Trends
1900 - 1939

1933, Hawthorne Studies, Mayo (1933, 1945)

Between 1927 and 1933, landmark research called the Hawthorne studies was conducted at the Hawthorne Works of the Western Electric Company (Mayo, 1933, 1945). While the studies were designed to measure how the physical characteristics of the work environment affected worker productivity, an unexpected finding was that performance tended to increase when a group was being studied by management. This pointed to the possibility that the manager's (leader's) behavior might influence follower performance.

1938, Executive Functions, Barnard (1938)

Chester Barnard was president of the New Jersey Bell Telephone Company. In 1938, Barnard wrote an influential book entitled *The Functions of the Executive.* Barnard summarized the functions of the executive as follows:

Establishing and Maintaining a System of Communication
Securing Essential Services from Other Members
Formulating Organizational Purposes and Objectives

Barnard's writings can be seen as a step away from a mechanistic view of organizations toward a more organic view.

He envisioned the manager-employee relationship as one in which workers decide what range of authority they will allow the organization to exercise over them. This range is influenced by multiple factors including compensation, the degree to which the followers believe the requests made of them are aligned with the organization's mission and the degree to which they believe the manager directing them has what we would today call referent versus legitimate power.

To that extent, Barnard distinguished between *Authority of Position* and *Authority of Leadership* "whose knowledge and understanding regardless of position command respect."

"Thus men impute authority to communications from superior positions, provided they are reasonably consistent with advantages of scope and perspective that are credited to those positions. This authority is to a considerable extent independent of the personal ability of the incumbent of the position. It is often recognized that though the incumbent may be of limited personal ability his advice may be superior solely by reason of the advantage of position. This is the authority of position.

But it is obvious that some men have superior ability. Their knowledge and understanding regardless of position command respect. Men impute authority to what they say in an organization for this reason only. This is the authority of leadership."[4]

The Era of Leadership Traits
Societal Trends
1940 - 1949

1940 to 1949

The impact on the Great Depression influenced attitudes about many things, including the nature of work, leadership and followership. As an example, the Worldcat database indicates that between 1900 and 1939, approximately 600 books, dissertations and theses were published within the narrow classification of *Leadership and Business*.

Approximately 22% of these 600 leadership and business publications were about the intersection of socialism, the labor movement and business. Between 1940 and 1949, the concomitant percentage had risen to 33%. By contrast, the current percentage is about 4%. Ideas such as safeguarding the rights of workers and emphasizing a collective distribution of profits were increasing in popularity during this post-depression period. One place this increased emphasis can be seen is in the percent of workers joining unions.

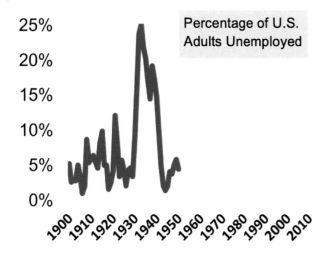

Percentage of U.S. Adults Unemployed

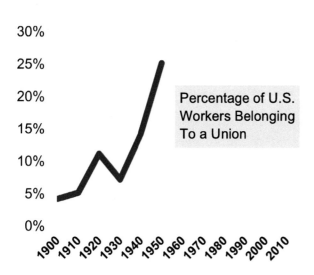

Percentage of U.S. Workers Belonging To a Union

The Era of Leadership Traits

Societal Trends
1940 - 1949

In 1940, there were about 500 thousand U.S. men and women in the military. In 1945, there were 12 million. World War II required a rapid expansion in the number of members in the military. The massive growth in the military-industrial complex required to transport these 12 million service members to different places around the world and then house, clothe, equip and care for them influenced a variety of changes in the workforce.

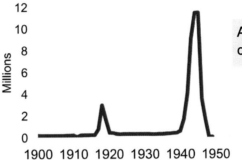

Active-Duty Members of the U.S. Military

At the beginning of the century about 44% of single women worked outside of the home compared to only 6% of married women. By 1949, the percentage of married women counted in labor force participation surveys had more than tripled.

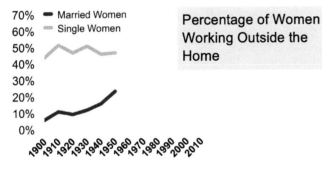

Percentage of Women Working Outside the Home

Because of increasing mechanization, the percentage of workers involved in acquiring raw materials continued to decrease and the number of tertiary workers increased. Professional workers typically required more education than workers in the primary occupations. Thanks partly to the government's *G. I. Bill*, but also in response to the changing needs of the workplace, we see the percentage of adults holding bachelor's degrees rising. In 1900, 27,410 U.S. adults walked across a stage to receive a bachelor's degree. In 1949, that number was 365,492.

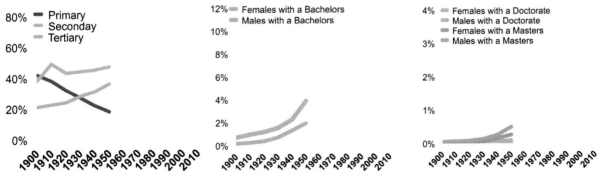

1947, Administrative Behavior in Organizations, Simon (1947), March and Simon (1958)

Simon's 1947 book covered a range of topics. He is likely best remembered, however, for his idea of bounded rationality or satisficing.

Simon argued that rational decision-making would require us to have a complete knowledge of the consequences that would follow for each choice we make. This however is much too complicated for most of us to do, as we are confronted with thousands of decisions throughout our day. To deal with this complexity, we create heuristics, or rules of thumb, to use for most decisions. This extends to decisions leaders make in organizations.

So, in the course of a day, leaders are required to make many decisions. We feel, however, that we don't have enough time to make optimal decisions for each challenge.

Rather than allocate all of our time and energy to one decision, and push everything else to the side, we search for decisions for most of these challenges that are *good enough*, called satisficing. Simon's prescient observation was that organizations typically run on a collection of decisions that were good enough rather than optimal. His ideas continued to erode the imagery of organizations as well-oiled machines and added to a more organic view of organizations.

1949, Principles of Management, Fayol (1949)

In 1949, Henry Fayol[5] captured much of the dominant management thought of the 1940's. In his book, *General and Industrial Management,* Fayol advanced the five functions and 14 principles of management that are still widely referenced in the management literature.

Five Functions of Management

Planning by identifying and selecting appropriate organizational goals, developing strategic objectives and courses of action.

Organizing teams and materials according to the plan. Assigning work, authority and responsibility to followers and coordinating resources.

Staffing by recruiting, selecting, training and developing employees.

Directing (Leading) by guiding the performance of workers to achieve goals by communicating and motivating.

Controlling by monitoring results against goals and taking any corrective actions necessary.

Fourteen Principles of Management[6]

Division of Labor Having followers specialize in certain skills should increase efficiency.

Authority and Responsibility Managers have the right to give orders and the power to exhort subordinates for obedience.

Discipline Managers must be willing to give workers warnings, fines and suspensions in order to promote order.

Unity of Command An employee should receive orders from only one manager or leader.

Order There should be a place for everything and everything should be in its place.

Unity of Direction The organization should have a coordinated effort linked to a common goal.

Scalar Authority Communication should occur up and down the hierarchy.

Centralization Authority should be concentrated as high as needed for the environment in which the organization functions.

Initiative Employees should have enough freedom to execute plans.

Equity All organizational members should be treated with both consideration and justice.

Remuneration of Personnel Employee rewards should be based on well-directed efforts and be fair to both the employee and organization.

Stability of Tenure of Personnel Creating long-term employees increases the chances for maximum performance.

Subordination of Individual Interests to the Common Interest The collective interests of the organization outweigh those of individuals.

Esprit de Corps Harmony should be fostered and conflict minimized in order to develop a sense of camaraderie to a common cause.

The Era of Leadership Traits
Leadership Traits

1948, Leader Traits, 1904 to 1948, Stogdill (1948)

Low Follower Focus		High Follower Focus	
Low Leader Focus		High Leader Focus	
Low Relationship		High Relationship	
Low Task		High Task	
Autocratic		Democratic	
Theoretical		Research Based	

The search for the elusive list of traits that could explain what made leaders different from non-leaders, was studied throughout the period of 1900 to 1948. In 1948, Stogdill meta-analyzed 128 of these published studies concerning traits of leaders. Stogdill's primary technique was to create frequency counts of which traits were included in each article.

Unfortunately, there were so many traits identified in the studies he reviewed, that one overall conclusion was that a simple list couldn't be developed. "The evidence suggests that leadership is a relationship between persons in a social situation, and that persons who are leaders in one situation may not necessarily be leaders in other situations." (1948, p. 64)

The table below is how Stogdill summarized the body of trait studies. The column with a "+" indicates a positive relationship. A "-" symbol indicates either a negative or non-relationship.[7]

	+	-		+	-
Physical Characteristics			**Personality (continued)**		
Activity, Energy	5		Emotional Balance	11	8
Age	10	8	Extroversion	5	6
Appearance, Grooming	13	3	Originality, Creativity	7	
Height	9	4	Personal Integrity	6	
Weight	7	4	Self-Confidence	17	
Social Background			Strength of Conviction	7	
Education	22	5	**Task-Related Characteristics**		
Social Status	15	2	Achievement Drive	7	
Mobility	5		Drive for Responsibility	12	
Intelligence and Ability			Persistence	12	
Intelligence	23	10	Responsible	17	
Judgment, Decisiveness	9		Task Orientation	6	
Knowledge	11		**Social Characteristics**		
Fluency of Speech	13		Enlisting Cooperation	7	
Personality			Cooperativeness	11	
Adaptability	10		Popularity, Prestige	10	
Alertness	6		Sociability	14	
Ascendance, Dominance	11	6	Social Participation	20	

The Era of Leadership Traits
Summary

Summary

As former President Clinton famously illustrated, words can have multiple meanings, depending on the context in which they are used. During grand jury testimony, President Clinton explained:

> "It depends on what the meaning of the word "is" is….if "is" means is and never has been…that is one thing. If it means there is none, that was a completely true statement….Now, if someone had … asked me a question in the present tense, I would have said no. And it would have been completely true."

The study of leadership traits likely suffered from a similar challenge. In the period of 1900 through 1949 the search was for traits "in general."

That search eventually became a bit more specific in the forms of personality traits and intelligence. Those research areas continue to be active in predicting various aspects of leadership.

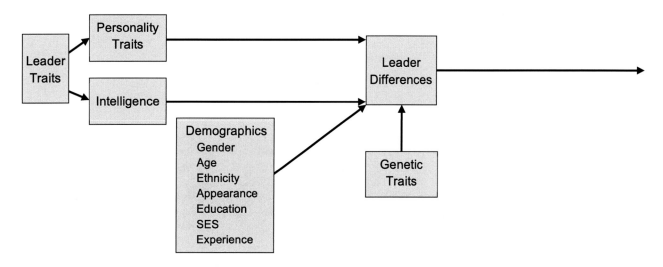

Both personality and intelligence research have contributed to a more recent line of study called emotional intelligence. Emotional intelligence is also an active line of research in the area of leadership.

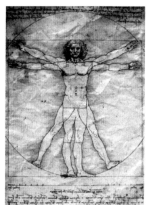

Additionally, a body of research has also grown on how both biological and other types of demographics impact things such as leadership style and leadership outcomes.

The search for things that explain differences between who does and does not emerge as a leader; and effective and ineffective leaders is still an active line of research. We now think of it more as "leader differences" research than trait research.

The Era of Leadership Traits
Summary

An important observation is that most of what was reviewed in this chapter is, at best, interesting history to most workers and leaders today. Leaders and followers in organizations who are in their 60's are members of the Baby Boomer generation. Many of these individuals likely entered the workforce during the late 1960's and 1970's at a time in which Fayol's ideas about principles of scientific management were beginning to fade.

Leader traits were still being studied, but the theory was also lessening in relevance. Baby Boomer leaders may have studied these theories in a formal collegiate or leadership training program, but there is also a likelihood they have not encountered them or skimmed those sections of a textbook.

Leaders and followers who are in their 40's and 50's typically entered the workforce in the late 1970's and beyond. For them, the theories covered in this chapter are probably as remote as discussions of the Great Depression or World War I. For leaders and followers in their 30's and younger, these theories are all ancient history.

Leader and Follower Age			70		55	40		25	
Began Work	1930's 1940's 1950's	1960's	1970's	1980's	1990's	2000's	2010's	2020's

Began Work									
	1930's	1940's	1950's	1960's	1970's	1980's	1990's	2000's	2010's	2020's
Scientific Mgt									
Satisficing									
Principles Mgt									

Leadership Theories									
	1930's	1940's	1950's	1960's	1970's	1980's	1990's	2000's	2010's	2020's
Traits									

The Era of Leadership Traits
Key Points

Prior to the 20th century, the dominant theory of leadership was called "the Great Man" (person) approach, in which the belief was that certain individuals were born to be great.

Between 1900 and 1948, this theory eventually gave way to the search for traits such as appearance, personality, intelligence and social background. In his 1948 review of 128 published studies concerning traits of leaders, Stogdill concluded that "The evidence suggests that leadership is a relationship between persons in a social situation, and that persons who are leaders in one situation may not necessarily be leaders in other situations." (1948, p. 64)

In the early part of the 20th century, the industrial revolution was influencing how we envisioned management and leadership. The dominant view from this era is called mechanistic.

Mechanistic structures strive for efficiency by emphasizing a highly centralized hierarchy in which both roles and job tasks are clearly delineated and in which workers are closely supervised. A common metaphor for a mechanistic view of organizations is envisioning workers as interchangeable parts in a well-oiled machine.

Taylor's (1911) theory of scientific management emphasized studying the way workers perform their tasks, gathering all of the informal job knowledge that workers possess and experimenting with ways of improving the manner in which tasks are performed. New methods of performing tasks are codified into written rules and standard operating procedures.

The Era of Leadership Traits
Key Points

The Hawthorne Studies by Mayo (1933, 1945) pointed to the possibility that the manager's (leader's) behavior might influence follower performance.

An early precursor to a more organic view of organizations is seen in Barnard's (1938) writings about the importance of communication in organizations, and a view in which workers decide what range of authority they will allow the organization to exercise over them.

The influence of the massive mobilization for World War II, coupled with the aura that that effort saved the world had a great deal of influence over ideas about leadership and management.

Those ideas were captured in Fayol's 14 principles of management.

In 1900, 1,405 men and 339 women earned master's degrees in the United States. Only 334 men and 31 women earned doctorates that year.

In 1949, 38,133 men and 16,094 women earned a masters degree. That year 5,433 men and 593 women earned a doctorate. Despite this increase, less that one percent of U.S. adults held graduate degrees in 1949.

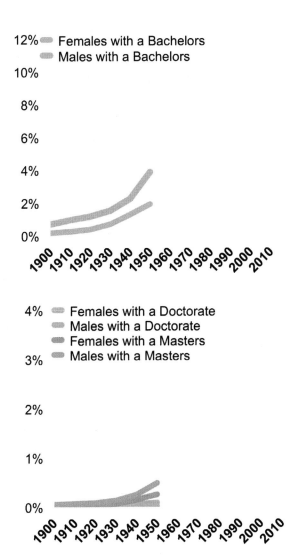

12% Females with a Bachelors
Males with a Bachelors

4% Females with a Doctorate
Males with a Doctorate
Females with a Masters
Males with a Masters

The Era of Leadership Traits
Notes

[1] The data for the three graphs on this page come from the years indicated from that year's *Statistical Abstract of the United States.*

[2] These estimates were calculated by using data from Snyder, T. D. and National Center for Education Statistics. (1993). *120 years of American education: A statistical portrait.* Washington, DC: U.S. Dept. of Education, Office of Educational Research and Improvement, National Center for Education Statistics and the *Statistical Abstracts of the United States.*

[3] Taken from Taylor, F. W. (1911). *The principles of scientific management.* New York: Norton.

[4] Barnard, C. I. (1953). *The functions of the executive.* Cambridge, Mass: Harvard University Press. p. 174.

[5] These were first written in 1916, but became more widely known in 1947. Fayol, H. (1916), *Administration industrielle et générale; prévoyance, organisation, commandement, coordination, controle* (in French), Paris, H. Dunod et E. Pinat; Fayol, H. (1949). *General and industrial management.* London: Pitman.

[6] Ibid.

[7] Taken from Stogdill, R. M. (1948). Personal factors associated with leadership: A survey of the literature. *Journal of Psychology,* 25, 35– 71.

Chapter 4
The Era of Leadership Behaviors

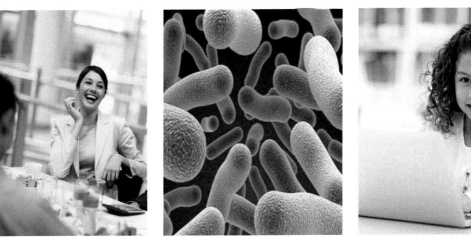

The Era of Leadership Behaviors
Predominant Management and Leadership Theories

Although the search for traits that distinguished leaders from non-leaders didn't end in 1949, a shift began to occur in the 1950's, in which researchers analyzed what leaders did and how they interacted with followers, more than who the leaders were.

Five management theories developed during this era are considered influential by the sources described in chapter 2. Those theories are shown in grey.

The six theories shown in beige have served as important influences on proceeding leadership theories. Each of these will be reviewed in about a page.

Those shown in light blue form the body of theories we can broadly group into the leadership models that emphasize both *Task* and *Relationship*. Each will be reviewed in this chapter in about a page. Volume 2 of the third edition of this book series discusses those theories shown in blue in greater detail.

The Era of Leadership Behaviors		
1954	Maslow's Hierarchy	Maslow (1954, 1962, 1965)
1954	Management by Objectives	Drucker (1954)
1955	Ohio State Studies	Fleishman, Harris and Burtt (1955) Hemphill and Coons (1957), Stogdill (1963)
1956	Five Bases of Social Power	French (1956), French and Raven (1959)
1957	Personality and Organization	Argyris (1957, 1964, 1973)
1959	Motivation Hygiene Theory	Herzberg (1959, 1966, 1976)
1960	Theory X and Theory Y	McGregor (1960, 1966)
1960	University of Michigan Studies	Katz and Kahn (1952) Cartwright and Zander (1960), Likert (1961)
1961	Management Systems	Likert (1961, 1967), Likert and Likert (1976)
1961	Mechanistic and Organic Systems	Burns and Stalker (1961)
1963	Behavioral Theory of the Firm	Cyert and March (1963)
1964	Managerial Grid	Blake and Mouton (1964, 1965, 1972, 1978)
1964	Contingency Theory	Fiedler (1964, 1966, 1967, 1971) Fiedler and Mahar (1979), Fiedler and Chemers (1974) Fiedler, Chemers and Mahar (1976) Fiedler and Garcia (1987)
1966	Four-Factor Theory	Bowers and Seashore (1966)
1965	Technological Determinism	Woodward (1965, 1970)
1966	Social Psychology of Organizations	Katz and Kahn (1966, 1978)
1969	Situational Theory	Hersey and Blanchard (1969, 1977)

The Era of Leadership Behaviors
Societal Influences

1950-1969

In the 1950's and 1960's, we see the percentage of the workforce employed in tertiary professions rising significantly, with a concomitant decline in the percentage of the workforce involved in primary occupations. To some degree, this reflects the growing complexity of the workplace and the need for higher percentages of workers to plan, organize, analyze, manage and lead.[1]

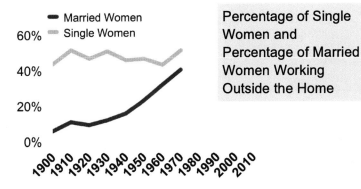

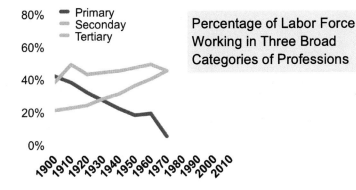

Percentage of Labor Force Working in Three Broad Categories of Professions

We also see a sharp rise in the percentage of married women working outside the home.

Percentage of Single Women and Percentage of Married Women Working Outside the Home

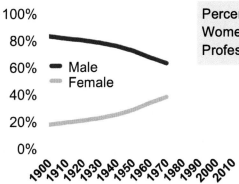

We also see a continued rise in the percentage of women comprising the category of professional workers.

Percentage of Men and Women Classified as Professional Workers

71

The Era of Leadership Behaviors
Societal Influences

This time period also witnessed a rapid expansion in the percentage of homes with a telephone, radio and television.

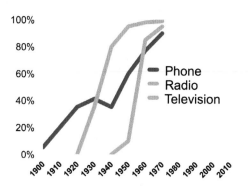

Percentage of Homes with a Telephone Radio and Television

- Phone
- Radio
- Television

We also see that society was becoming more mobile. The chart below shows the number of vehicles per 1,000 people in the United States. By 1969, there was one vehicle for about every two people in the United States.

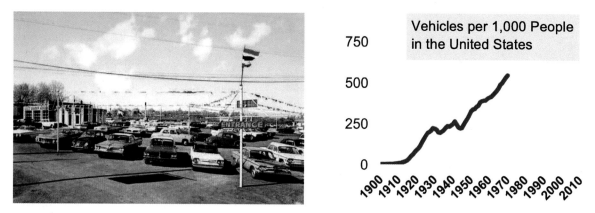

Vehicles per 1,000 People in the United States

We also see that education levels continued to increase. By 1969, about 6% of men and 4% of women in the United States held a bachelors degree. About 2% of adults held a masters degree, but less than 0.5% held a doctorate.

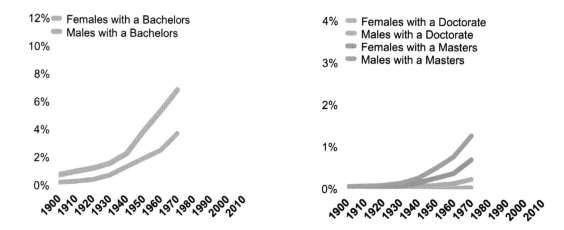

- Females with a Bachelors
- Males with a Bachelors

- Females with a Doctorate
- Males with a Doctorate
- Females with a Masters
- Males with a Masters

The Era of Leadership Behaviors
Technological Influences

Technological Influences 1950 to 1969

One of the major technological impacts during this time was the mechanization of the manufacturing process. The assembly line that had provided the munitions for World War II evolved from war manufacturing to commercial production.

Previously, machines were used to support the manufacturing process by automating somewhat simple tasks. During this era, machinery became more complex.

More sophisticated machines allowed for the automation of more complex tasks that, previously, had to be performed by hand. Partially because of improved machinery, the workforce transitioned from performing specialized tasks on a line to the roles of machine operator, maintenance and quality control for the new mechanized processes.

The most impactful post-war changes came from the commercial use of computer technology. Prior to the 1950's, computational devices were the domains of the military and select academic organizations. The equipment's limited application, lack of infrastructure support, tremendous size and extreme cost prohibited widespread commercial and private applications.

This changed with the development of programming languages that allowed programmers to customize the functionality of the devices. Programmable computers created a demand for software engineers, programmers and computer technicians. Larger, private and commercial organizations found a wide range of uses for the new technology such as payroll, inventory, billing, accounting and a myriad of statistical processing and research tasks.

Between 1960 and 1969, the government continued to fuel innovation through massive spending on research and support of the "space race."

During this era, the goal of "going to the moon" fueled developments in a wide array of computer and satellite applications.

The Era of Leadership Behaviors
Somewhat Influential Management and Leadership Theories

Six theories from this era have had some impact on the development of subsequent theories of leadership. Using the salad analogy from chapter 2, these theories are not as important as lettuce, tomatoes, olives and cheese to the success of the organizational leadership salad. Similar to wonderful spices, though, these theories have added improvements to our understanding of organizational leadership.

Somewhat Influential Theories		
1957	Personality and Organization	Argyris (1957, 1964, 1973, 1983)
1961	Management Systems	Likert (1961, 1967), Likert and Likert (1976)
1961	Mechanistic and Organic Systems	Burns and Stalker (1961)
1963	Behavioral Theory of the Firm	Cyert and March (1963)
1965	Technological Determinism	Woodward (1965, 1970)
1966	Social Psychology of Organizations	Katz and Kahn (1966, 1978)

1957, Personality and Organization, Argyris (1957, 1964, 1973, 1983)

Argyris argued that a fundamental conflict exists in organizations. Organizations typically structure followers' roles and direct their work in order to achieve organizational objectives. Followers, on the other hand, generally want to be self-directive and to feel fulfilled through exercising initiative and responsibility. Argyris explained the conflict as follows.

1. The lower one goes down the choice of command, the less the control and the fewer the abilities that may be used by an employee.

2. The more that leadership is directive, the more dependence or the less control the employee will tend to experience.

3. The more managerial controls are unilateral, the more dependence or the less control the employee will tend to experience.

4. This means that the general tendency will be for lower-level employees to react to try to overcome frustration or conflict.

5. Or to fight the organization by trying to redesign it and gain more control by, for example, creating a union. (Argyris, 1957, 1973).[2]

In 1983, Argyris described what he called single-loop (top-down) and double-loop (top-down and bottom-up) systems.

Single-Loop Learning
  Top-Down Control
  Win-Or-Lose Orientation toward Others
  Concealment of Feelings
  Rational Censoring of Information, Freedom and Risk

Double-Loop Learning
  Learning Orientation
  A Low-Defensive, High-Information Environment
  Joint Control by the More and Less Powerful

1961, Mechanistic and Organic Systems, Burns and Stalker (1961)

Burns and Stalker used the terms mechanistic and organic to describe two different organizational forms and philosophies. It is important to emphasize that a mechanistic organization is not a bad thing. These types of organizations tend to evolve when the work followers perform doesn't change much from week to week and the organization's competitive environment requires the organization to emphasize efficiency.

Organic organizations tend to evolve when the work requires a great deal of input from a variety of workers throughout the organization in order to tackle problems that may be new to the organization. Here effectiveness is emphasized more than efficiency.[3]

 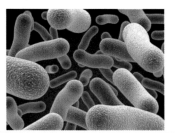

	Mechanistic	Organic
Tends to Evolve	Under Stable Conditions in Which Work Can Be Relatively Easily Codified and Measured	Under Changing Conditions in Which the Nature of Work Changes Frequently
Nature of Work	More Emphasis on Efficiency	More Emphasis on Effectiveness
Distribution of Work	Problems and Tasks Facing the Organization as a Whole Are Broken Down into Small, Measurable Parts	Problems are Seen More Globally and Are More Difficult to Break Down into Simpler Tasks
Structure and Control	Hierarchical, Transactional	Networked, Based on Common Interests
Communication	Top-Down, Leader to Follower	Lateral Communication Across Departments and Hierarchical Levels, Resembling Consultation
Who Defines Work Tasks	Immediate Superiors in the Hierarchy	There is Adjustment and Continual Re-Definition of Individual Tasks Through Interactions with Others
Location of Knowledge	Top of the Hierarchy	Can Be Located Anywhere in the Organization
Values	Insistence on Loyalty and Obedience to Superiors as a Condition of Membership	Commitment to the Organization is More Highly Valued Than Loyalty and Obedience to Superiors
Prestige	Greater Importance and Prestige are Attached to Internal (Local) Than to General Knowledge, Experience and Skills	Greater Importance and Prestige are Attached to Activities External to the Organization Than to Internal (Local) Knowledge, Experience and Skills

1961, Management Systems, Likert (1961, 1967); Likert and Likert (1976)

Likert developed and administered an instrument called the *Profile of Organizational Characteristics* to employees in a variety of organizations. Based on his research he described four types of leadership/management styles. There is some support for the belief that moving from the left to the right across the table below increases both follower satisfaction and productivity.[4]

	Exploitive Authoritative	Benevolent Authoritative	Consultative	Participative
Followers	Directed	Directed	Consulted	Participate
Responsibility	Senior Levels	Managerial Levels	Dispersed	Widespread
Trust	Very Little	Limited	Mutual	Mutual
Decisions	Announced	Centralized	Somewhat Decentralized	Decentralized
Motivational Mechanisms	Fear and Punishment	System of Rewards	Intrinsic Rewards	Intrinsic Rewards
Communication	Top Down	Top Down	Both Directions	Both Directions
Satisfaction				
Productivity				

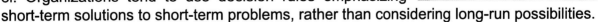

1963, Behavioral Theory of the Firm, Cyert and March (1963)

Cyert and March built on the theories of *Administrative Behavior in Organizations* (Simon, 1947, Simon and March, 1958) described in chapter 3. While the Cyert and March theory is quite complex, the points below capture some of the important aspects.[5]

Quasi-Resolution of Conflict

Organizations are coalitions of individuals whose individual goals often conflict. How this conflict is resolved is determined by the organization's acceptable bargaining process. This process is constrained by past behaviors and decisions.

Bounded Rationality or Satisficing

Organizations have multiple, competing goals and will accept suboptimal outcomes if they are above a minimum level. Organizations tend to use decision rules emphasizing short-term solutions to short-term problems, rather than considering long-run possibilities.

Problemistic Searching

Problem solving is usually triggered by a specific problem and the goal is to solve that one problem. As a result, the alternatives the organizational decision-makers consider are limited in scope. Solutions ultimately accepted are often those endorsed by a dominant coalition. The effect is that organizational policies will change only incrementally.

Slack Resources

Occasionally, organizations find themselves with excess or slack resources. It is during these periods, when they are not engaged in (problemistic) problem solving, that innovation may occur.

1965, Technological Determinism, Woodward (1965, 1970)

 In the early 1960's, Woodward was studying organizational structure and strategy. She concluded that the technology an organization used seemed to influence the type of structure the organization employed. This idea came to be known as technological determinism, connoting that, to some degree, technology determines organizational structure. Woodward developed a 10-level continuum of technological complexity, and then grouped those 10 levels into the three categories shown.[6]

The Woodward model was designed to explain how technology impacts organizational design in manufacturing environments rather than service environments. The fundamental idea, however, that the technology organizations use impacts multiple aspects of how those organizations plan and organize is readily apparent in the twenty-first century.

	Small Batch and Unit Production	Large Batch and Mass Production	Continuous Process Production
Example	Small Machine Shop	Automobile Assembly Line	Chemical Plant
Production	One at a Time	Produce a Large Number of the Same Items at the Same Time	Continuous Transformation Process
Workers	Use Technology from Start to Finish	Division of Labor	Oversight of the Technology
Organizational Design	Tends to Be Organic	Tends to Be Mechanistic	Tends to Be Organic
Level of Complexity	Low	Medium	High
Formalization	Less Formalized	More Formalized	Less Formalized

1966, Social Psychology of Organizations, Katz and Kahn (1966, 1978)

 Katz and Kahn are remembered for bringing the ideas of open and closed systems to organizational theory. A closed system doesn't interact with its environment in order to function. While the nuances of whether there is truly anything that is completely immune from its external environment can be debated, a clock is a good visual. Assuming the clock has a great battery, it can function for a long period of time with no input from outside its case.

Open systems, however, acquire inputs, transform those inputs and provide outputs. A houseplant illustrates an open system. The plant takes in light, water, carbon dioxide and nutrients, transforms them and outputs new growth and oxygen.

Katz and Kahn were among the first theorists to encourage managers and leaders to envision workplace organizations as open rather than closed systems.

The Era of Leadership Behaviors
Very Influential Management and Leadership Theories

Eleven theories from this era have had a great deal of impact on the development of subsequent theories of leadership. Using the salad analogy from chapter 2, these theories are lettuce, tomatoes, olives and cheese in the organizational leadership salad.

Very Influential Theories		
1954	Maslow's Hierarchy	Maslow (1954, 1962, 1965)
1954	Management by Objectives	Drucker (1954)
1955	Ohio State Studies	Fleishman, Harris and Burtt (1955) Hemphill and Coons (1957), Stogdill (1963)
1956	Five Bases of Social Power	French (1956), French and Raven (1959)
1959	Motivation Hygiene Theory	Herzberg (1959, 1966, 1976)
1960	Theory X and Theory Y	McGregor (1960, 1966)
1960	University of Michigan Studies	Katz and Kahn (1952) Cartwright and Zander (1960), Likert (1961)
1964	Managerial Grid	Blake and Mouton (1964, 1965, 1972, 1978)
1964	Contingency Theory	Fiedler (1964, 1966, 1967, 1971), Fiedler and Mahar (1979), Fiedler and Chemers (1974) Fiedler, Chemers and Mahar (1976) Fiedler and Garcia (1987)
1966	Four-Factor Theory	Bowers and Seashore (1966)
1969	Situational Theory	Hersey and Blanchard (1969, 1977)

The Era of Leadership Behaviors
Maslow's Hierarchy of Needs

1954, Maslow's Hierarchy of Needs (1954, 1962, 1965)

Low Follower Focus		High Follower Focus
Low Leader Focus		High Leader Focus
Low Relationship		High Relationship
Low Task		High Task
Autocratic		Democratic
Theoretical		Research Based

Maslow developed his hierarchy of needs by studying individuals who he believed were self-actualized, such as Lincoln, Jefferson and Einstein. His hierarchy of needs is well known. Less frequently presented, however, are his characteristics of self-actualized people.

1. They perceive reality efficiently and tolerate uncertainty
2. They accept themselves and others for what they are
3. They are spontaneous, resulting in appreciating most things
4. They are problem-centered
5. They seek solitude in order to search for serenity
6. They emphasize inner satisfaction over external rewards
7. They have peak or mystical experiences
8. They seek connections with humanity
9. They are humble
10. They have clear ethical beliefs
11. They often have unusual senses of humor
12. They are often creative
13. They often resist enculturation

Self-Actualization
Esteem
Belongingness and Love
Safety
Biological and Physiological

There has been very little direct, empirical research on Maslow's hierarchy. It has, however, served as a foundation for several psychological, emotional intelligence and spirituality theories that have been empirically tested. In the field of leadership, the idea of self-actualization influenced conceptualizations of transformational leadership by authors such as Burns (1978) and Bass (1985). The graphs remind us that the theory is still popular in the peer-reviewed literature, as a subject of doctoral dissertations and as a source of ideas in books.[7]

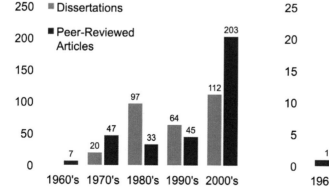

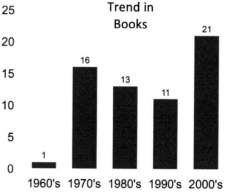

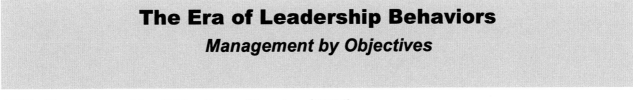

The Era of Leadership Behaviors
Management by Objectives

1954, Management by Objectives, Drucker (1954)

Low Follower Focus		High Follower Focus
Low Leader Focus		High Leader Focus
Low Relationship		High Relationship
Low Task		High Task
Autocratic		Democratic
Theoretical		Research Based

In his 1954 book, *The Practice of Management*, Peter Drucker provided several generations of managers and leaders a widely used method for establishing objectives with followers.

Management by objectives (MBO) is based on six steps related to establishing mission-related objectives for followers to pursue. The objectives themselves should be what Drucker called SMART – specific, measureable, agreed upon, realistic and time related.

1. Set or Review Organizational Objectives
2. Cascade Objectives Down to Employees
    a. Specific
    b. Measurable
    c. Agreed to by Manager (Leader) and Follower
    d. Realistic
    e. Time Related
3. Encourage Participation in Goal Setting
4. Monitor Progress
5. Evaluate and Reward Performance
6. Repeat the Cycle

Despite being over 60 years old, management by objectives is still popular. Even though the theory peaked in popularity in the 1970's, since 2000 there have been over 35 books, 125 articles and 35 dissertations written about MBO.[8]

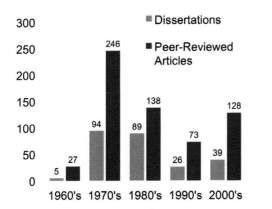

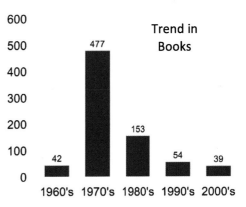

The Era of Leadership Behaviors
The Ohio State Studies

1955, The Ohio State Studies, Fleishman, Harris and Burtt (1955)
Hemphill and Coons (1957), Stogdill (1963)

Low Follower Focus		High Follower Focus
Low Leader Focus		High Leader Focus
Low Relationship		High Relationship
Low Task		High Task
Autocratic		Democratic
Theoretical		Research Based

Following Stogdill's assessment of trait theory, researchers began to focus a bit less on leaders as individuals and a bit more on followers' perceptions of leaders.

In seminal studies, researchers at Ohio State University began interviewing followers, asking about the behaviors in which effective leaders engaged.

Over 1,800 descriptions of leader behaviors were eventually synthesized down to 100 questions to measure 12 dimensions of leadership on the 1963 version of the *Leader Behavior Description Questionnaire XII* (XII connoting 12 subscales). Of these 12 dimensions, two have become foundational aspects of leadership: initiation of structure and consideration.

The *LBDQ* manual (Stogdill, 1963) defines these two primary leader behaviors as:

Initiation of Structure   **Low ◄─────────► High**
Clearly defines own role, and lets followers know what is expected

Consideration   **Low ◄─────────► High**
Regards the comfort, well-being, status, and contributions of followers

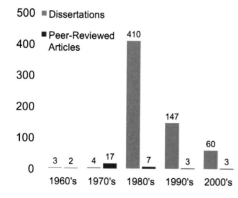

The *Leader Behavior Description Questionnaire XII* has been used in over 30 peer-reviewed articles and over 600 dissertations. While interest in the constructs measured by the various versions of the *LBDQ* peaked in the 1970's, it is still in use.[9]

A review of the instrument is included in volume 2 of this book series.

The Era of Leadership Behaviors
The Five Bases of Social Power

1956, The Five Bases of Social Power, French (1956), French and Raven (1959)

Low Follower Focus	High Follower Focus
Low Leader Focus	High Leader Focus
Low Relationship	High Relationship
Low Task	High Task
Autocratic	Democratic
Theoretical	Research Based

While French and Raven's sources of power are not a pure leadership theory, they are often related to discussions of how leaders exercise power. French and Raven (1959) define the five bases of power as follows.[10]

The **legitimate power** of a leader is power that stems from internalized values that a leader has a legitimate right to influence a follower and the follower has an obligation to accept this influence.

The **expert power** of a leader is related to the extent of the knowledge or perception of knowledge that a follower attributes to a leader.

The **referent power** of a leader has its basis in the identification of the follower with the leader such as a feeling of oneness with the leader or a desire for such an identity.

Reward power is the ability to reward a follower.

Coercive power stems from the expectation on the part of a follower that she/he will be punished by a leader for failing to conform to an influence attempt.

The first graph shows peer-reviewed articles and dissertations specifically using French and Raven's model.[11] Of these, more than 70% are empirical studies. It is difficult to pinpoint the number of books written that employ French and Raven's ideas, as a title such as "social power" has many connotations. The second graph shows books on social power in general, excluding areas such as nuclear, clean or green energy (power).[12]

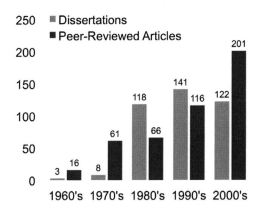

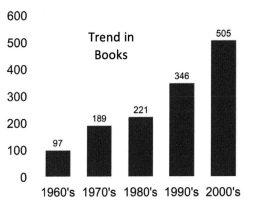

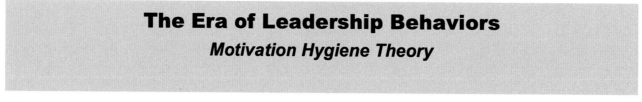

The Era of Leadership Behaviors
Motivation Hygiene Theory

1959, Motivation Hygiene Theory, Herzberg (1959, 1966, 1976)

Low Follower Focus	High Follower Focus
Low Leader Focus	High Leader Focus
Low Relationship	High Relationship
Low Task	High Task
Autocratic	Democratic
Theoretical	Research Based

Hertzberg originally interviewed 200 engineers and accountants about work situations in which they felt very happy as well as very unhappy. He then asked the participants what events might help them to change their feelings. The interviews lead to two classifications of events.

Dissatisfiers or Hygiene Factors are considered foundational, but don't motivate followers. The easiest ways to envision dissatisfiers in the 21st century are the Internet and air conditioning. If we go to work on a summer day and the air conditioning and the Internet are working, we don't suddenly become more motivated – these are expectations or dissatisfiers. If, however, we go to work and the air conditioning and Internet are not working, our motivation will almost assuredly fall.

Satisfiers or Motivators, however, motivate followers.[13]

Dissatisfiers or Hygiene Factors	Satisfiers or Motivators
Company Policies	Achievement
Supervision	Recognition
Relationship with Supervisor and Peers	The Work Itself
Work Conditions	Responsibility
Salary	Advancement
Status, Security	Growth

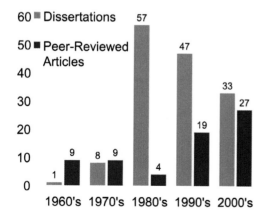

It is difficult to determine how many peer-reviewed articles have used Herzberg's motivation hygiene theory, as those words as well as "satisfier" are very generic.

Using "dissatisfier" in either the title or abstract, we see that at least 65 peer-reviewed articles have been published on the topic.[14] Of these, over a quarter are empirical studies.

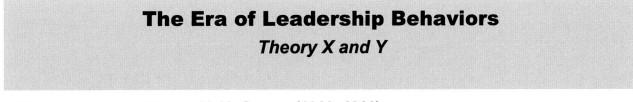

The Era of Leadership Behaviors
Theory X and Y

1960, Theory X and Theory Y, McGregor (1960, 1966)

Low Follower Focus		High Follower Focus
Low Leader Focus		High Leader Focus
Low Relationship		High Relationship
Low Task		High Task
Autocratic		Democratic
Theoretical		Research Based

McGregor added to our repertoire the idea of two fundamentally different attitudes leaders might hold toward followers, called *Theory X* and *Theory Y*. We can see the evolution of this type of distinction within the full range model of leadership in dimensions such as management by exception-active compared to intellectual stimulation.

Theory X Assumptions	Theory Y Assumptions
The Average Follower is Lazy, Dislikes Work, and Will Try to Do as Little as Possible	Followers Want Responsibility
These Followers Need to Be Closely Monitored	Followers Are Capable of Self-Control and Self-Direction
The Monitoring Should Include Strict Work Rules and Clear Reward and Punishment Procedures	Followers Can Handle Responsibility, as Most Individuals Have Some Levels of Creativity and Ingenuity

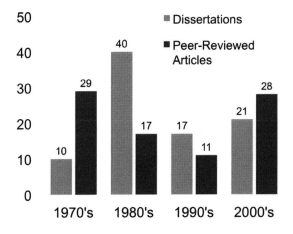

Chart: Dissertations and Peer-Reviewed Articles by decade
- 1970's: Dissertations 10, Peer-Reviewed Articles 29
- 1980's: Dissertations 40, Peer-Reviewed Articles 17
- 1990's: Dissertations 17, Peer-Reviewed Articles 11
- 2000's: Dissertations 21, Peer-Reviewed Articles 28

There have been over 80 peer-reviewed articles using the idea of theory X and Y.[15] It is difficult to estimate the number of books on the subject, as the phrase "theory X" is used in many disciplines.

While popular in casual conversation, such as "she's a theory X manager (leader)," the theory has suffered from the lack of a specific instrument to measure the constructs (Kopelman, 2008). Less than 10 percent of the peer-reviewed articles are empirical studies.

The Era of Leadership Behaviors
The University of Michigan Studies

1960, The University of Michigan Studies, Katz and Kahn (1952)
Cartwright and Zander (1960), Likert (1961)

Low Follower Focus	High Follower Focus
Low Leader Focus	High Leader Focus
Low Relationship	High Relationship
Low Task	High Task
Autocratic	Democratic
Theoretical	Research Based

Researchers at the University of Michigan found somewhat similar dimensions of effective leadership behaviors as those at Ohio State University.

What the Ohio State studies labeled, *Initiating Structure*, researchers at the University of Michigan labeled *Production Orientation*. Similarly, what Ohio State researchers labeled *Consideration*, Michigan researchers called *Employee Orientation*.

Ohio State

The Ohio State studies viewed initiation of structure and consideration as two separate constructs.

Initiation of Structure   Low ←——————→ High

Clearly defines own role, and lets followers know what is expected

Consideration   Low ←——————→ High

Regards the comfort, well-being, status, and contributions of followers

University of Michigan

Unlike the Ohio State researchers, however, the researchers at the University of Michigan originally conceived of these constructs as opposite ends of a continuum.

Production Orientation
Emphasize the task or production aspects of the job and getting things done

←——————→

Employee Orientation
Emphasize a concern for interpersonal relations and the personal needs of followers

The Era of Leadership Behaviors
The Managerial Grid

1964, The Managerial Grid, Blake and Mouton (1964, 1965, 1972, 1978)

Low Follower Focus	High Follower Focus
Low Leader Focus	High Leader Focus
Low Relationship	High Relationship
Low Task	High Task
Autocratic	Democratic
Theoretical	Research Based

Both the Ohio State and Michigan streams of research conceived of dimensions of leadership related to *Taking Care of Business* (initiating structure, production orientation) and *Taking Care of Followers* (consideration, employee orientation).[16]

Blake and Mouton used similar dimensions of leader behavior but called them *Concern for Production* and *Concern for People*.

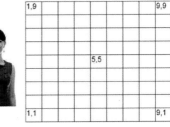

The authors assigned the dimensions to a grid with the X-axis describing concern for production and the Y-axis concern for people. The grid axes are numbered 1 through 9.

A leader who is very focused on *Taking Care of Business* (initiating structure, production) and struggles with *Taking Care of Followers* (consideration, employee orientation, concern for people), for example, would be said to have a 9,1 style of leadership, while a leader high on both dimensions would be said to have a 9, 9 style.

There have been nearly 40 peer-reviewed articles and 100 books written using the managerial grid. A large number of the articles are empirically based. Over 50 of the books are credited to Blake and represent the translations and expansion of the theory to more than 11 languages.[17]

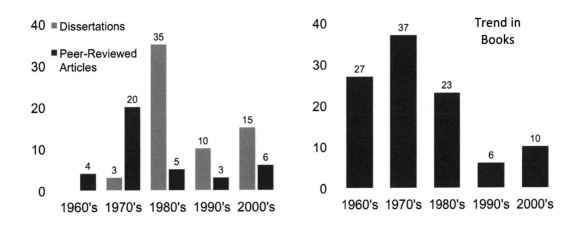

The Era of Leadership Behaviors
Contingency Theory

1964, Contingency Theory, Fiedler (1964, 1966, 1967, 1971)

Low Follower Focus		High Follower Focus
Low Leader Focus		High Leader Focus
Low Relationship		High Relationship
Low Task		High Task
Autocratic		Democratic
Theoretical		Research Based

Fiedler's contingency theory melds four variables into one theory: the nature of the leader-member relationship, how structured the task is, the level of position power the leader holds, how much relationship orientation (called being a high LPC leader) and how much task orientation (called being a low LPC leader) the leader should engage in. Based on eight octants, Fiedler theorized combinations of these four variables that would result in the most favorable outcomes.[18]

Leader-Member Relationship	Good				Poor			
Task Structure	High		Low		High		Low	
Position Power	Strong	Weak	Strong	Weak	Strong	Weak	Strong	Weak
Octant	1	2	3	4	5	6	7	8
Recommended Leadership Style	Medium to High Task Orientation / Low to Medium Relationship Orientation				High Relationship Orientation / Low Task Orientation			High Task Orientation / Low Relationship Orientation

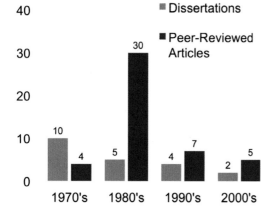

The instrument most associated with contingency theory is the *Least Preferred Coworker Scale*. The trends in peer-reviewed articles and dissertations using this instrument are on the decline.[19]

- Dissertations
- Peer-Reviewed Articles

40
30
20
10
0

10 4 5 30 4 7 2 5

1970's 1980's 1990's 2000's

The Era of Leadership Behaviors
The Four-Factor Theory

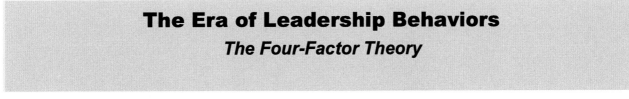

1966, The Four-Factor Theory, Bowers and Seashore (1966)

Low Follower Focus		High Follower Focus
Low Leader Focus		High Leader Focus
Low Relationship		High Relationship
Low Task		High Task
Autocratic		Democratic
Theoretical		Research Based

Bowers and Seashore's primary contribution to leadership theory was to propose an integrative framework for understanding similarities among leadership research that had been conducted prior to 1966.[20] Bowers and Seashore's theory itself didn't evolve as a line of research, but influenced proceeding theories such as path-goal theory.

Support and **Goal Emphasis** are similar to the Ohio State constructs of initiating structure and consideration.

Interaction Facilitation connotes encouraging followers to communicate and build mutually satisfying relationships.

Work Facilitation is the leader behavior of efficient planning, scheduling, coordinating and resource allocation.

	Support	Goal Emphasis	Interaction Facilitation	Work Facilitation
Katz et al. (1950)	Employee Orientation	Production Orientation		Production Orientation
Katz and Kahn (1951)	Employee Orientation		Group Relationships	Differentiation of Supervisory Role
Hemphill and Coons (1957)	Maintenance of Membership	Objective Attainment	Group Interaction Facilitation	Objective Attainment
Halpin and Winer (1957)	Consideration	Production Emphasis	Sensitivity	Initiating Structure
Kahn (1958)	Providing Direct Need Satisfaction	Structuring Path to Goal Attainment		Enabling Goal Achievement
Cartwright and Zander (1960)	Group Maintenance Functions	Goal-Achievement Functions	Group Maintenance Functions	Goal-Achievement Functions
Likert (1961)	Supportive Relationships	High-Performance Goals	Group Methods of Supervision	Technical Knowledge, Planning, Scheduling
Mann (1962)	Human Relations Skills	Administrative Skills	Human Relations Skills	Technical Skills

The Era of Leadership Behaviors
Situational Leadership

1969, Situational Leadership, Hersey and Blanchard (1969, 1977)

Low Follower Focus		High Follower Focus
Low Leader Focus		High Leader Focus
Low Relationship		High Relationship
Low Task		High Task
Autocratic		Democratic
Theoretical		Research Based

Building on the models from Ohio State, Michigan and Blake and Mouton, Hersey and Blanchard's situational leadership also uses a two-dimensional grid. Their leadership dimensions are *Supportive* and *Directive* behavior.

Beyond the two leader dimensions, however, Hersey and Blanchard posit that leaders should adjust their styles of leading based on two dimensions related to followers: the follower's capability to do a particular task/job and the follower's commitment to do that task/job.

For followers who are **Highly Competent** and **Highly Committed**, the leader should delegate to those followers, engaging in **minimal amounts** of both **Directive** and **Supportive Behaviors**.

For followers who are **Low on Competence** and **Highly Committed**, the leader should direct those followers through **High Directing** and **Low Supporting Behaviors**.

For followers who are **Highly Competent** and **Low on Commitment**, the leader should support those followers through **Low Directing** and **High Supporting Behaviors**.

For followers who have **Some Competence** and **Some Commitment**, the leader should coach those followers through **High Directing** and **High Supporting Behaviors**.

There is limited quantitative research on situational leadership. It does have, however, intuitive appeal.[21]

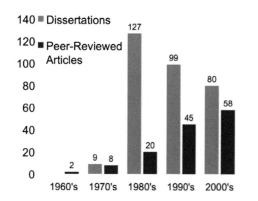

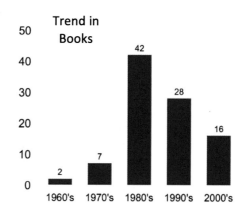

The Era of Leadership Behaviors
Summary

Following the era of leadership traits, two fundamental leadership behaviors were explored, emphasizing task oriented behaviors and relationship oriented behaviors. One branch of this line of research included one or more situational aspects. The three most enduring theories from that branch are contingency, path-goal and situational leadership theories. Of the theories without a situational element, the managerial (leadership) grid is the most enduring theory.

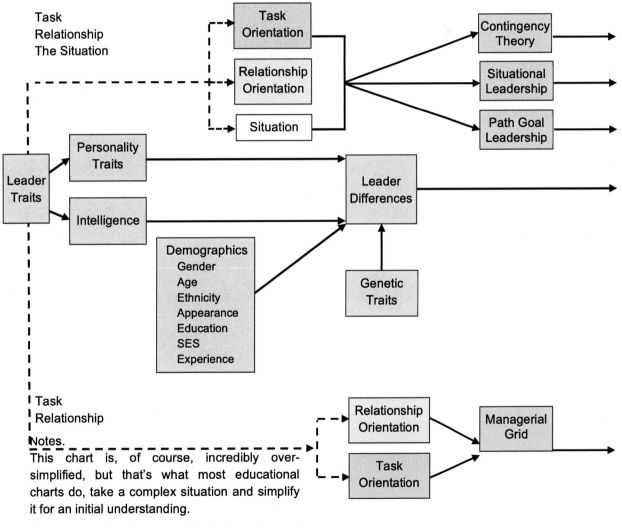

Notes.

This chart is, of course, incredibly over-simplified, but that's what most educational charts do, take a complex situation and simplify it for an initial understanding.

To create a chart that would be both legible and fit on one page, it wasn't possible to calibrate boxes to exact points in time. See the timeline in chapter 2 for that detail.

While the chart is original work, the inspiration came from Derue, Nahrgang, Wellman and Humphrey (2011).

The Era of Leadership Behaviors
Summary

The chart below illustrates that the ideas of the bases of social power, satisficing and Maslow's hierarchy of needs are lilkely familiar theories to most managers and leaders.

Organic and mechanistic organizations, open versus closed systems, satisfiers and dissatisfiers and theory X and Y are likely familiar terms to managers and leaders in their late 30's and older.

Of the leadership theories from this era, the managerial grid and path-goal theory are likely familiar to managers and leaders older than 30, and situational leadership may well be quite familiar to most leaders and managers.

Leader and Follower Age			70		55		40		25	
Began Work	1930's	1940's	1950's	1960's	1970's	1980's	1990's	2000's	2010's	2020's

Management Theories										
	1930's	1940's	1950's	1960's	1970's	1980's	1990's	2000's	2010's	2020's
Scientific Mgt										
Satisficing										
Principles Mgt										
Organic/Mech										
Open Systems										
Dissatisfiers										
Theory X/Y										
Maslow's Hierarchy										
Bases of Power										

Leadership Theories										
	1930's	1940's	1950's	1960's	1970's	1980's	1990's	2000's	2010's	2020's
Traits										
Managerial Grid										
Path-Goal										
Contingency										
Situational										

The Era of Leadership Behaviors
Key Points

In the 1950's and 1960's, the percentage of the workforce employed in tertiary professions rose significantly. To some degree, this reflected the growing complexity of the workplace, and the need for higher percentages of workers to plan, analyze, manage and lead. We also see that this time period witnessed a rapid expansion in the percentage of homes with a telephone, radio and television.

During this era, there was a movement away from viewing organizations as highly mechanistic structures and toward viewing them as more organic. Burns and Stalker (1961) introduced the organic terminology, and Katz and Kahn (1966) added the terms open and closed systems to this line of thought. Argyris (1957) introduced the idea that a fundamental conflict exists in organizations. Organizations typically structure followers' roles and direct their work in order to achieve organizational objectives. Followers, on the other hand, generally want to be self-directive and to feel fulfilled through exercising initiative and responsibility.

Likert (1961) described four types of leadership/management styles: exploitive, authoritative benevolent, authoritative consultative and participative. There is some evidence that consultative and participative leadership styles increase follower satisfaction and productivity more than exploitive or authoritative benevolent.

Cyert and March (1963) introduced the idea of problemistic searching in which problem solving is usually triggered by a specific problem and the goal is to solve that one problem. As a result, the alternatives the organizational decision-makers consider are limited in scope. Solutions ultimately accepted are often alternatives endorsed by a dominant coalition. The effect of problemistic searching is that organizational policies will change only incrementally.

The Era of Leadership Behaviors
Key Points

While it lacks an empirical base, Maslow's hierarchy of needs is still very popular. Over 200 peer-reviewed articles have incorporated the theory since the year 2000. The theory posits that individuals progress through five levels of need: biological and physiological, safety, belongingness and love, esteem and self-actualization.

Drucker's (1954) theory of management by objectives emphasized setting or reviewing organizational objectives and cascading those objectives down to employees. The objectives should be specific, measurable, agreed to by the manager (leader) and follower, realistic and time related.

Studies done at Ohio State, Fleishman, Harris and Burtt (1955) Hemphill and Coons (1957), Stogdill (1963) identified two primary dimensions of leader behavior. Initiation of structure is leader behavior that clearly defines roles and lets followers know what is expected of them. Consideration consists of regarding the comfort, well-being, status and contributions of followers.

French and Raven (1959), explained five types of social power: legitimate power, reward power, coercive power, expert power and referent power.

Hertzberg (1959, 1966, 1976) developed a theory of aspects of work. He distinguished between factors that motivate followers and hygiene factors or dissatisfiers. Although dissatisfiers don't motivate followers, their absence lowers motivation.

McGregor (1960, 1966) developed the concept of theory X and theory Y attitudes about followers. A theory X view is that the average follower is lazy, dislikes work and will try to do as little as possible. A theory Y view is that followers want responsibility.

The Era of Leadership Behaviors
Key Points

The University of Michigan studies, Katz and Kahn (1952), Cartwright and Zander (1960), Likert (1961) described somewhat similar dimensions of leadership as those at Ohio State University. Production orientation emphasized the task or production aspects of the job and getting things done. Employee orientation emphasized a concern for interpersonal relations and the personal needs of followers.

Blake and Mouton (1964, 1965, 1972, 1978) used similar dimensions of leader behavior as the Ohio State and Michigan studies but called their dimensions concern for production and concern for people. The authors laid the two dimensions onto a grid with the X-axis describing concern for production and the Y-axis concern for people. The grid axes are numbered 1 through 9.

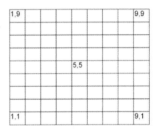

Fiedler's contingency theory (1964, 1966, 1967, 1971) begins with the premise that leaders have relatively consistent leadership styles, based on the dimensions of task or relationship orientation.

Fiedler's model provides eight scenarios, based on: leader-follower relationship, the structure of the task at hand and how much position power the leader holds.

Bowers and Seashore (1966) proposed a framework for understanding similarities of earlier research. Their four dimensions were support, goal emphasis, interaction facilitation and work facilitation.

Hersey and Blanchard's (1969, 1977) situational leadership theory used a two-dimensional grid with leadership dimensions of supportive and directive behavior. Beyond the two leader behavior dimensions, Hersey and Blanchard posited that leaders should adjust their styles of leading based on two dimensions related to followers: the follower's capability to do a particular task/job and the follower's commitment to do that task/job.

The Era of Leadership Behaviors
Graduate Education

Between 1950 and 1969, education levels in the United States continued to increase. By 1969, about 6% of men and 4% of women held a bachelors degree. About 2% of adults held a masters degree, but less than 0.5% held a doctorate. Possessing a graduate degree was still a rare accomplishment.

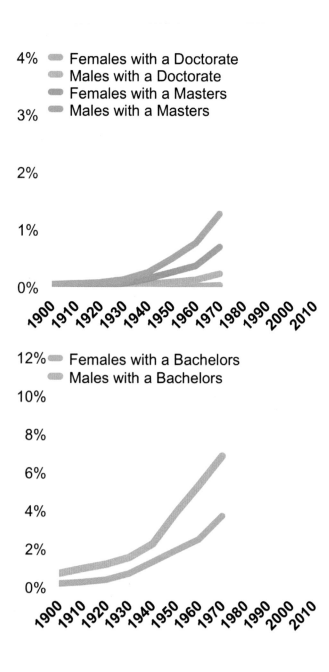

The Era of Leadership Behaviors
Notes

About the Publication Graphs Used in this Book

Generally, the search terms were placed in quotation marks for all searches. This often resulted in fewer returned results, but the results were a bit more specific.

This method likely undercounted some articles based on authors' language used in a title or abstract. As an example, not putting *transformational leadership* in quotations would have counted an article that might have only used the words transformational and leadership in an abstract such as "school leadership is facing a brave new world. The introduction of distance education is a transformational paradigm for learning…"

The graphs used in these chapters depicting trends in publication are not designed to account for every single book, article or dissertation related to a topic. Rather, they are designed to provide a sense of the changes in the growth and decline in the popularity of a theory. There are likely a few more documents in each category that used more creative titles, but were not included in the graph counts. It is doubtful, however, that the shape of the overall trends in popularity would change much.

Peer-Reviewed Literature – Abbreviated AD for Academic Databases
For a review of the peer-reviewed literature, the following databases were searched:

Academic Search Complete, Agricola, Alt HealthWatch, Business Source Complete, CI-NAHL Plus with Full Text, Computer Source, Economía y Negocios, ERIC, Fuente Académica, Health Source - Consumer Edition, Health Source: Nursing/Academic Edition, Information Science & Technology Abstracts (ISTA), Internet and Personal Computing Abstracts, Legal Collection, Library, Information Science & Technology Abstracts, MAS Ultra - School Edition, MasterFILE Premier, MedicLatina, Middle Search Plus, Military & Government Collection, MLA Directory of Periodicals, MLA International Bibliography, Primary Search, Professional Development Collection, Psychology and Behavioral Sciences Collection, Religion and Philosophy Collection, Research Starters - Business, Research Starters - Education, SocINDEX with Full Text, Teacher Reference Center, The Serials Directory, TOPICsearch, Vocational and Career Collection, World History Collection, Chicano Database, Legal Source, GreenFILE, MEDLINE, Science & Technology Collection.

The "peer-reviewed" limiter was selected. An important note, however, is that the number of "hits" one receives from an initial search typically will be reduced by up to 20% by using the brute force method of clicking through each page of displayed records until one reaches the end of the list.

In EBSCOHost, in 2014, this process seemed to force the elimination of duplicate records beyond the removal of duplicates performed by checking that option on the menu.

The Era of Leadership Behaviors
Notes

Dissertations – Abbreviated PD for ProQuest Dissertations and Theses A&I

Trends for dissertations are based on the ProQuest Dissertations and Theses A&I database. Typically, the name of the theory was entered in quotations as a search term in the title or abstract of the dissertation. It appeared that ProQuest's database of dissertations published in the 1960's and 1970's is smaller than the population of dissertations from those decades. The trends in dissertations for the 1980's through the present are informative. Readers, though, should avoid concluding "wow did the number of dissertations jump from the 1970's to the 1980's." This may or not have been the case, based on what seems to be a few limitations of the database.

Books – Abbreviated WC for Worldcat Database

Typically, the name of the theory was entered in quotations as a search term in the title of the book. All book results returned were displayed. This included paper and e-book versions as well as all international language versions.

[1] The first five graphs are derived from the *Statistical Abstract of the United States.*

[2] These points were summarized from Argyris, C. (1957). *Personality and organization.* New York: Harper.

[3] This table is based on Burns and Stalker's 1961 work. The language they use, however, doesn't translate well to twenty-first century organizations. As an example, they use the word "a concern" for what, today we would call an organization. Some of their words were translated into more modern parlance for this table while remaining true to their ideas.

[4] Summarized from Likert, R. (1961). *New patterns of management.* New York: McGraw-Hill.

[5] The book is more complex than what is shown, but these four points come from Cyert, R. M., and March, J. G. *A behavioral theory of the firm.* Englewood Cliffs, N. J.: Prentice Hall, 1963.

[6] Based on Woodward, J. (1965). *Industrial organization: theory and practice.* London: Oxford University Press.

[7] The data for the dissertations were obtained by entering Maslow and Hierarchy in the title or abstract of PD. The data for peer-reviewed articles were obtained by entering Maslow and Hierarchy in the title or abstract of AD. The data for books were obtained by entering Maslow and Hierarchy in the title of WC.

[8] "Management by Objectives" in the title or abstract of AD and PD, title of WC.

[9] "Leader Behavior Description Questionnaire" or *LBDQ* in the title or abstract of AD and PD.

[10] These were taken almost verbatim from French, J. R. and Raven, B. H. (1959), "The Bases of Social Power," in Cartwright, D. (Ed.), *Studies of Social Power,* Institute for Social Research, Ann Arbor, Michigan.

[11] "Expert Power" or "Referent Power" or "Coercive Power" or "Reward Power" or "Legitimate Power" in the title or abstract in AD.

[12] ti:"social power" - nuclear - green - solar in the title of WC.

[13] Based on Herzberg, F. (1959). *The motivation to work.* New York: Wiley.

[14] "Dissatisfier*" in the title or abstract of AD and PD.

[15] "Theory Y" in the title or abstract of AD and PD. In the 2000's, about 10 studies were removed from the total because they used "Theory Y" in a different way.

[16] These two terms, *Task* and *Relationship* will be used from here forward as a generic description of the dimensions of (Initiating Structure, Production, Directing and so forth) and (Consideration, Employee Orientation, Concern for People, Supporting and so forth).

[17] "Managerial Grid" or "Leadership Grid" in the title or abstract of AD and PD, title of WC.

[18] Based on Fiedler, F. E. (1967). *A theory of leadership effectiveness.* New York: McGraw–Hill.

[19] "Least Preferred Coworker" in the title or abstract of AD and PD.

[20] The table is from Bowers, D. G. and Seashore, S. E. (1966). Predicting organizational effectiveness with a four-factor theory of leadership. *Administrative Science Quarterly*, 11, 238– 263. Small edits were made to consolidate space, the table transposed and put into chronological order.

[21] "Situational Leadership" in the title or abstract of AD and PD, title of WC.

Chapter 5
The Era of Transforming Followers

The Era of Transforming Followers
Predominant Management and
Leadership Theories

The predominant theories of the 1950's and 60's were those based on the dimensions of task and relationship. The relationship aspects of those theories carried into theories covered in this chapter such as path-goal, leader-member exchange and charismatic leadership.

Several theories during the 1970's and 1980's, however, advocated leader behaviors that were stronger than the relational aspects from the previous era. Servant leadership, transformational leadership and the full range model of leadership challenged leaders to assist in *transforming followers* into not only better workers but also better persons in general.

Interspersed in this era were six management theories that also influenced how we envision leadership.

Finally, the trait approach was re-examined in 1974 and 1986 meta-analyses.

The Era of Transforming Followers		
1970	Servant Leadership	Greenleaf (1970, 1972, 1974, 1977, 1979)
1971	Path-Goal Theory	Evans (1970) House (1971, 1996)
1973	Normative Theory	Vroom and Yetton (1973) Vroom and Jago (1978, 1988)
1974	Traits Continued	Stogdill (1974)
1975	Leader-Member Exchange Theory	Dansereau, Graen and Haga (1975) Graen and Uhl-Bien (1991, 1995)
1977	Charismatic Theory	House (1975, 1977, 1992)
1978	Theory Z	Ouchi and Jaeger (1978), Ouchi (1981, 1984)
1978	Substitutes for Leadership	Kerr and Jermier (1978)
1978	Transformational Leadership	Burns (1978)
1981	Six Sigma	Motorola (1981), General Electric (1995)
1982	In Search of Excellence	Peters and Waterman (1982)
1985	Full Range Model of Leadership	Bass (1995, 1998, 1999) Bass and Avolio (1994, 1995, 1996, 1997, 2002) Bass, Avolio and Jung (1999)
1986	Total Quality Management	Deming (1986)
1986	Traits Continued	Lord, de Vader and Alliger (1986)

1970 - 1989

In the 1970's and 1980's, we see that the percentage of the workforce employed in tertiary professions continued to rise, while the percentage working in primary professions continued to drop.

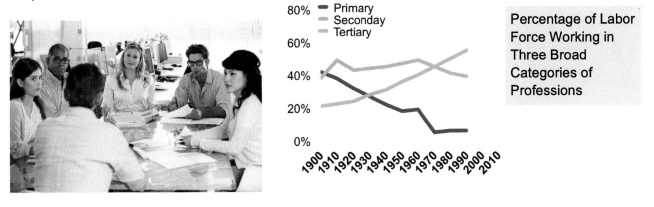

Percentage of Labor Force Working in Three Broad Categories of Professions

We also see a continued rise in the percentage of women working outside the home.

Percentage of Single Women and Percentage of Married Women Working Outside the Home

We also see a continued rise in the percentage of women comprising the category of professional workers.

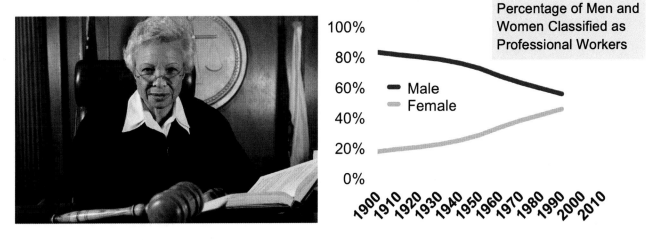

Percentage of Men and Women Classified as Professional Workers

The Era of Transforming Followers
Societal Influences

During this time period, most homes in the United States had a telephone, radio and television. Television, however, was limited to just a few channels. The introduction of cable television was also occurring and growing rapidly.[1] In the 1980's, the introduction of the personal computer began. All of these devices provided more information to more people.

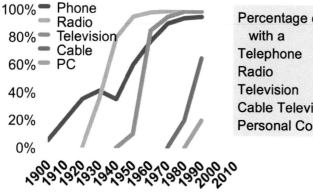

Percentage of Homes
  with a
Telephone
Radio
Television
Cable Television
Personal Computer

The unemployment rate was slowly rising during this period, reaching 9.6% in 1982. Union membership however was gradually declining from its peak in the early 1960's.

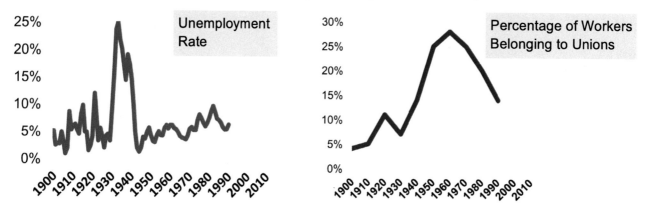

We also see that education levels continued to increase. By 1989, about 9% of men and 7% of women in the United States held a bachelors degree. About 4% of adults held a masters degree, but less than 0.6% a doctorate.

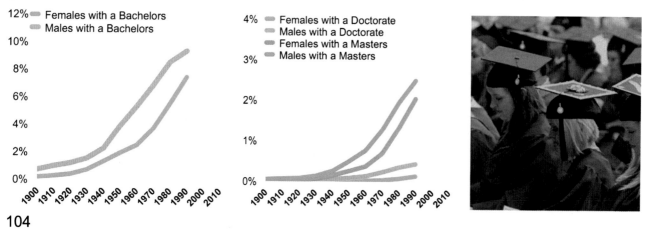

104

Technological Influences

This era can also be defined by rapid improvements in computer technology and its adoption by organizations of all sizes. Up to this point, several limitations impeded the widespread adoption of what we today call computers.

During the 1970's and 1980's, equipment became more powerful while simultaneously becoming smaller and less expensive. Additionally, the keyboard and the mouse were added as a way to interact with devices, culminating in the first microcomputer and subsequent generations of the personal computer.

Other advancements were made in the programming languages utilized by these computers. Because programmers created a wider spectrum of applications, computers were able to complete a more diverse array of functions.

Yet, the general population lacked the education and understanding of the technology needed to incorporate it into their workplaces or households. Even though the community of users, programmers and developers expanded at a rapid pace, the computer primarily remained in the domains of engineers and enthusiasts.

The development of a "visual" operating system changed this paradigm, making the computer accessible to a wider spectrum of users. Apple and Microsoft both introduced versions of operating systems that overlaid visual representations of concepts on top of the traditional computer architecture making them more accessible to the casual user.

Building on this new operating system, several productivity applications were developed including spreadsheet, word processing and presentation software. The ability of the computer to perform multiple productivity functions and store data internally/externally made the technology increasingly more attractive for both personal and business use.

Computer skills became an increasingly important requirement of the workforce. This began the transition away from typewriters to word processors. As a reflection of this, by 1989 15% of households had a personal computer while during the 1950's and 1960's only larger organizations could afford, house and utilize this technology.

The Era of Transforming Followers
Somewhat Influential Management and Leadership Theories

Four theories from this era had some impact on the development of subsequent theories of leadership. Using the salad analogy from chapter 2, these theories are less important than lettuce, tomatoes, olives or cheese to the success of the organizational leadership salad. Similar to wonderful spices, though, these theories have added improvements to our understanding of organizational leadership.

Somewhat Influential Theories		
1973	Normative Theory	Vroom and Yetton (1973) Vroom and Jago (1978, 1988)
1978	Theory Z	Ouchi and Jaeger (1978), Ouchi (1981, 1984)
1978	Substitutes for Leadership	Kerr and Jermier (1978)
1982	In Search of Excellence	Peters and Waterman (1982)

The Era of Transforming Followers
Normative Theory

1973, Normative Theory, Vroom and Yetton (1973), Vroom and Jago (1978, 1988)

Low Follower Focus		High Follower Focus	
Low Leader Focus		High Leader Focus	
Low Relationship		High Relationship	
Low Task		High Task	
Autocratic		Democratic	
Theoretical		Research Based	

Vroom, Yetton and Jago are known for their work in decision-making. Their theory used seven questions, which could lead to five types of leader decision-making approaches. There have been about 10 peer-reviewed articles on the model, but only about two since 1990.

Is There a Quality Requirement	Is There Sufficient Information	Is the Problem Structured	Is Follower Acceptance Critical	Would a Unilateral Decision Be Accepted	Do Followers Share Goals Represented	Is Follower Conflict Likely

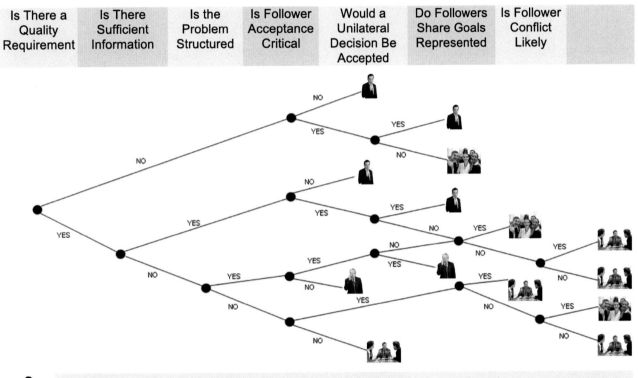

 **Autocratic Type 1** – The leader <u>makes the decision alone</u>.

 Autocratic Type 2 – The leader collects information from followers, then <u>makes the decision alone</u>.

Consultative Type 1 – The leader discusses the problem with <u>relevant followers individually</u> and then makes the decision alone.

Consultative Type 2 – The leader discusses the problem with <u>relevant followers as a group</u> and then makes the decision alone.

 Group-based – The leader discusses the problem with <u>relevant followers as a group</u>; the decision is then a group decision.

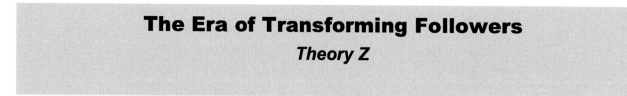

The Era of Transforming Followers
Theory Z

1978, Theory Z, Ouchi and Jaeger (1978), Ouchi (1981, 1984)

Low Follower Focus	High Follower Focus
Low Leader Focus	High Leader Focus
Low Relationship	High Relationship
Low Task	High Task
Autocratic	Democratic
Theoretical	Research Based

In 1978, Ouchi contrasted what he described as a typical set of American leadership/work assumptions with those that might be typical Japanese assumptions. He then proposed a hybrid set of assumptions that he labeled type Z. This slowly became known as theory Z.[2]

Area	Type A (American)	Type J (Japanese)	Type Z (Modified American)
Employment	Short-Term Employment	Lifetime Employment	Long-Term Employment
Decision Making	Individual Decision-Making	Consensual Decision-Making	Consensual Decision-Making
Responsibility	Individual Responsibility	Collective Responsibility	Individual Responsibility
Promotion	Rapid Evaluation and Promotion	Slow Evaluation and Promotion	Slow Evaluation and Promotion
Control	Explicit, Formalized Control	Implicit, Informal Control	Implicit, Informal Control With Explicit, Formalized Measures
Career Path	Specialized Career Path	Non-Specialized Career Path	Moderately Specialized Career Path
Areas of Concern	Segmented Concern	Holistic Concern	Holistic Concern, Including Family

The popularity of theory Z peaked in the 1980's. There is still, however, some peer-reviewed literature written on the topic.

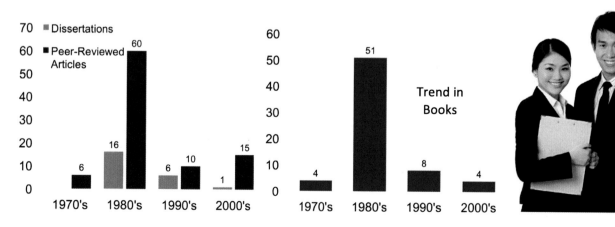

Trend in Books

The Era of Transforming Followers
Substitutes for Leadership

1978, Substitutes for Leadership, Kerr and Jermier (1978)

Low Follower Focus		High Follower Focus
Low Leader Focus		High Leader Focus
Low Relationship		High Relationship
Low Task		High Task
Autocratic		Democratic
Theoretical		Research Based

In 1978, Kerr and Jermier asked whether certain factors could lessen the need for leadership. They divided possible substitutes into three sources: followers, the tasks being done and the organization.[3]

Follower Characteristics	Task Characteristics	Organizational Characteristics
Abilities	Routine, Methodologically Invariant Tasks	The Degree of Organizational Formalization
Experience, Training and Knowledge	Intrinsically Satisfying Tasks	Inflexibility of Rules
Need for Independence	Task Feedback	Cohesiveness of Work Groups
Professional Orientation		Amount of Staff and Advisory Support
Indifference Toward Rewards		Organizational Rewards Not Controlled by the Leader
		The Spatial Distance Between Supervisors and Their Subordinates

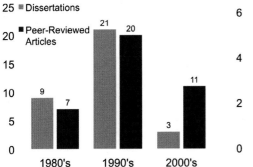

Dissertations / Peer-Reviewed Articles

	1980's	1990's	2000's
Dissertations	9	21	3
Peer-Reviewed Articles	7	20	11

Trend in Books

	1970's	1980's	1990's	2000's
Books	2	4	1	2

Interest in substitutes for leadership seems to have peaked in the 1990's. There have been, however, over 35 peer-reviewed articles and over 30 dissertations done on the idea.

The Era of Transforming Followers
In Search of Excellence

1982, in Search of Excellence, Peters and Waterman (1982)

Low Follower Focus		High Follower Focus
Low Leader Focus		High Leader Focus
Low Relationship		High Relationship
Low Task		High Task
Autocratic		Democratic
Theoretical		Research Based

Peters and Waterman reported what they believed were practices among excellent Fortune 500 companies. They classified a company as excellent if it was in the top half of its industry on at least four of six performance measures for each year between 1961 and 1980.[4] They then summarized the themes below as common among these excellent companies.[5]

Bias for Action A preference for doing things.

Close to the Customer Customer satisfaction is an "obsession."

Autonomy and Entrepreneurship Breaking a large organization into smaller elements and encouraging each element to think independently and competitively.

Productivity through People Treating lower level employees well.

Hands-on, Value-driven "Walking the walk" in leadership positions.

Stick to the Knitting Concentrating on the things the organization does well.

Simple Form, Lean Staff This includes lean staff within the executive offices.

Simultaneous Loose-tight Properties This combines the first seven principles.

In Search of Excellence has been an influential book. Unfortunately, the authors didn't provide replicable details on how they selected the companies for their research. Aupperle, Acar and Booth (1986) performed an empirical analysis attempting to replicate some of the selection criteria used by Peters and Waterman. Aupperle, Acar and Booth concluded that companies in the upper-quartile means of the *Forbes* 1,000 consistently outperformed on ROE, ROA, sales growth and market valuation, over two different five-year periods, than the *excellent* firms studied in *In Search of Excellence*. Still, the eight principles seem sensible and have almost assuredly been adopted by legions of leaders and managers.

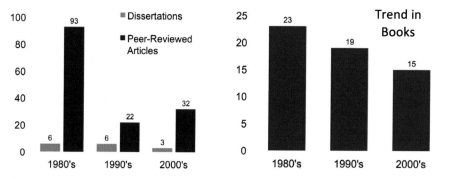

The Era of Transforming Followers
Very Influential Management and Leadership Theories

Ten theories from this era have had a great deal of impact on the development of subsequent theories of leadership. Using the salad analogy from chapter 2, these theories are lettuce, tomatoes, olives and cheese in the organizational leadership salad.

Very Influential Theories		
1970	Servant Leadership	Greenleaf (1970, 1972, 1974, 1977, 1979)
1971	Path-Goal Theory	Evans (1970) House (1971, 1996)
1974	Traits Continued	Stogdill (1974)
1975	Leader-Member Exchange Theory	Dansereau, Graen and Haga (1975) Graen and Uhl-Bien (1991,1995)
1977	Charismatic Theory	House (1975, 1977, 1992)
1978	Transformational Leadership	Burns (1978)
1981	Six Sigma	Motorola (1981), General Electric (1995)
1985	Full Range Model of Leadership	Bass (1995, 1998, 1999) Bass and Avolio (1994, 1995, 1996, 1997, 2002) Bass, Avolio and Jung (1999)
1986	Total Quality Management	Deming (1986)
1986	Traits Continued	Lord, de Vader and Alliger (1986)

The Era of Transforming Followers
Servant Leadership

1970, Servant Leadership, Greenleaf, (1970, 1972, 1974, 1977, 1979)

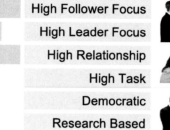

Low Follower Focus		High Follower Focus
Low Leader Focus		High Leader Focus
Low Relationship		High Relationship
Low Task		High Task
Autocratic		Democratic
Theoretical		Research Based

The phrase servant leadership was developed by Greenleaf (1970). In *The Servant as Leader*, Greenleaf explained: "The servant-leader is a servant first... It begins with the natural feeling that one wants to serve, to serve first. Then conscious choice brings one to aspire to lead. That person is sharply different from one who is a leader first."[6]

Multiple writers have added structure to what dimensions of servant leadership entail. The table below summarizes some of the regularly discussed aspect of servant leadership. There is a great deal of overlap between servant leadership constructs and those found in both transformational and authentic leadership. The table below captures some of the more unique aspects of servant leadership.

Related to the Leader	Related to the Follower	Related to the Community
Spirituality	Healing	Stewardship
Altruism	Empowerment	Building Community

The graphs indicate that interest in servant leadership is growing at a rapid pace. Most writings on servant leadership are currently theoretical, but several instruments have recently been developed that show promise toward developing an empirical base for servant leadership.[7]

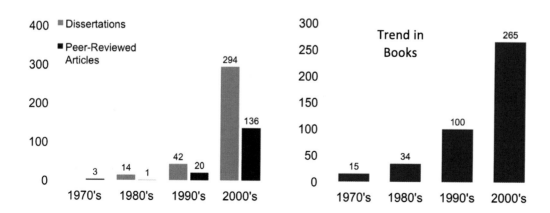

The Era of Transforming Followers
Path-Goal Theory of Leadership

1971, Path-Goal Theory, Evans (1970), House (1971, 1996)

Low Follower Focus		High Follower Focus
Low Leader Focus		High Leader Focus
Low Relationship		High Relationship
Low Task		High Task
Autocratic		Democratic
Theoretical		Research Based

Path-goal theory has gone through several iterations. The last update was by House in 1996. Four broad, leader behaviors are included in the essence of path-goal theory.

Directive Path-Goal Clarifying Leader Behavior provides psychological structure for subordinates. This involves letting subordinates know what they are expected to do, scheduling and coordinating work.

Supportive Leader Behavior displays concern for subordinates' welfare and creates a friendly and psychologically supportive work environment.

Participative Leader Behavior encourages subordinate influence on decision-making and work unit operations. This involves consulting with subordinates and taking their opinions and suggestions into account.

Achievement Oriented Behavior encourages performance excellence. This involves setting challenging goals, seeking improvement, emphasizing excellence in performance and showing confidence in subordinates.[8]

While slightly more complex than the flowchart shown, Neider and Schriesheim (1988) provided a model with some of the elements that capture the idea of a path toward a goal.

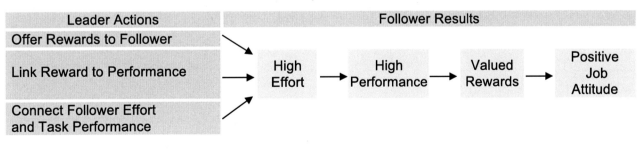

Leader Actions	Follower Results
Offer Rewards to Follower	
Link Reward to Performance	High Effort → High Performance → Valued Rewards → Positive Job Attitude
Connect Follower Effort and Task Performance	

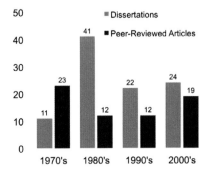

There have been only a handful of books written on path-goal theory. It is, however, still popular in both the peer-reviewed literature as well as a topic of dissertations.

1974, Traits Continued, Stogdill (1974)

Low Follower Focus	
Low Leader Focus	
Low Relationship	
Low Task	
Autocratic	
Theoretical	

High Follower Focus	
High Leader Focus	
High Relationship	
High Task	
Democratic	
Research Based	

In 1974, Stogdill performed a second review of trait studies. The table on the right shows his findings. *Pos* indicates positively related, and *0/-* indicates not or negatively related. The table below is Stogdill's synopsis of traits frequently appearing in studies. He grouped these traits into three categories: leadership skills, relationship with the group and personal characteristics.[9]

Leadership Skills
Social and interpersonal skills
Technical skills
Administrative skills
Intellectual skills
Leadership effectiveness and achievement
Social nearness, friendliness
Group task supportiveness
Task motivation and application
Relationship With the Group
Maintaining a cohesive work group
Maintaining coordination and teamwork
Maintaining standards of performance
Informal group control (group freedom)
Nurturant behavior
Personal Characteristics of the Leader
Willingness to assume responsibility
Emotional balance and control
Ethical conduct, personal integrity
Communicative, verbal ability
Ascendance, dominance
Personal soundness, good character
Physical energy
Experience and activity
Mature, cultured
Courage, daring
Aloof, distant
Creative, independent
Conforming

	1948 Pos	1948 0/-	1974 Pos
Physical Characteristics			
Activity, energy	5		24
Age	10	8	6
Appearance, grooming	13	3	4
Height	9	4	
Weight	7	4	
Social Background			
Education	22	5	14
Social status	15	2	19
Mobility	5		6
Intelligence and Ability			
Intelligence	23	10	25
Judgment, decisiveness	9		6
Knowledge	11		12
Fluency of speech	13		15
Personality			
Adaptability	10		
Adjustment, normality			11
Aggressiveness			12
Alertness	6		4
Ascendance, dominance	11	6	31
Emotional balance, control	11	8	14
Enthusiasm			3
Extroversion	5	6	1
Independence, nonconformity			13
Objectivity, tough minded			7
Originality, creativity	7		13
Integrity, ethical conduct	6		9
Resourcefulness			7
Self-confidence	17		28
Strength of conviction	7		
Tolerance of stress			9
Task-Related Characteristics			
Achievement, desire to excel	7		21
Drive for responsibility	12		17
Enterprise, initiative			10
Persistence against obstacles	12		
Responsible	17		6
Task orientation	6		13
Social Characteristics			
Ability to enlist cooperation	7		3
Administrative ability			16
Attractiveness			4
Cooperativeness	11		5
Nurturance			4
Popularity, prestige	10		1
Sociability, interpersonal skills	14		35
Social participation	20		9
Tact, diplomacy	8		4

The Era of Transforming Followers
Leader-Member Exchange Theory

1975, Leader-Member Exchange Theory, Dansereau, Graen and Haga (1975)
Graen and Uhl-Bien (1991,1995)

Low Follower Focus		High Follower Focus
Low Leader Focus		High Leader Focus
Low Relationship		High Relationship
Low Task		High Task
Autocratic		Democratic
Theoretical		Research Based

The idea of leader-member exchange theory has been slowly evolving. Graen and Uhl-Bien (1995) explained that the theory originally confirmed that leaders form different relationships with different followers within the same work areas – often called out-groups and in-groups. Based on this, the theory evolved to describe three stages of leader-follower development.[10]

Characteristic	Stranger	Acquaintance	Maturity
Relationship Building Phase	Role Finding	Role Making	Role Implementation
Type of Reciprocity	Cash and Carry	Mixed	In-Kind
Time Span of Reciprocity	Immediate	Some Delay	Indefinite
Leader-Member Exchange	Low	Medium	High
Incremental Influence	None	Limited	Almost Unlimited

LMX theory is very popular. Over 500 peer-reviewed articles and dissertations have been published on the theory since 2000.[11]

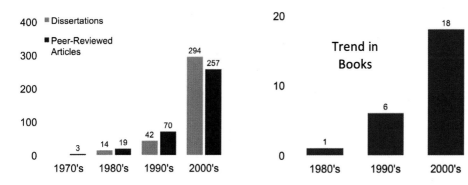

The Era of Transforming Followers
Charismatic Leadership

1977, House (1975, 1977, 1992), House, Woycke and Fodor (1988)
House, Howell and Shamir (1992), House and Shamir (1993)

Low Follower Focus		High Follower Focus
Low Leader Focus		High Leader Focus
Low Relationship		High Relationship
Low Task		High Task
Autocratic		Democratic
Theoretical		Research Based

Based on his work between 1975 and 1993, House and others developed explanations of the personal characteristics and behaviors of charismatic leaders and the effects charismatic leadership has on followers. Highlights from those articles are shown in the table below.[12]

Personality	Leader Behaviors	Effects on Followers
Extremely High Levels of Self-Confidence	Relieves Followers from Experiences of Stress and Alienation	Trust in the Leader's Ideology
Desire to Influence	Articulates Ideological Goals	Identification with the Leader
Strong Conviction in the Moral Righteousness of His/Her Beliefs	Causes Followers to Model Their Behaviors, Feelings and Cognitions after the Leader	Belief Similarity Between the Leader and the Follower
Dominant	Motivates Followers to Transcend Their Own Self-Interests for the Sake of the Team, the Organization or the Larger Collective	Unquestioning Acceptance
Expresses Confidence	Arouses Motives Relevant to the Accomplishment of the Mission	Affection Toward the Leader
	Raises Followers to Higher Levels of Morality	Obedience Toward the Leader
	Defines These Goals in Appealing Ideological Terms	Emotional Involvement with the Leader
		Belief That They Can Contribute to Goal Accomplishment
		Strive to Meet Specific and Challenging Performance Standards
		A Positive Transforming Effect on the Organizations That They Lead as Well as on Their Followers

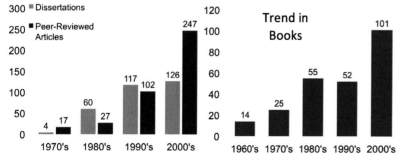

There has been a steady increase in publications on charismatic leadership in dissertations, peer-reviewed articles and books.

Since 2000, there have been over 360 peer-reviewed journal articles and dissertations and over 100 books published on the topic.

The Era of Transforming Followers
Transformational Leadership

1978, Transformational Leadership, Burns (1978)

Low Follower Focus	High Follower Focus
Low Leader Focus	High Leader Focus
Low Relationship	High Relationship
Low Task	High Task
Autocratic	Democratic
Theoretical	Research Based

While there have been many contributions to the idea of transformational leadership, the theory was first fully described in 1978 by Burns. Burns envisioned transformational and transactional leadership as separate entities.[13]

	Transformational Leadership	Transactional Leadership
Goals	The Leader and Follower Are Presently or Potentially United in the Pursuit of "Higher" Goals	The Leader and Follower Have Separate and Possibly Unrelated Goals
Interests	There is the Achievement of Significant Change That Represents the Collective or Pooled Interests of Leaders and Followers	There is a Bargain to Aid the Individual Interests of Persons or Groups Going Their Separate Ways
Relationship	The Leader Shapes, Alters and Elevates the Motives, Values and Goals of Followers Through the Vital Teaching Role of Leadership	Two Persons May Exchange Goods, Services or Other Things in Order to Realize Independent Objectives
Measures of Success	The End Results of the Transformational Relationship Are "Higher" Goals Such as Liberty, Justice and Equality	The Interactions Comprising the Exchange Have Characteristics Such as Honesty, Responsibility, Fairness and the Honoring of Commitments

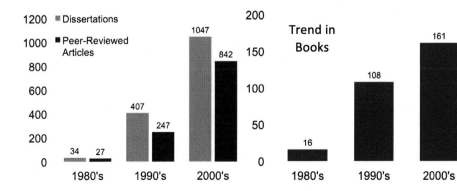

It is almost impossible to separate the results of these searches from those that include the full range model of leadership.

Nonetheless, interest in transformational leadership is still growing.

The Era of Transforming Followers
Six Sigma

1981, Six Sigma, Motorola (1981), General Electric (1995)

Low Follower Focus	High Follower Focus
Low Leader Focus	High Leader Focus
Low Relationship	High Relationship
Low Task	High Task
Autocratic	Democratic
Theoretical	Research Based

The term six sigma refers to a standard of quality that equates to 3.4 defects per one million opportunities (DPMO). This equates to 99.997% "quality." There are multiple methodologies and tools related to striving for this level of quality. Motorola, beginning in the 1980's and General Electric thereafter, each pioneered this quality technique. While methodologies vary, the chart below gives a sense of the quality tools used at each of

Performance	Defects Per Million	Sigma
30.9000%	690,000.0	1
69.2000%	308,000.0	2
93.3000%	66,800.0	3
99.4000%	620.0	4
99.9800%	320.0	5
99.9997%	3.4	6

five stages called DMAIC: define opportunities, measure performance, analyze opportunities, improve performance and control performance.[14]

Stage	Goal	Typical Statistical and Quality Tools
Define Opportunities	Identify a Long-term Quality Problem	Stakeholder Analysis, Work Breakdown Structure, Surveys, Process Charts, SIPOC Diagrams (Suppliers, Inputs, Processes, Outputs, Customers, Requirements), CTQ (Critical to Quality)
Measure Performance	Measure the Problem on a Long-Term Basis	Process Flowcharts, Benchmarking, Measurement Systems Analysis, Pareto Charts, Histograms, Process Capabilities, Control Charts, Process Sigma Calculations
Analyze Opportunities	Identify and Verify Significant Root Causes	Experimental Designs, Scatter Plots, Correlations, Time Series Charts, Pareto Charts, Cause and Effect/Fishbone Diagrams, Multiple Regression, Analyses of Variance, Cause and Effect Matrices, Failure Mode and Effect Analyses
Improve Performance	Experiment with Solutions and Validate a Solution	Experimental Designs, Criteria Based Matrices (Selecting Best Solution) Failure Mode and Effect Analyses, Poka-Yoke (Mistake-Proofing), Simulations
Control Performance	Develop a Plan to Ensure Control	Control Charts, Control Plans, Process Standardization and Documentation, New Six Sigma Calculations

	1980's	1990's	2000's
Dissertations	0	9	184
Peer-Reviewed	0	35	1,358
Books	5	199	5,072

The rise in dissertations, peer-reviewed articles and books from the 1980's through the first decade of the twentieth century has been so dramatic that the data are shown in tabular rather than graphic form.

The Era of Transforming Followers
The Full Range Model of Leadership

1985, Full Range Model of Leadership, Bass (1985, 1998, 1999)
Bass and Avolio (1994, 1995, 1996, 1997, 2002), Bass, Avolio and Jung (1999)

Low Follower Focus		High Follower Focus
Low Leader Focus		High Leader Focus
Low Relationship		High Relationship
Low Task		High Task
Autocratic		Democratic
Theoretical		Research Based

The full range model of leadership has gone through several evolutions over the past three decades. Bass (1985) built on Burns' work. Whereas Burns envisioned transformational and transactional leadership as separate entities, Bass envisioned them on a continuum. By 1991, a nine-component model was advanced and was supported by the *Multifactor Leadership Questionnaire 5X*. By 2009, the model was refined by creating a second-order component called passive-avoidant leadership.[15]

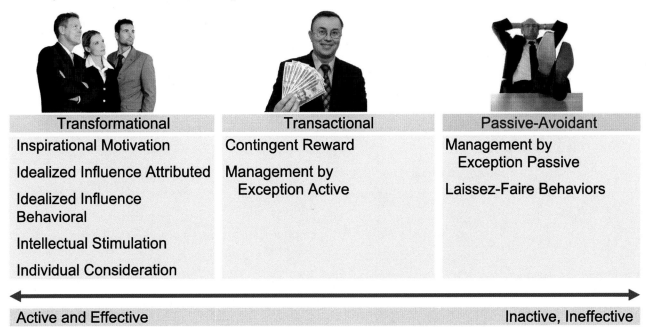

Transformational	Transactional	Passive-Avoidant
Inspirational Motivation	Contingent Reward	Management by Exception Passive
Idealized Influence Attributed	Management by Exception Active	Laissez-Faire Behaviors
Idealized Influence Behavioral		
Intellectual Stimulation		
Individual Consideration		

Active and Effective   **Inactive, Ineffective**

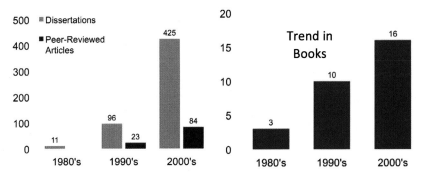

Data shown earlier for transformational leadership are different than these data. These graphs are based on the phrases "Full Range Model of Leadership" or "Multifactor Leadership Questionnaire."

Even this narrower search shows a dramatic rise in publications.

The Era of Transforming Followers
Total Quality Management

1986, Total Quality Management, Deming (1986)

Low Follower Focus	High Follower Focus
Low Leader Focus	High Leader Focus
Low Relationship	High Relationship
Low Task	High Task
Autocratic	Democratic
Theoretical	Research Based

Total quality management is a phrase used to describe various quality initiatives suggested by Deming and others. The methods were highly influenced by Japanese manufacturing methods. Deming is remembered for his 14 points from chapter 2 of his book *Out of the Crisis*.[16] The graphs below provide a sense of the widespread popularity of total quality management.

Deming's 14 Points	
Create Constancy of Purpose Toward Improvement of Products and Services	Drive out Fear
Adopt the New Economic Philosophy	Break Down Barriers Between Departments
Cease Dependence on Inspection to Achieve Quality	Eliminate Slogans, Exhortations and Targets for Workers. The Bulk of the Causes of Low Quality and Production Belong to the System Not individual Workers
End the Practice of Awarding Business (Solely) on the Basis of Price Tag	Remove Barriers That Rob Hourly Workers of Their Rights to Pride of Work
Improve Constantly and Forever the System of Production and Service, to Improve Quality and Productivity	Remove Barriers that Rob People in Management and Engineering of Their Rights to Pride of Work
Institute Training on the Job	Institute a Vigorous Program of Education and Self-Improvement
Institute Leadership to Help People, Machines and Gadgets to Do a Better Job	Put Everybody in the Company to Work to Accomplish the Transformation

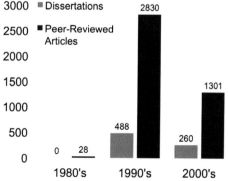

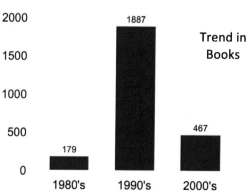

The Era of Transforming Followers
Leadership Traits Continued

1986, Traits Continued, Lord, de Vader and Alliger (1986)

Low Follower Focus		High Follower Focus
Low Leader Focus		High Leader Focus
Low Relationship		High Relationship
Low Task		High Task
Autocratic		Democratic
Theoretical		Research Based

Earlier research on leader traits tended to report the frequency of traits found in various studies. One of the problems with this approach is that a study with 50 participants carries as much weight in an analysis as a study with 5,000 participants. Each is given a frequency of 1.

Another problem with using frequency counts is that there is no sense of how strong the opinions were. If, for example, on a 5-point Likert scale, the participants in one study, on average, rated a particular trait as a 4.90 in importance, and a second study had a mean rating of 3.01, both results might be counted as reporting that that trait was important and given a frequency count of 1 – yet there is a difference in the strength of the ratings given to that trait.

Lord, de Vader and Alliger used the Schmidt-Hunter validity generalization technique in order to conduct a more sophisticated analysis than Stogdill performed, called a meta-analysis. This technique takes into account the sample size of the various studies, the strengths of the relationships found in each study as well as five other sources of "error" in studies. In order to conduct this type of meta-analysis, however, studies analyzed must include a certain minimum amount of statistical results in the article.

In the table below, k represents the number of studies meta-analyzed and N represents the total sample represented by those k studies. The *True r* (which is corrected for range restriction and unreliability) reported by Lord, de Vader and Alliger is a number between -1 and +1. In this case, all six *True r* correlations were "positive" indicating that as the variable named in each column increased, the perception of the leader improved.

Leader Traits and Leader Performance						
	Intelligence	Masculinity Femininity	Adjustment	Dominance	Extroversion	Conservatism
k	18	4	11	11	13	2
N	2,239	293	1,085	1,660	1,701	125
True r	.50	.34	.24	.13	.26	.22

k is the number of studies analyzed. For example, 18 empirical trait studies were analyzed that reported the statistical association between leader intelligence and leader performance. If we added all of the participants from those 18 studies together, there would be 2,239 participants. The *True r* indicates that the more intelligent the leader was, the higher the participants' perceptions of the leader (*True r* = .50).

121

The Era of Transforming Followers
Summary

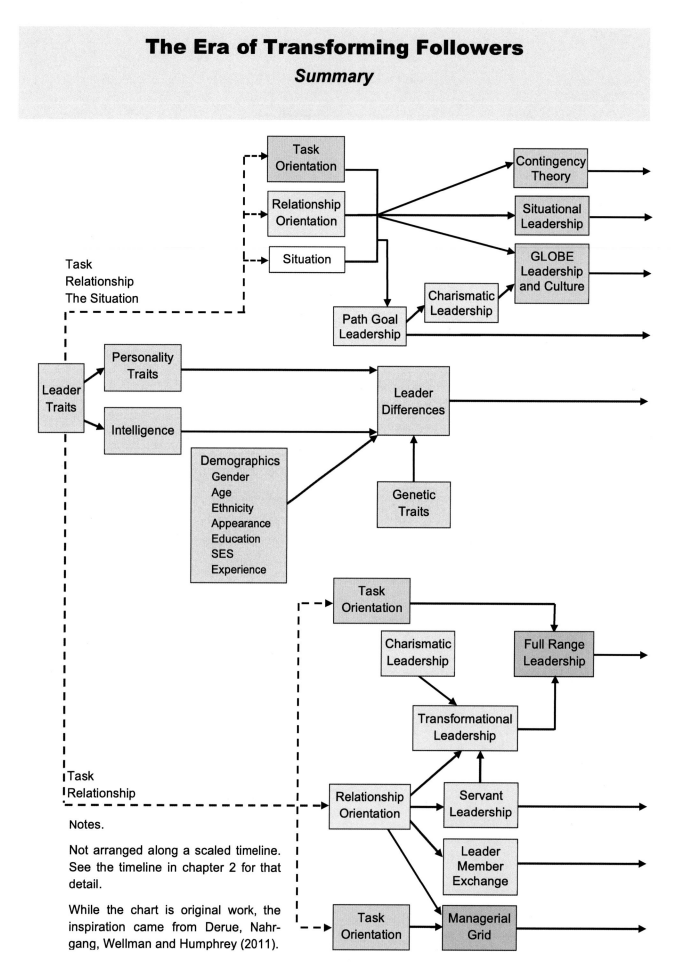

Task
Relationship
The Situation

Task
Relationship

Notes.

Not arranged along a scaled timeline. See the timeline in chapter 2 for that detail.

While the chart is original work, the inspiration came from Derue, Nahrgang, Wellman and Humphrey (2011).

The Era of Transforming Followers

Summary

The model on the opposite page builds on the model from chapter 4. As we recall, after interest in trait theory waned, interest turned to leader behaviors.

Two "branches" occurred. One group of theories tended to focus on leader emphases on tasks and relationships. The other branch added to those dimensions, some aspect of the situation in which the leader and follower relationship exists.

The branch that includes a situational element, includes contingency, situational and path-goal theories of leadership. Each theory became quite popular. House (1992) has indicated that much of his work on path-goal theory influenced his ideas on charismatic leadership. We see charismatic leadership, in turn, influencing those aspects of leadership studied in the GLOBE study. In the case of the GLOBE study, the situational element was organizational culture.

The second branch consists primarily of theories without a strong situational element. The emphases on relationships influenced leader-member exchange theory as well as servant leadership.

We see that relationship orientation, charismatic leadership and servant leadership influenced transformational leadership.

When combined with an emphasis on tasks in the form of transactional leadership, those strands influenced the full range model of leadership.

The Era of Transforming Followers
Summary

The graph below reminds us that total quality management is slowly fading in popularity while interest in six sigma is growing rapidly. Five leadership theories covered in this chapter are still very popular: leader member exchange (LMX), charismatic leadership, transformational leadership, servant leadership and the full range model of leadership.

Leader and Follower Age				70		55		40		25	
Began Work	1930's	1940's	1950's	1960's	1970's	1980's	1990's	2000's	2010's	2020's

Management Theories

	1930's	1940's	1950's	1960's	1970's	1980's	1990's	2000's	2010's	2020's
Scientific Mgt										
Satisficing										
Principles Mgt										
Organic/Mech										
Open Systems										
Dissatisfiers										
Theory X/Y										
Maslow's Hierarchy										
Bases of Power										
Total Quality Mgt										
Six Sigma										

Leadership Theories

	1930's	1940's	1950's	1960's	1970's	1980's	1990's	2000's	2010's	2020's
Traits										
Managerial Grid										
Path-Goal										
Contingency										
Situational										
Servant										
LMX										
Charismatic										
Transformational										
Full Range Model										

The Era of Transforming Followers
Key Points

In the 1970's and 1980's, the percentage of the workforce employed in tertiary professions continued to rise significantly. Most U.S. homes had a telephone, radio and television. The birth of the personal computer was just beginning. This era also witnessed a continued rise in the percentage of women in the workforce, as well as a rise in the percentage of women working in professional positions.

Several management theories had some influence on subsequent leadership and management practices. Vroom, Yetton and Jago introduced a decision matrix with seven leadership questions and suggested appropriate leadership behaviors. In 1978, Kerr and Jermier asked whether certain factors could lessen the need for leadership. They divided possible substitutes into three sources: followers, the tasks being done and the organization.

In 1978, Ouchi contrasted what he described as a typical set of American leadership/work assumptions with those that might be typical Japanese assumptions. He then proposed a hybrid set that he labeled type Z assumptions. This slowly became known as theory Z. In 1982, Peters and Waterman's bestselling book, *In Search of Excellence*, advocated taking care of both customers and followers as key ingredients of excellence.

Two management theories were extremely influential during this era. Total quality management emphasizes an array of quality initiatives. Some of the philosophies of TQM can be seen in Deming's 14 points.

Six sigma refers to a standard of quality that equates to 3.4 defects per one million opportunities (DPMO). While methodologies vary, six sigma initiatives often have five stages called DMAIC: define opportunities, measure performance, analyze opportunities, improve performance and control performance.

The Era of Transforming Followers
Key Points

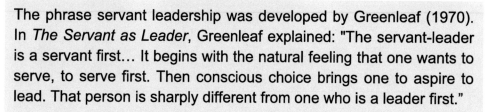

The phrase servant leadership was developed by Greenleaf (1970). In *The Servant as Leader*, Greenleaf explained: "The servant-leader is a servant first... It begins with the natural feeling that one wants to serve, to serve first. Then conscious choice brings one to aspire to lead. That person is sharply different from one who is a leader first."

House's (1971, 1996) path-goal theory advocates that leaders assist followers in determining their desired goals. Leaders assist the followers by using one or more of the following behaviors: directive path-goal clarifying leader behavior, supportive leader behavior, participative leader behavior and achievement oriented behavior.

Leader-member exchange theory, Graen and Uhl-Bien (1975), pointed out that leaders form different relationships with different followers within the same work areas – often called out-groups and in-groups. Based on this line of research, the authors identified three stages through which leader-follower relationships might progress: stranger, acquaintance and mature partnership.

While the study of charismatic leadership is not a new phenomenon, House, developed a model to explain charismatic leadership that included aspects of leader personality, leader behaviors and the effects on followers. Leader personality characteristics include: extremely high levels of self-confidence; a desire to influence others; a strong conviction in the moral righteousness of his/her beliefs; being dominant and expressing confidence.

Burns (1978) envisioned transformational and transactional leadership as separate entities. In transactional leadership, the leader and follower have separate and possibly unrelated goals. Conversely, in transformational leadership the leader and follower are presently or potentially united in the pursuit of "higher" goals.

The Era of Transforming Followers
Key Points

Whereas Burns envisioned transformational and transactional leadership as separate entities, Bass envisioned them on a continuum. By 1991, a nine-component model was advanced and was supported by the *Multifactor Leadership Questionnaire 5X*. By 2009, the model was refined by creating transformational, transactional and passive-avoidant leadership.

In 1978, Stogdill conducted a second analysis of trait studies. He found that three types of traits seemed to be related to leadership ratings: leadership skills, relationship with the group and personal characteristics. In 1986, Lord, de Vader and Alliger used the Schmidt-Hunter validity generalization technique in order to conduct a meta-analysis. They concluded that leadership perceptions were related to leader traits of intelligence, masculinity-femininity, dominance, adjustment, extroversion and conservatism.

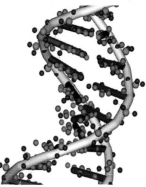

The Era of Transforming Followers
Graduate Education

By 1989 about 18% of U.S. adults held a bachelor's degree, about 4% held a masters degree and about 0.7% held a doctorate. In 1989, obtaining a graduate degree was still a rarity.

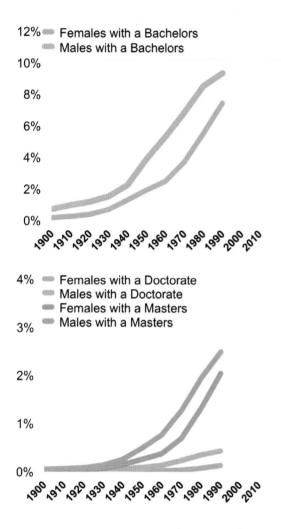

The Era of Transforming Followers
Notes

[1] Based on the Wall Street Journal article, (1998). Tuning In: Communications Technologies Historically Have Had Broad Appeal for Consumers, Wall Street Journal, Classroom Edition

[2] Based on Ouchi, W. (1981). Going from A to Z: Thirteen steps to a Theory Z organization. *Management Review*, 70(5), 8. and Daft, R. L. (2004). Theory Z: Opening the Corporate Door for Participative Management. *The Academy of Management Executive*, 18, 4, 117.

[3] Summarized from Kerr, S. and Jermier, J. (1978). Substitutes for leadership: Their meaning and measurement. *Organizational Behavior and Human Performance*, 22, 374– 403.

[4] The measures used were return on assets (ROA), return on equity (ROE), return on sales (ROS), growth in terms of assets and equity and market valuation. An additional screening was conducted for company innovation through extensive interviews in 21 of the organizations and briefer interviews in the remaining 22. Peters and Waterman advanced eight principles they believed made these organizations excellent.

For the peer reviewed and dissertation graphs "In Search of Excellence" in title or abstract and Peters in abstract of AD and PD. For books, "In Search of Excellence" in title of WC.

[5] Summarized from Peters, T. J. and Waterman, R. H. (1982). *In search of excellence: Lessons from America's best-run companies*. New York: Harper & Row.

[6] http://www.greenleaf.org/whatissl/

[7] "Servant Leadership" or "Servant Leader" in the title or abstract of AD, PD, in the title of WC.

[8] All four definitions as well as the information for the table are from House, R. J. (1996). Path-goal theory of leadership: Lessons, legacy and a reformulated theory. *Leadership Quarterly*. 323 - 340.

[9] Stogdill, R. M. (1974). *Handbook of leadership: A survey of theory and research*. New York: Free Press.

[10] Based on Graen, G. B. and Uhl-Bien, M. (1991). The transformation of professionals into self-managing and partially self-designing contributions: Toward a theory of leadership making. *Journal of Management Systems*, 3(3), 33– 48.

[11] "Leader-Member Exchange" or "Leader Member Exchange" in the title or abstract of AD, PD, in the title of WC.

[12] House, R. J. (1977) A 1976 theory of charismatic leadership. In J. G. Hunt and L. L. Larson (eds.), *Leadership: The cutting edge.* Carbondale, IL: Southern Illinois University Press.

House, R. J., Howell, J. M., Shamir, B., et al. (1992). Charismatic leadership: A 1992 theory and five empirical tests. Unpublished manuscript.

"Charismatic Leadership" or "Charismatic Leader" in title or abstract of AD, PD, in title of WC.

[13] The information for this table was garnered from pp. 425 – 427 of Burns, J. M. (1978). *Leadership.* New York: Harper & Row. Burns didn't provide a table, but these contrasts are interwoven in those pages.

The charts were obtained by putting "Transformational Leadership" or "Transformational Leader" in the title or abstract of AD and PD, and the title of WC.

[14] This table was compiled from Moosa, K. and Sajid, A. (2010). Critical analysis of Six Sigma implementation. *Total Quality Management & Business Excellence*, 21(7), 745-759 and isixsigma.com

[15] "Full Range Model of Leadership" or "Full Range Leadership" or "Multifactor Leadership Questionnaire" in the title or abstract of AD and PD, and the title of WC.

[16] These principles are almost verbatim from Deming.org. In a few cases, a word was deleted in a sentence to assist in getting all 14 points onto one page.

Chapter 6
The Search for the Successor to Transformational Leadership

The Search for the Successor to Transformational Leadership
Predominant Management and Leadership Theories

Transformational leadership was an extraordinarily popular leadership paradigm in the 1980's. This popularity, however, also continued into the 1990's and the first decade of the twenty-first century.

During the era of the 1990's and 2000's two new leadership theories, the implicit dimensions of leadership measured by project GLOBE and authentic leadership influenced attitudes about leadership. Personality and emotional intelligence were also increasingly used to measure associations with effective leadership. Additionally, the idea of innate traits began re-emerging as a result of studies of heredity and the human genome.

The radical ways in which the Internet changed how we communicate and work influenced ideas posited in several best-selling management/leadership books. These books challenged managers and leaders to reengineer their processes with an eye on the disruptive technologies of the future. Ideas by Hammer and Champy, Collins and Porras, Hamel and Prahalad, and Collins will each be summarized in the first part of this chapter.

Senge's ideas about learning organizations and those theories shown in blue will be reviewed in the second part of the chapter.

The Search for the Successor to Transformational Leadership		
1990	Big-Five Personality	McCrae and Costa (1987, 1990, 2010)
1990	Emotional Intelligence	Salovey and Mayer (1990), Goleman (1995) Bar-On (1997), Mayer, Salovey and Caruso (2004)
1990	Learning Organizations	Senge (1990)
1993	Reengineering	Hammer (1990), Hammer and Champy (1993)
1994	Built to Last	Collins and Porras (1994, 1996)
1996	Competing for the Future	Hamel and Prahalad (1994,1996)
2001	Good to Great	Collins (2001)
2004	The Global Leadership and Organizational Behavior Effectiveness (GLOBE) Project	Den Hartog, House, Hanges, Ruiz-Quintanilla, Dorfman, Ashkanasy and Falkus (1999) House and GLOBE Research Team (2004, 2012)
2007	Authentic Leadership	Avolio, Gardner and Walumbwa (2007), Walumbwa, Avolio, Gardner, Wernsing and Peterson (2008)
2011	Traits Continued	Derue, Nahrgang, Wellman and Humphrey (2011)
2000's	Genetic Studies	Li, Arvey, Zhang and Song (2011) Chaturvedi, Arvey, Zhangmand and Christoforou (2011) Loehlin, McCrae, Costa and John (1998)

1990 - 2009

In the period between 1990 and 2009, we see a decline in the percentage of the workforce who worked in primary (those acquiring raw materials) and secondary occupations (those converting, distributing and repairing things made from raw materials) and a rise in the percentage of the workforce who worked in tertiary occupations (professionals, technical workers and service workers)[1]

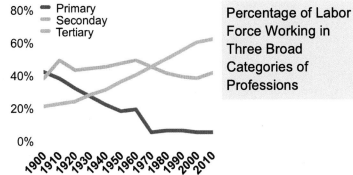

Percentage of Labor Force Working in Three Broad Categories of Professions

By 2009, approximately 71% of men and 58% of women were working outside the home.

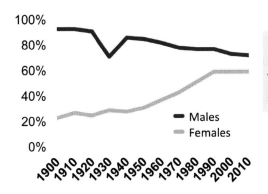

Percentage of Men and Percentage of Women Working Outside the Home

Approximately 62% of married and 64% of single women worked outside the home.

Percentage of Single Women and Percentage of Married Women Working Outside the Home

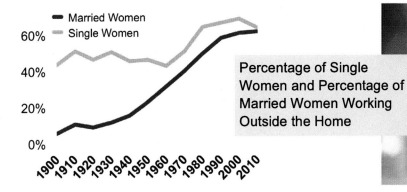

135

The Search for the Successor to
Transformational Leadership
Societal Influences

By 2009, we also see what is often called the digital convergence, in which the lines between what is a computer, phone, video source and so forth became a bit blurred. By 2010, most U.S. households had a cell phone and cable television. About 80% had some form of computer and about 77% had Internet access.[2]

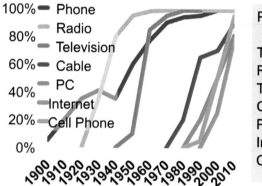

Legend:
- Phone
- Radio
- Television
- Cable
- PC
- Internet
- Cell Phone

Percentage of
Homes with a
Telephone
Radio
Television
Cable Television
Personal Computer
Internet Access
Cell Phone

By 2009, the unemployment rate was nearing 9%. The participation rate in labor unions had become steady at around 12%.

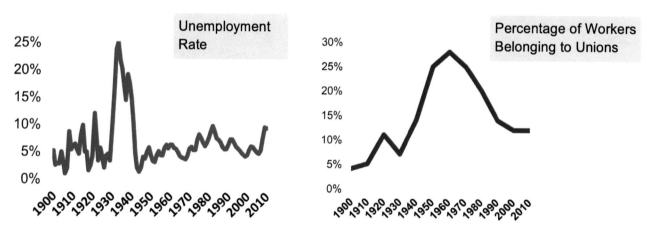

Unemployment Rate

Percentage of Workers Belonging to Unions

By 2009, approximately 21% of US adults held a bachelors degree. A little over 7% held a masters degree and less than 1% a doctorate.

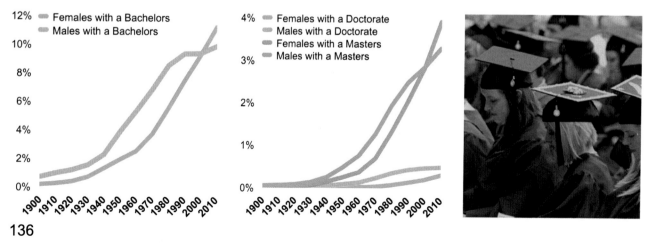

Legend (left chart):
- Females with a Bachelors
- Males with a Bachelors

Legend (right chart):
- Females with a Doctorate
- Males with a Doctorate
- Females with a Masters
- Males with a Masters

The Search for the Successor to Transformational Leadership
Technological Influences

1982	1992	2002	2012
Mobira Senator	Nokia 1011	Blackberry 5810	IPhone 5
Approximately	Approximately	Approximately	Approximately
$6,000	$600	$500	$200

Although we instinctively know that technology regularly becomes more powerful and less expensive, it helps to stop and actually envision that trend.

In 1982, the first "cell-phone" weighed 21 pounds and cost approximately $6,000, 1982 dollars. By contrast, the IPhone 5 weighed 4 ounces and cost approximately $200, 2013 dollars.

What we think of as a computer also made the same transition from slow and expensive to powerful and inexpensive. The use of the computer transitioned from an isolated portion of the workforce performing specialized tasks to general use by the majority of the workforce. Additional components were added to the PC that allowed computers to transmit and receive data from other connected computers. Collaborative tools such as email and instant messaging were also created. A desktop computer didn't change much in appearance. We still had monitors, mice and keyboards, but the speed/power increased dramatically.

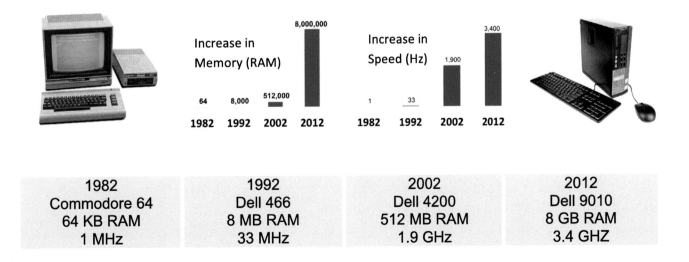

1982	1992	2002	2012
Commodore 64	Dell 466	Dell 4200	Dell 9010
64 KB RAM	8 MB RAM	512 MB RAM	8 GB RAM
1 MHz	33 MHz	1.9 GHz	3.4 GHZ

The Search for the Successor to Transformational Leadership
Technological Influences

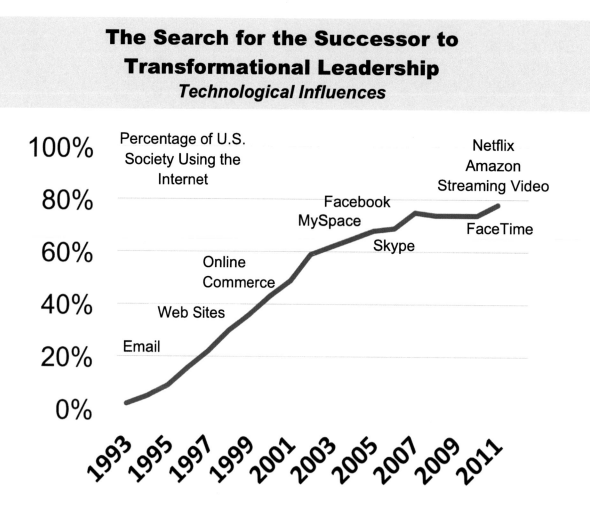

The most dramatic revolution during this era was that of connectivity. In 1990, the "Internet" was primarily a text-based connection of academic and scientific computers designed to share research types of data.

By the early 1990's, "modems" allowed individual users to connect their home or business computers to their telephone line and connect to the Internet.

Very quickly, both telephone and cable companies began increasing the capacity to carry digital information into households and workplaces.

In the latter-half of the 1990's, companies that were early innovators such as Amazon began selling products on-line.

By 2003, popular "social media" sites such as MySpace and Facebook began.

By 2005, early video-conferencing technologies such as Skype entered the marketplace, followed by Apple's FaceTime in 2012.

Although the technology for streaming video over the Internet existed in the mid-1990's, bandwidth into homes was insufficient to exploit this technology. By 2011, though, major providers such as Netflix and Amazon began streaming content across the Internet to televisions and portable devices.

The Search for the Successor to Transformational Leadership
Somewhat Influential Management and Leadership Theories

Four theories from this era have had some impact on the development of subsequent theories of leadership. All four were books written as the Internet and e-business revolution was changing many of the challenges confronting leaders and managers.

Somewhat Influential Theories		
1993	Reengineering	Hammer and Champy (1990, 1993)
1994	Built to Last	Collins and Porras (1994, 1996)
1996	Competing for the Future	Hamel and Prahalad (1994, 1996)
2001	Good to Great	Collins (2001)

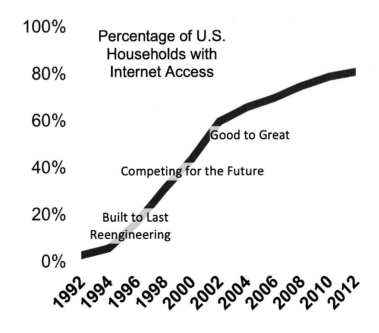

The Search for the Successor to
Transformational Leadership
Reengineering the Corporation

1993, Reengineering the Corporation, Hammer (1990)
Hammer and Champy (1993)

Low Follower Focus		High Follower Focus
Low Leader Focus		High Leader Focus
Low Relationship		High Relationship
Low Task		High Task
Autocratic		Democratic
Theoretical		Research Based

Reengineering the Corporation was the first of a series of books imploring leaders and managers to change their methods, called processes, as a result of the Internet revolution. Hammer described reengineering as "the notion of discontinuous thinking - of recognizing and breaking away from the outdated rules and fundamental assumptions that underlie operations." (1990, p. 107)

In his 1990 *Harvard Business Review* article, Hammer provided the following seven principles for how to reengineer business processes.

Organize around outcomes, not tasks.

Have those who use the output of the process perform the process.

Subsume information-processing work into the real work that produces the information.

Treat geographically dispersed resources as though they were centralized.

Link parallel activities instead of integrating their results.

Put the decision point where the work is performed and build control into the process.

Capture information once and at the source.

It is difficult to separate articles, dissertations and books specifically referencing Hammer and Champy's methodology from the more general idea of reengineering. However, using the term reengineering in the title, only one article was published before 1990.[3]

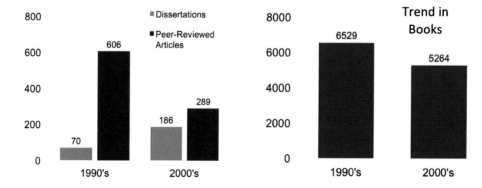

The Search for the Successor to Transformational Leadership
Built to Last

1994, Built to Last, Collins and Porras (1994, 1996)

Low Follower Focus		High Follower Focus
Low Leader Focus		High Leader Focus
Low Relationship		High Relationship
Low Task		High Task
Autocratic		Democratic
Theoretical		Research Based

Collins and Porras studied 36 companies. They classified within different industries, a visionary company contrasted with a company that might be successful, but was not visionary. They broadly defined visionary as a) a premier institution in its industry, b) widely admired by knowledgeable businesspeople, c) made an indelible imprint on the world in which we live, d) had multiple generations of chief executives, e) had been through multiple product (or service) life cycles and f) was founded before 1950.

Based on their analysis of the differences between the visionary and non-visionary companies, Collins and Porras developed what they called *Twelve Shattered Myths*.

1. It takes a great idea to start a great company.
2. Visionary companies require great and charismatic visionary leaders.
3. The most successful companies exist first and foremost to maximize profits.
4. Visionary companies share a common subset of "correct" core values.
5. The only constant is change.
6. Blue-chip companies play it safe.
7. Visionary companies are great places to work, for everyone.
8. Highly successful companies make their best moves by brilliant and complex strategic planning.
9. Companies should hire outside CEO's to stimulate fundamental change.
10. The most successful companies focus primarily on beating the competition.
11. You can't have your cake and eat it too.
12. Companies become visionary primarily through "vision statements."

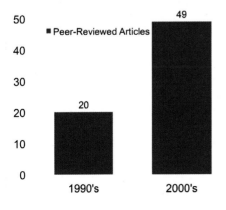

No dissertations using *Built to Last* in the title and connoting the Collins and Porras model were located. Although approximately 30 books were found that used the term *Built to Last* in their title, none besides versions of the Collins and Porras book(s) were related to this theory. About 70 peer-reviewed articles, however, have been written about this particular theory.

The Search for the Successor to Transformational Leadership
Competing for the Future

1996, Competing for the Future, Hamel and Prahalad (1994, 1996)

Low Follower Focus			High Follower Focus	
Low Leader Focus			High Leader Focus	
Low Relationship			High Relationship	
Low Task			High Task	
Autocratic			Democratic	
Theoretical			Research Based	

Hamel and Prahalad's article in *Harvard Business Review*, and subsequent best-selling book,[4] were targeted toward senior executives. The book provided ideas about how to think strategically about a rapidly changing world. One of the arguments Hamel and Prahalad made was what they called the 40/30/20 rule.

Looking Outward		Looking Inward
> 3 Years	< 3 Years	
Not Collective		

Their beliefs are that about 40% of a senior executive's time is devoted to looking outward. About 30% of that time is spent peering three or more years into the future. Of the time spent looking forward, no more than 20% is devoted to building a collective view of the future (the other 80% is spent considering the future of the manager's particular business). Hamel and Prahalad used the table below to explain competing for the future.

Not Only	But Also
The Competitive Challenge	
Reengineering Processes	Regenerating Strategies
Organizational Transformation	Industry Transformation
Competing for Market Share	Competing for Opportunity Share
Finding the Future	
Strategy is Learning	Strategy is Forgetting
Strategy is Positioning	Strategy is Foresight
Strategic Plans	Strategic Architecture
Mobilizing for the Future	
Strategy as Fit	Strategy as Stretch
Strategy as Resource Allocation	Strategy as Resource Accumulation and Leverage
Getting to the Future First	
Competing Within an Existing Industry Structure	Competing to Shape Future Industry Structure
Competing for Product Leadership	Competing for Core Competence
Competing as a Single Entity	Competing as a Coalition
Maximizing the Ratio of New Products	Maximizing the Rate of New Market Learning
Minimizing Time to Market	Minimizing Time to Global Preemption

The Search for the Successor to Transformational Leadership
Good to Great

2001, Good to Great, Collins (2001)

Low Follower Focus		High Follower Focus
Low Leader Focus		High Leader Focus
Low Relationship		High Relationship
Low Task		High Task
Autocratic		Democratic
Theoretical		Research Based

Collins compared companies that had made a leap from being good to being great. The appendix to his book provided details of the various selection criteria he used in the study. As part of the study, Collins identified what he called *Level 5 Executives* (leaders). These leaders were often able to move organizations from good to great.

Level 5 Leader	Builds Enduring Greatness Through a Paradoxical Blend of Personal Humility and Professional Will
Effective Leader	Catalyzes Commitment To and Vigorous Pursuit of a Clear and Compelling Vision, Stimulating Higher Performance Standards
Competent Manager	Organizes People and Resources Toward the Effective and Efficient Pursuit of Predetermined Objectives
Contributing Team Member	Contributes Individual Capabilities To the Achievement of Group Objectives and Works Effectively With Others in a Group Setting
Highly Capable Individual	Makes Productive Contributions through Talent, Knowledge, Skills and Good Work Habits

Collins suggested that the characteristics of professional will and personal humility were vital to becoming a *Level 5 Leader*. About 60 peer-reviewed articles have been published on these ideas.

Professional Will	Personal Humility
Creates Superb Results, a Clear Catalyst in the Transition from Good to Great	Demonstrates a Compelling Modesty, Shunning Public Adulation; Never Boastful
Demonstrates an Unwavering Resolve to Do Whatever Must be Done to Produce the Best Long-Term Results, No Matter How Difficult	Acts with Quiet, Calm Determination; Relies Principally on Inspired Standards, Not Inspiring Charisma, to Motivate
Sets the Standard of Building an Enduring Great Company; Will Settle for Nothing Less	Channels Ambition into the Company, Not the Self; Sets Up Successors for Even Greater Success in the Next Generation
Looks in the Mirror, Not out the Window to Apportion Responsibility for Poor Results, Never Blaming Other People, External Factors or Bad Luck	Looks Out the Window, Not in the Mirror to Apportion Credit for the Success of the Company to Other People, External Factors and Good Luck

The Search for the Successor to
Transformational Leadership
Very Influential Management and Leadership Theories

Using the salad analogy from chapter 2, the theories below are lettuce, tomatoes, olives and cheese in the organizational leadership salad.

	Very Influential Theories	
1990	Big-Five Personality	McCrae and Costa (1990), Goldberg (1990) Costa and McCrae (1992)
1990	Learning Organizations	Senge (1990)
1995	Emotional Intelligence	Salovey and Mayer (1990), Goleman (1995) Bar-On (1997), Mayer, Salovey, and Caruso (2004)
2004	The Global Leadership and Organizational Behavior Effectiveness (GLOBE) Project	Den Hartog, House, Hanges, Ruiz-Quintanilla, Dorfman, Ashkanasy and Falkus (1999) House and GLOBE Research Team (2004, 2012)
2007	Authentic Leadership	Avolio, Gardner and Walumbwa (2007), Walumbwa, Avolio, Gardner, Wernsing and Peterson (2008)
2011	Traits Continued	Derue, Nahrgang, Wellman and Humphrey (2011)
2000's	Genetic Studies	Li, Arvey, Zhang and Song (2011) Chaturvedi, Arvey, Zhangmand and Christoforou (2011) Loehlin, McCrae, Costa and John (1998)

The Search for the Successor to Transformational Leadership
Personality

1990, McCrae and Costa (1987, 1990, 2010)

Low Follower Focus		High Follower Focus
Low Leader Focus		High Leader Focus
Low Relationship		High Relationship
Low Task		High Task
Autocratic		Democratic
Theoretical		Research Based

Hundreds of researchers have contributed to our understanding of personality. Over the past few decades, a model has evolved that describes personality using five factors. The general term for this description of personality is the five-factor model (FFM) or the big five model of personality.

Extraversion	Agreeableness	Openness to New Experiences	Conscientiousness	Neuroticism
Warmth	Trust	Fantasy	Competence	Anxiety
Gregariousness	Straight	Aesthetics	Order	Hostility
Assertiveness	Forwardness	Feelings	Dutifulness	Depression
Activity	Altruism	Actions	Achievement	Self-
Excitement	Compliance	Ideas	Striving	Consciousness
Seeking	Modesty	Values	Self-Discipline	Impulsiveness
Positive Emotions	Tendermindedness		Deliberation	Vulnerability

Personality has been studied so extensively that there are over 90 meta-analyses on things that are related to personality. Leadership researchers, of course, have also studied leader personality. Generally, extraversion, agreeableness and openness are often associated with effective leadership, and neuroticism and lack of conscientiousness with ineffective leadership.

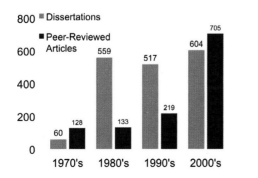

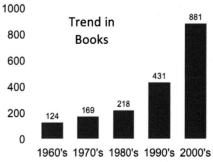

The Search for the Successor to Transformational Leadership
The Fifth Discipline and The Learning Organization

1990, The Fifth Discipline and The Learning Organization, Senge (1990)

Low Follower Focus		High Follower Focus
Low Leader Focus		High Leader Focus
Low Relationship		High Relationship
Low Task		High Task
Autocratic		Democratic
Theoretical		Research Based

Senge defined learning organizations as "organizations where people continually expand their capacity to create the results they truly desire, where new and expansive patterns of thinking are nurtured, where collective aspiration is set free, and where people are continually learning how to learn together." He argued that five disciplines help to create a learning organization.[5]

Systems Thinking	Using Tools to Develop a Conceptual Framework Using a Body of Knowledge to Make Full Patterns Clearer Thinking About How to Change Patterns Effectively
Personal Mastery	Continually Clarifying and Deepening Our Personal Vision Focusing Our Energies, Developing Patience, Seeing Reality Objectively Personal Mastery is the Cornerstone of the Learning Organization Personal Mastery is the Learning Organization's Spiritual Foundation
Mental Models	Deeply Ingrained Assumptions and Generalizations Pictures or Images That Influence How We Understand the World
Shared Vision	Unearthing Shared "Pictures of the Future" Fostering Genuine Commitment Rather Than Compliance

Team Learning	Developing Group Problem Solving and Learning
	Individual Members Grow More Rapidly than on Their Own
	Dialogue, Which Consists of:
	    The Capacity of Members of a Team to Suspend
	        Assumptions and Enter into a Genuine "Thinking Together"
	    Learning How to Recognize the Patterns of Interaction in
	        Teams That Undermine Learning

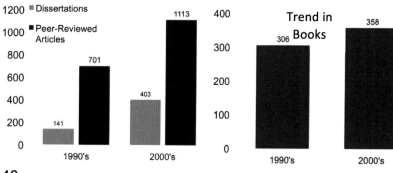

Senge's ideas continue to be very popular. Over 1,800 peer-reviewed articles and 650 books have been published on the topic.[6]

The Search for the Successor to Transformational Leadership
Emotional Intelligence

1990, Emotional Intelligence, Salovey and Mayer (1990), Goleman (1995) Bar-On (1997), Mayer, Salovey and Caruso (2004)

Low Follower Focus		High Follower Focus
Low Leader Focus		High Leader Focus
Low Relationship		High Relationship
Low Task		High Task
Autocratic		Democratic
Theoretical		Research Based

There are several models of emotional intelligence. Two popular approaches are those of Mayer, Salovey and Caruso and those of Bar-On. The Bar-On *Emotional Quotient Inventory* (EQ-i)[7] is a five-dimension model[8] and the *Mayer-Salovey-Caruso Emotional Intelligence Test* (MSCEIT)[9] is a four-dimension model.

Mayer, Salovey and Caruso Four Dimension Model, Measured by the MSCEIT
Perceiving Emotions
The Ability to Perceive Emotions in Oneself and Others as Well as in Objects, Art, Stories, Music and Other Stimuli
Facilitating Emotions
The Ability to Generate, Use, and Feel Emotion as Necessary to Communicate Feelings or Employ Them in Other Cognitive Processes
Understanding Emotions
The Ability to Understand Emotional Information, to Understand How Emotions Combine and Progress Through Relationship Transitions and to Appreciate Such Emotional Meanings
Managing Emotions
The Ability to Be Open to Feelings, and to Modulate Them in Oneself and Others so as to Promote Personal Understanding and Growth

Bar-On Five Dimension Model, Measured by the Bar-On EQ-i	
Intrapersonal	
Self-Regard Emotional Self-Awareness	Assertiveness Independence Self-Actualization
Interpersonal	
Empathy Social Responsibility	Interpersonal Relationship
Adaptability	
Problem Solving Reality Testing	Flexibility
Stress-Management	
Stress Tolerance Impulse Control	
General Mood	
Happiness Optimism	

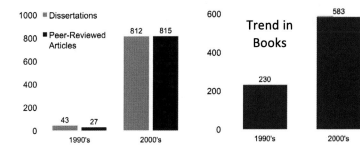

The increase in peer-reviewed articles, dissertations and books on the subject of emotional intelligence in the period between 2000-2009 was dramatic.

The Search for the Successor to Transformational Leadership
The GLOBE Project

2004, The Global Leadership and Organizational Behavior Effectiveness (GLOBE) Project, House et al., (1999, 2004, 2012)

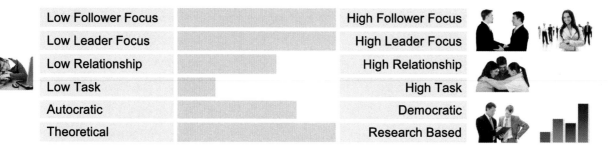

Low Follower Focus	High Follower Focus
Low Leader Focus	High Leader Focus
Low Relationship	High Relationship
Low Task	High Task
Autocratic	Democratic
Theoretical	Research Based

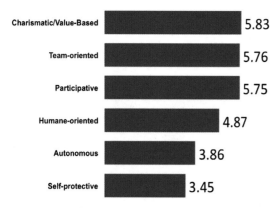

Charismatic/Value-Based	5.83
Team-oriented	5.76
Participative	5.75
Humane-oriented	4.87
Autonomous	3.86
Self-protective	3.45

The GLOBE project asked 17,370 middle managers from 951 organizations in 62 societies to indicate the degree to which different leadership behaviors contributed to or inhibited outstanding leadership.

On a scale of 1 – 7, charismatic/value-based, team-oriented and participative leadership were considered important worldwide. Conversely, self-protective leader behaviors were believed to inhibit being an outstanding leader.[10]

Project GLOBE Leadership Dimensions	
Charismatic/ Value-Based Leadership	Is the ability to inspire, to motivate and to expect high performance outcomes from others on the basis of firmly held core beliefs. These leaders are visionary, inspirational, engage in self-sacrifice, demonstrate integrity and are decisive and performance-oriented.
Team-Oriented Leadership	Emphasizes effective team building and implementation of a common purpose or goal among team members. Team-oriented leaders are collaborative integrators who are diplomatic, benevolent, administratively competent and procedural.
Participative Leadership	Is the degree to which leaders involve others in making and implementing decisions. Participative leaders emphasize democratic and participative decision-making.
Humane-Oriented Leadership	Reflects supportive and considerate leadership, but also includes compassion, modesty, generosity and an emphasis on being humane.
Autonomous Leadership	Refers to independent and individualistic leadership attributes. Autonomous leaders emphasize individualism, independence and autonomy and have unique attributes.
Self-Protective Leadership	Focuses on ensuring the safety and security of the individual and group through status enhancement and face saving.

The Search for the Successor to Transformational Leadership
Authentic Leadership

2007, Authentic Leadership, Avolio, Gardner and Walumbwa (2007)
Walumbwa, Avolio, Gardner, Wernsing and Peterson (2008)

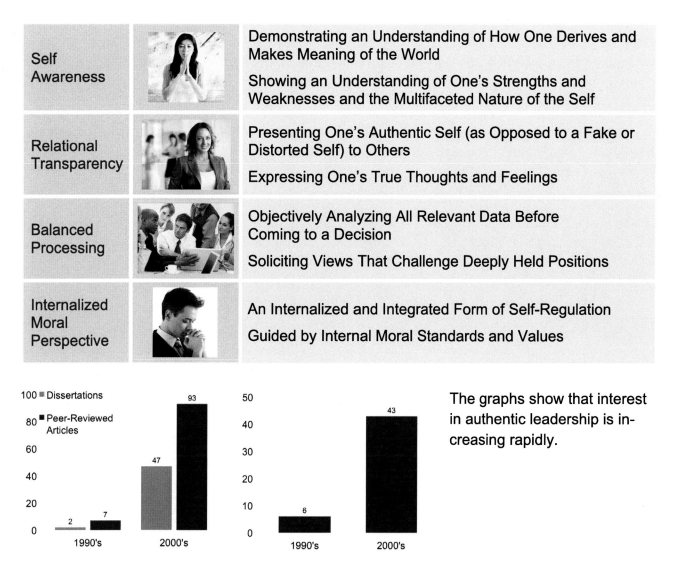

Low Follower Focus		High Follower Focus
Low Leader Focus		High Leader Focus
Low Relationship		High Relationship
Low Task		High Task
Autocratic		Democratic
Theoretical		Research Based

Empirical models to describe being an authentic leader are still evolving, and it is difficult to pinpoint the exact origins of the idea.[11] A leading instrument to measure authentic leadership is the *Authentic Leadership Questionnaire*, by Avolio, Gardner and Walumbwa.[12]

Self Awareness		Demonstrating an Understanding of How One Derives and Makes Meaning of the World
		Showing an Understanding of One's Strengths and Weaknesses and the Multifaceted Nature of the Self
Relational Transparency		Presenting One's Authentic Self (as Opposed to a Fake or Distorted Self) to Others
		Expressing One's True Thoughts and Feelings
Balanced Processing		Objectively Analyzing All Relevant Data Before Coming to a Decision
		Soliciting Views That Challenge Deeply Held Positions
Internalized Moral Perspective		An Internalized and Integrated Form of Self-Regulation
		Guided by Internal Moral Standards and Values

The graphs show that interest in authentic leadership is increasing rapidly.

- 100 ■ Dissertations
- 80 ■ Peer-Reviewed Articles

1990's	2000's
2, 7	47, 93

1990's	2000's
6	43

The Search for the Successor to Transformational Leadership
Traits Continued

2011, Traits Continued, Derue, Nahrgang, Wellman and Humphrey (2011)

Derue, Nahrgang, Wellman and Humphrey added two points of clarity to discussions about leader traits. First, they proposed an *Integrated Model of Leader Traits, Behaviors and Effectiveness*. As part of this model, they proposed a broad category called *Leader Traits and Characteristics*, which includes the three categories below.

Demographics	Task Competence	Interpersonal Attributes
Gender	Intelligence	Extraversion
Age	Conscientiousness	Agreeableness
Ethnicity	Openness to Experience	Communication Skills
Height	Emotional Stability	Emotional Intelligence
Weight	Technical Knowledge	Political Skills
Education	Leadership Self-Efficacy	
Social Status		

Second, they performed a multiple regression, not on data from a single study, but on the variables below that had previously been analyzed. Their study used 59 studies consisting of 13 previous meta-analyses and 46 primary studies. This resulted in 143 bivariate relationships that were used in the multiple regressions to predict leader effectiveness, follower job satisfaction and follower satisfaction with their leader.

Their results pointed to leader behaviors, particularly consideration, transformational leadership, contingent reward and not being passive-avoidant, as more important in predicting leadership outcomes than leader personality, intelligence or gender.[13]

Leader Trait/Behavior	Leader Effectiveness Total R^2 = .58	Follower Job Satisfaction Total R^2 = .56	Satisfaction with Leader Total R^2 = .92
Consideration	11.9% (Positively Related)	15.5% (Positively Related)	41.7% (Positively Related)
Contingent Reward	15.8% (Positively Related)	38.7% (Positively Related)	8.3% (Positively Related)
Transformational	14.5% (Positively Related)	17.7% (Positively Related)	15.1% (Positively Related)
Initiating Structure	7.8% (Positively Related)	3.0% (Positively Related)	6.3% (Positively Related)
Conscientiousness	6.0% (Positively Related)	3.7% (Negatively Related)	6.3% (Negatively Related)
Extraversion	7.0% (Positively Related)	0.7% (Positively Related)	4.3% (Positively Related)
Openness	6.2% (Positively Related)	0.2% (Positively Related)	0.5% (Positively Related)
Emotional Stability	3.9% (Positively Related)	0.2% (Positively Related)	0.4% (Positively Related)
Laissez-Faire	20.0% (Negatively Related)	3.7% (Negatively Related)	3.7% (Negatively Related)
MBE Passive	1.7% (Negatively Related)	13.6% (Negatively Related)	3.7% (Negatively Related)

Other Variables with Little Influence: Agreeableness, Gender, Intelligence and MBE Active[14]

Genetic Studies

To estimate the impact of heredity on our behaviors, a frequently used method is to study twins.

An advantage of using twins is that a reasonable assumption is that, for twins raised in the same household, environmental factors for each twin, such as attractiveness, their home life, pre-college schools attended and so forth are often similar for both twins.

Large sample sets of twins are studied. If the *Identical* (monozygotic) twins, on average, tend to be different on a measure of interest than the *Fraternal* (dizygotic) twins, the influences can be estimated for both the environmental experiences after the twins became adults and led somewhat separate lives as well as the genetic effects.

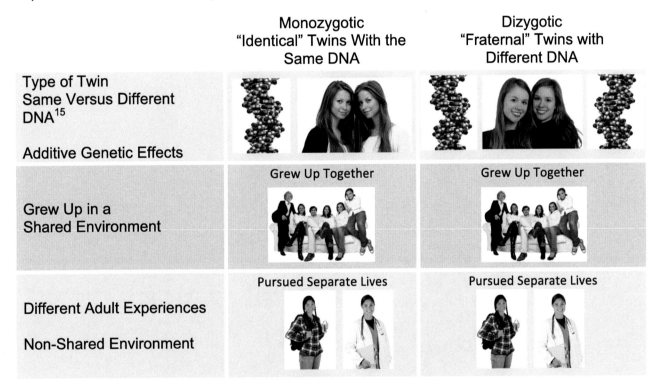

	Monozygotic "Identical" Twins With the Same DNA	Dizygotic "Fraternal" Twins with Different DNA
Type of Twin Same Versus Different DNA[15] Additive Genetic Effects		
Grew Up in a Shared Environment	Grew Up Together	Grew Up Together
Different Adult Experiences Non-Shared Environment	Pursued Separate Lives	Pursued Separate Lives

The results of twin studies have estimated that somewhere around 50% of the variance in both personality and transformational leadership can be explained by genetic factors.[16]

	Transformational Leadership (TF)	Leadership Role Occupancy (LRO)	LRO and TF	Personality
Hereditability Estimate	48% Li et al., 2012	30% Arvey et al., 2006		50% Loehlin et al., 1998
	59% Johnson et al., 1998			
	49% Chaturvedi et al., 2011			
Same Genetic Factors			13% Li et al., 2012	

The Search for the Successor to Transformational Leadership
Summary

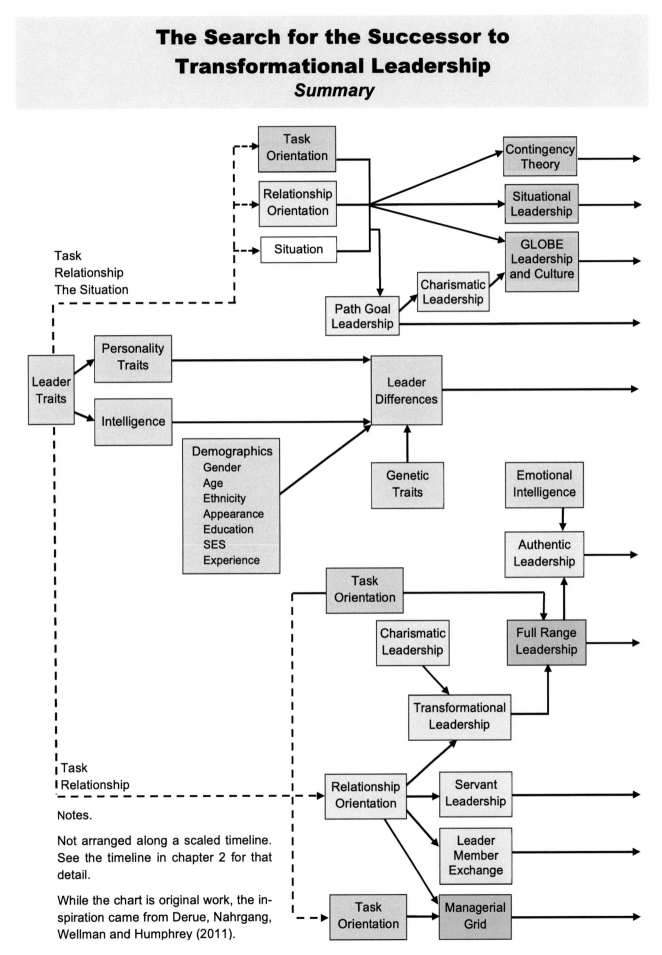

Notes.

Not arranged along a scaled timeline. See the timeline in chapter 2 for that detail.

While the chart is original work, the inspiration came from Derue, Nahrgang, Wellman and Humphrey (2011).

The Search for the Successor to Transformational Leadership
Summary

The graph below reminds us that the most enduring new management theory from this era was Senge's fifth discipline and learning organizations.

Leader and Follower Age				70		55		40		25	
Began Work	1930's	1940's	1950's	1960's	1970's	1980's	1990's	2000's	2010's	2020's

Management Theories										
	1930's	1940's	1950's	1960's	1970's	1980's	1990's	2000's	2010's	2020's
Scientific Mgt										
Satisficing										
Principles Mgt										
Organic/Mech										
Open Systems										
Dissatisfiers										
Theory X/Y										
Maslow's Hierarchy										
Bases of Power										
Total Quality Mgt										
Six Sigma										
Learning Orgs										

The Search for the Successor to Transformational Leadership
Summary

Four noteworthy areas of research in leadership emerged during this era.

Big-five personality research on leaders continues to be very popular.

Project GLOBE's seminal research on attitudes about leadership and culture around the planet was a landmark study. Recently, the third stage of GLOBE research has been completed, which analyzed CEO leadership around the planet.

Authentic leadership is the focus of a great deal of current research.

Research on the genetic contribution to leader emergence, style and effectiveness is in its infancy but will undoubtedly grow over the next few decades.

Leader and Follower Age				70		55	40		25	
Began Work	1930's	1940's	1950's	1960's	1970's	1980's	1990's	2000's	2010's	2020's

Leadership Theories										
Began Work	1930's	1940's	1950's	1960's	1970's	1980's	1990's	2000's	2010's	2020's
Traits										
Managerial Grid										
Path-Goal										
Contingency										
Situational										
Servant										
LMX										
Charismatic										
Transformational										
Full Range Model										
Personality										
Project GLOBE										
Authentic										
Genetics										

The Search for the Successor to
Transformational Leadership
Key Points

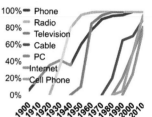

By 2009, we saw what is often called the digital convergence, in which the lines between what is a computer, phone, video source and so forth became a bit blurred. By 2009, most U.S. households had a cell phone and cable television. About 80% had some form of computer and about 77% had Internet access.

By 2009, approximately 21% of U.S. adults held a bachelors degree. About 7% held a masters degree and less than 1% a doctorate. More members of US society were working in tertiary professions and more women were working outside the home.

Reengineering (1993) emerged at the time that the Internet revolution was challenging us to move from paper-oriented forms to digital processes. Collins and Porras (1994) and Collins (2001) compared companies across different types of industries to determine what made some companies be built for lasting greatness. As part of that research, they described what they considered to be aspects of successful *Level 5 Leadership*. Hamel and Prahalad (1996) argued that about 40% of a senior executive's time is devoted to looking outward and about 30% of that time is spent peering three or more years into the future. Of the time spent looking forward, no more than 20% is devoted to building a collective view of the future.

The field of personality has been studied so extensively that there are over 90 meta-analyses on things that are related to personality. Leadership researchers have also studied leader personality.

Generally, extraversion, agreeableness and openness are often associated with effective leadership, and neuroticism and lack of conscientiousness with ineffective leadership.

The Search for the Successor to Transformational Leadership
Key Points

Senge (1990) argued that leaders of learning organizations engage in five disciplines: systems thinking, personal mastery, mental models, shared vision and team learning.

Mayer, Salovey and Caruso developed a four-dimension model of emotional intelligence that is measured by the MSCEIT. Their four dimensions are perceiving emotions, facilitating emotions, understanding emotions and managing emotions. Bar-On developed a five-dimension model of emotional intelligence that is measured by the EQ-i. His five dimensions are: intrapersonal, interpersonal, adaptability, stress-management and general mood.

The GLOBE project asked 17,370 middle managers from 951 organizations in 62 societies to indicate the degree to which different leadership behaviors contributed to or inhibited outstanding leadership.

Charismatic/value-based, team-oriented and participative leadership were considered important worldwide. Conversely, self-protective leader behaviors were believed to inhibit being an outstanding leader.

Empirical models to describe being an authentic leader are still evolving, and it is difficult to pinpoint the exact origins of the idea. A leading instrument to measure authentic leadership is the *Authentic Leadership Questionnaire*, by Avolio, Gardner and Walumbwa. In their article describing the instrument, they describe authentic leadership as consisting of four components: self-awareness, relational transparency, balanced processing and internalized moral perspective.

The results of twin studies have estimated that somewhere around 50% of the variance in both personality and transformational leadership can be explained by genetic factors.

The Search for the Successor to
Transformational Leadership
Graduate Education

By 2009, approximately 21% of U.S. adults held a bachelors degree. A little over 7% held a masters degree and less than 1% a doctorate. By 2009, more women were earning degrees than men. The charts shown are not percentages earned per year, but estimates of the percentage of adults in the United States holding those degrees. For both undergraduate and masters degrees, by 2009 a higher percentage of women than men held those degrees.

Earning a graduate degree was still a significant accomplishment.[17]

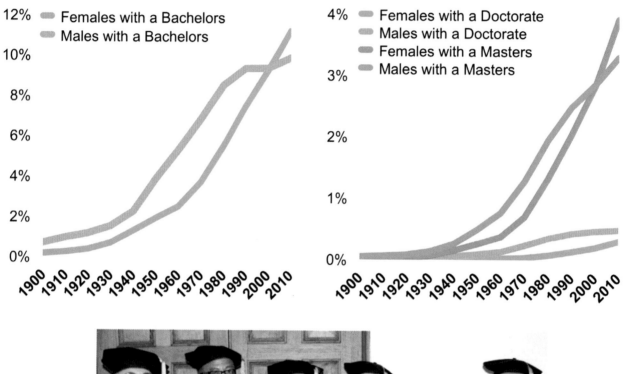

The Search for the Successor to Transformational Leadership
Notes

[1] The data for the three graphs on this page come from the years indicated from that year's *Statistical Abstract of the United States*.

[2] Based on the Wall Street Journal article, (1998). *Tuning In: Communications Technologies Historically Have Had Broad peal for Consumers, Wall Street Journal, Classroom Edition*. The 2010 data are from the US Census Bureau. The term "cable" includes satellite television and cable television. The term "PC" includes traditional computers, laptops and tablets.

[3] Reengineer* in tile for AD and PD. Reengineer* -software in title of WC.

[4] Hamel and Prahalad did not have this figure in their article or book. I created it to try to illustrate their 40/30/20 rule. The information comes from page 24 of their book. Hamel, G. and Prahalad, C. K. (1994). *Competing for the future*. Boston, Mass: Harvard Business School Press; Hamel, G., and Prahalad, C. K. (1994). Competing for the Future. *Harvard Business Review*, 72(4), 122.

[5] The data from this table come from pages 1 – 14 in Senge, P. M. (1990). *The fifth discipline: The art and practice of the learning organization*. New York: Doubleday/Currency. The definition of a learning organization is from page 3.

[6] "Learning Organization" or "Fifth Discipline" in the title or abstract of AD and PD, in the title of WC.

[7] Bar-On, R. (2004). The Bar-On Emotional Quotient Inventory (EQ-i): Rationale, description and psychometric properties. In G. Geher (Ed.), *Measuring emotional intelligence: Common ground and controversy*. Hauppauge, NY: Nova Science.

[8] The EQ-I 2.0 contains a six-dimensions model. The EQ-I 2.0 is explained in volume 2 of this series.

[9] *Mayer-Salovey-Caruso Emotional Intelligence Test (MSCEIT),* by J. D. Mayer, P. Salovey, and D. R. Caruso, 2002, Toronto, Ontario: Multi-Health Systems, Inc.

[10] Oddly, the GLOBE research project book did not report single mean scores for the dimensions of leadership worldwide. These means are from Den, H. N., House, R. J., Hanges, P. J., Ruiz-Quintanilla, S. A., Dorfman, P. W., Brenk, K. M., Konrad, E., Sabadin, A. (1999). Culture specific and cross culturally generalizable implicit leadership theories: Are attributes of charismatic/transformational leadership universally endorsed? *The Leadership Quarterly, 10,* 2, 219-256. The means provided here, were reported in this article and represent a slightly smaller subset of the final GLOBE sample. "the analyses reported in the present paper are based on 15,022 middle managers from 60 different societies/cultures," p. 233.

[11] For a thorough review of authentic leadership, see Gardner, W. L., Cogliser, C. C., Davis, K. M. and Dickens, M. P. (2011). Authentic leadership: A review of the literature and research agenda. *The Leadership Quarterly, 22,* 6, 1120-1145.

[12] Walumbwa, F. O., Peterson S. J., Avolio B. J., Wernsing T. S. and Gardner W. L. (2008). Authentic leadership: Development and validation of a theory-based measure. *DigitalCommons@University of Nebraska - Lincoln.*

[13] The R^2's shown in each column refer to the amount of variance each predictor explained of the total R^2. For example, all of the predictor variables in the multiple regression explained 58% of the variance in leader effectiveness. Leader consideration explained 11.9% of the total 58%.

[14] In a multiple regression, these variables had little or no influence beyond the impact of the other variables shown in the table. In bivariate analyses, they are related to leadership outcomes.

[15] The question of just how identical, identical twins are has recently been questioned. Some studies indicate there may be small differences in certain portions of each twin's DNA. See, for example:

http://www.scientificamerican.com/article.cfm?id=identical-twins-genes-are-not-identical

[16] Li, W. D., Arvey, R. D., Zhang, Z. and Song, Z. (2011). Do leadership role occupancy and transformational leadership share the same genetic and environmental influences? *The Leadership Quarterly.* 3-23.

Arvey, R. D., Rotundo, M., Johnson, W., Zhang, Z. and McGue, M. (2006). The determinants of leadership role occupancy: Genetic and personality factors. *The Leadership Quarterly*, 17, 1–20.

Loehlin, J. C., McCrae, R. R., Costa, P. T. and John, O. P. (1998). Heritabilities of common and measure-specific components of the big five personality factors. *Journal of Research in Personality*, 32, 431– 453.

Johnson, A. M., Vernon, P. A., McCarthy, J. M., Molso, M., Harris, J. A. and Jang, K. J. (1998). Nature vs nurture: Are leaders born or made? A behavior genetic investigation of leadership style. *Twin Research*, 1, 216– 223.

Chaturvedi, S., Arvey, R., Zhang, Z. and Christoforou, P. (2011). Genetic underpinnings of transformational leadership: The mediating role of dispositional hope. *Journal of Leadership & Organizational Studies, 18,* 4, 469-479.

[17] From left to right, Dr.'s Richard Suttle, Earnest Thomas, Alicia Gonzalez-Quiroz, Patti Benitez, Debra Lopez and John Blumentritt earning their PhD's in Leadership Studies from Our Lady of the Lake University.

Summary

Organizational Leadership
Key Points

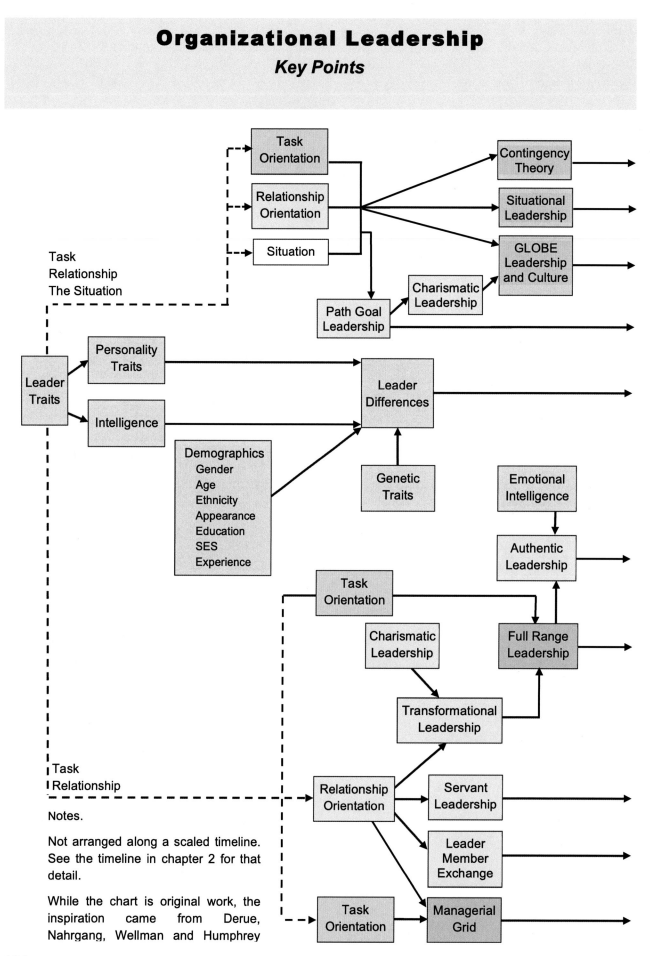

Task
Relationship
The Situation

Task
Relationship

Notes.

Not arranged along a scaled timeline. See the timeline in chapter 2 for that detail.

While the chart is original work, the inspiration came from Derue, Nahrgang, Wellman and Humphrey

The diagram on the opposite page reminds us that many of our current, popular theories of organizational leadership built on the work or earlier theories and research.

The Era of Leadership Traits

The first era discussed in this book was that of trait research. The primary research goal in this line of research was the search for a list of traits that explained why some individuals became leaders while others did not, or why some individuals succeeded as leaders while others did not.

Prior to the 20th century, the dominant theory of leadership was called "the Great Man" (person) approach, in which the belief was that certain individuals were born to be great.

Between 1900 and 1948, this theory eventually gave way to the search for traits such as appearance, personality, intelligence and social background. In his 1948 review of 128 published studies concerning traits of leaders, Stogdill concluded that "The evidence suggests that leadership is a relationship between persons in a social situation, and that persons who are leaders in one situation may not necessarily be leaders in other situations." (1948, p. 64)

In the early part of the 20th century, the industrial revolution was influencing how we envisioned management and leadership. The dominant view from this era is called mechanistic.

Mechanistic structures strive for efficiency by emphasizing a highly centralized hierarchy in which both roles and job tasks are clearly delineated and in which workers are closely supervised. A common metaphor for a mechanistic view of organizations is envisioning workers as interchangeable parts in a well-oiled machine.

Taylor's (1911) theory of scientific management emphasized studying the way workers perform their tasks, gathering all of the informal job knowledge that workers possess and experimenting with ways of improving the manner in which tasks are performed. New methods of performing tasks are codified into written rules and standard operating procedures.

The Era of Leadership Traits (Continued)

The Hawthorne Studies by Mayo (1933, 1945) pointed to the possibility that the manager's (leader's) behavior might influence follower performance.

An early precursor to a more organic view of organizations is seen in Barnard's (1938) writings about the importance of communication in organizations, and a view in which workers decide what range of authority they will allow the organization to exercise over them.

The influence of the massive mobilization for World War II, coupled with the aura that that effort saved the world had a great deal of influence over ideas about leadership and management.

Those ideas were captured in Fayol's 14 principles of management.

The Era of Leadership Behaviors
Key Points

The Era of Leadership Behaviors

Following the search for leader traits, in the post World War II era, researchers tended to focus more on what leaders did, rather than who they were.

In the 1950's and 1960's, the percentage of the workforce employed in tertiary professions rose significantly. To some degree, this reflected the growing complexity of the workplace, and the need for higher percentages of workers to plan, analyze, manage and lead. We also see that this time period witnessed a rapid expansion in the percentage of homes with a telephone, radio and television.

During this era, there was a movement away from viewing organizations as highly mechanistic structures and toward viewing them as more organic. Burns and Stalker (1961) introduced the organic terminology, and Katz and Kahn (1966) added the terms open and closed systems to this line of thought. Argyris (1957) introduced the idea that a fundamental conflict exists in organizations. Organizations typically structure followers' roles and direct their work in order to achieve organizational objectives. Followers, on the other hand, generally want to be self-directive and to feel fulfilled through exercising initiative and responsibility.

Likert (1961) described four types of leadership/management styles: exploitive, authoritative benevolent, authoritative consultative and participative. There is some evidence that consultative and participative leadership styles increase follower satisfaction and productivity more than exploitive or authoritative benevolent.

Cyert and March (1963) introduced the idea of problemistic searching in which problem solving is usually triggered by a specific problem and the goal is to solve that one problem. As a result, the alternatives the organizational decision-makers consider are limited in scope. Solutions ultimately accepted are often alternatives endorsed by a dominant coalition. The effect of problemistic searching is that organizational policies will change only incrementally.

The Era of Leadership Behaviors

Key Points

The Era of Leadership Behaviors

While it lacks an empirical base, Maslow's hierarchy of needs is still very popular. Over 200 peer-reviewed articles have incorporated the theory since the year 2000. The theory posits that individuals progress through five levels of need: biological and physiological, safety, belongingness and love, esteem and self-actualization.

Drucker's (1954) theory of management by objectives emphasized setting or reviewing organizational objectives and cascading those objectives down to employees. The objectives should be specific, measurable, agreed to by the manager (leader) and follower, realistic and time related.

Studies done at Ohio State, Fleishman, Harris and Burtt (1955) Hemphill and Coons (1957), Stogdill (1963) identified two primary dimensions of leader behavior. Initiation of structure is leader behavior that clearly defines roles and lets followers know what is expected of them. Consideration consists of regarding the comfort, well-being, status and contributions of followers.

French and Raven (1959), explained five types of social power: legitimate power, reward power, coercive power, expert power and referent power.

Hertzberg (1959, 1966, 1976) developed a theory of aspects of work. He distinguished between factors that motivate followers and hygiene factors or dissatisfiers. Although dissatisfiers don't motivate followers, their absence lowers motivation.

McGregor (1960, 1966) developed the concept of theory X and theory Y attitudes about followers. A theory X view is that the average follower is lazy, dislikes work and will try to do as little as possible. A theory Y view is that followers want responsibility.

The Era of Leadership Behaviors
Key Points

The Era of Leadership Behaviors

The University of Michigan studies, Katz and Kahn (1952), Cartwright and Zander (1960), Likert (1961) described somewhat similar dimensions of leadership as those at Ohio State University. Production orientation emphasized the task or production aspects of the job and getting things done. Employee orientation emphasized a concern for interpersonal relations and the personal needs of followers.

Blake and Mouton (1964, 1965, 1972, 1978) used similar dimensions of leader behavior as the Ohio State and Michigan studies but called their dimensions concern for production and concern for people. The authors laid the two dimensions onto a grid with the X-axis describing concern for production and the Y-axis concern for people. The grid axes are numbered 1 through 9.

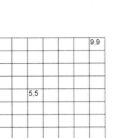

Fiedler's contingency theory (1964, 1966, 1967, 1971) begins with the premise that leaders have relatively consistent leadership styles, based on the dimensions of task or relationship orientation.

Fiedler's model provides eight scenarios, based on: leader-follower relationship, the structure of the task at hand and how much position power the leader holds.

Bowers and Seashore (1966) proposed a framework for understanding similarities of earlier research. Their four dimensions were support, goal emphasis, interaction facilitation and work facilitation.

Hersey and Blanchard's (1969, 1977) situational leadership theory used a two-dimensional grid with leadership dimensions of supportive and directive behavior. Beyond the two leader behavior dimensions, Hersey and Blanchard posited that leaders should adjust their styles of leading based on two dimensions related to followers: the follower's capability to do a particular task/job and the follower's commitment to do that task/job.

The Era of Transforming Followers
Key Points

The Era of Transforming Followers

In the 1970's and 1980's theories evolved that advocated serving followers and helping to transform them into better persons.

In the 1970's and 1980's, the percentage of the workforce employed in tertiary professions continued to rise significantly. Most U.S. homes had a telephone, radio and television. The birth of the personal computer was just beginning. This era also witnessed a continued rise in the percentage of women in the workforce, as well as a rise in the percentage of women working in professional positions.

Several management theories had some influence on subsequent leadership and management practices. Vroom, Yetton and Jago introduced a decision matrix with seven leadership questions and suggested appropriate leadership behaviors. In 1978, Kerr and Jermier asked whether certain factors could lessen the need for leadership. They divided possible substitutes into three sources: followers, the tasks being done and the organization.

In 1978, Ouchi contrasted what he described as a typical set of American leadership/work assumptions with those that might be typical Japanese assumptions. He then proposed a hybrid set that he labeled type Z assumptions. This slowly became known as theory Z. In 1982, Peters and Waterman's bestselling book, *In Search of Excellence*, advocated taking care of both customers and followers as key ingredients of excellence.

Two management theories were extremely influential during this era. Total quality management emphasizes an array of quality initiatives. Some of the philosophies of TQM can be seen in Deming's 14 points.

Six sigma refers to a standard of quality that equates to 3.4 defects per one million opportunities (DPMO). While methodologies vary, six sigma initiatives often have five stages called DMAIC: define opportunities, measure performance, analyze opportunities, improve performance and control performance.

The Era of Transforming Followers
Key Points

The Era of Transforming Followers

The phrase servant leadership was developed by Greenleaf (1970). In *The Servant as Leader*, Greenleaf explained: "The servant-leader is a servant first... It begins with the natural feeling that one wants to serve, to serve first. Then conscious choice brings one to aspire to lead. That person is sharply different from one who is a leader first."

House's (1971, 1996) path-goal theory advocates that leaders assist followers in determining their desired goals. Leaders assist the followers by using one or more of the following behaviors: directive path-goal clarifying leader behavior, supportive leader behavior, participative leader behavior and achievement oriented behavior.

Leader-member exchange theory, Graen and Uhl-Bien (1975), pointed out that leaders form different relationships with different followers within the same work areas – often called out-groups and in-groups. Based on this line of research, the authors identified three stages through which leader-follower relationships might progress: stranger, acquaintance and mature partnership.

While the study of charismatic leadership is not a new phenomenon, House, developed a model to explain charismatic leadership that included aspects of leader personality, leader behaviors and the effects on followers. Leader personality characteristics include: extremely high levels of self-confidence; a desire to influence others; a strong conviction in the moral righteousness of his/her beliefs; being dominant and expressing confidence.

The Era of Transforming Followers
Key Points

The Era of Transforming Followers

Burns (1978) envisioned transformational and transactional leadership as separate entities. In transactional leadership, the leader and follower have separate and possibly unrelated goals. Conversely, in transformational leadership the leader and follower are presently or potentially united in the pursuit of "higher" goals.

Whereas Burns envisioned transformational and transactional leadership as separate entities, Bass envisioned them on a continuum. By 1991, a nine-component model was advanced and was supported by the *Multifactor Leadership Questionnaire 5X*. By 2009, the model was refined by creating transformational, transactional and passive-avoidant leadership.

In 1978, Stogdill conducted a second analysis of trait studies. He found that three types of traits seemed to be related to leadership ratings: leadership skills, relationship with the group and personal characteristics. In 1986, Lord, de Vader and Alliger used the Schmidt-Hunter validity generalization technique in order to conduct a meta-analysis. They concluded that leadership perceptions were related to leader traits of intelligence, masculinity-femininity, dominance, adjustment, extroversion and conservatism.

The Search for the Successor to Transformational Leadership
Key Points

The Search for the Successor to Transformational Leadership

Transformational leadership continues to be the most popular theory of leadership. During the 1990's and 2000's emotional intelligence, the GLOBE project and authentic leadership emerged.

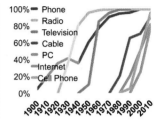

By 2009, we saw what is often called the digital convergence, in which the lines between what is a computer, phone, video source and so forth became a bit blurred. By 2009, most U.S. households had a cell phone and cable television. About 80% had some form of computer and about 77% had Internet access.

By 2009, approximately 21% of U.S. adults held a bachelors degree. About 7% held a masters degree and less than 1% a doctorate. More members of US society were working in tertiary professions and more women were working outside the home.

Reengineering (1993) emerged at the time that the Internet revolution was challenging us to move from paper-oriented forms to digital processes. Collins and Porras (1994) and Collins (2001) compared companies across different types of industries to determine what made some companies be built for lasting greatness. As part of that research, they described what they considered to be aspects of successful *Level 5 Leadership*. Hamel and Prahalad (1996) argued that about 40% of a senior executive's time is devoted to looking outward and about 30% of that time is spent peering three or more years into the future. Of the time spent looking forward, no more than 20% is devoted to building a collective view of the future.

The field of personality has been studied so extensively that there are over 90 meta-analyses on things that are related to personality. Leadership researchers have also studied leader personality.

Generally, extraversion, agreeableness and openness are often associated with effective leadership, and neuroticism and lack of conscientiousness with ineffective leadership.

The Search for the Successor to Transformational Leadership
Key Points

The Search for the Successor to Transformational Leadership

Senge (1990) argued that leaders of learning organizations engage in five disciplines: systems thinking, personal mastery, mental models, shared vision and team learning.

Mayer, Salovey and Caruso developed a four-dimension model of emotional intelligence that is measured by the MSCEIT. Their four dimensions are perceiving emotions, facilitating emotions, understanding emotions and managing emotions. Bar-On developed a five-dimension model of emotional intelligence that is measured by the EQ-i. His five dimensions are: intrapersonal, interpersonal, adaptability, stress-management and general mood.

The GLOBE project asked 17,370 middle managers from 951 organizations in 62 societies to indicate the degree to which different leadership behaviors contributed to or inhibited outstanding leadership.

Charismatic/value-based, team-oriented and participative leadership were considered important worldwide. Conversely, self-protective leader behaviors were believed to inhibit being an outstanding leader.

Empirical models to describe being an authentic leader are still evolving, and it is difficult to pinpoint the exact origins of the idea. A leading instrument to measure authentic leadership is the *Authentic Leadership Questionnaire*, by Avolio, Gardner and Walumbwa. In their article describing the instrument, they describe authentic leadership as consisting of four components: self-awareness, relational transparency, balanced processing and internalized moral perspective.

The results of twin studies have estimated that somewhere around 50% of the variance in both personality and transformational leadership can be explained by genetic factors.

Organizational Leadership
Key Points

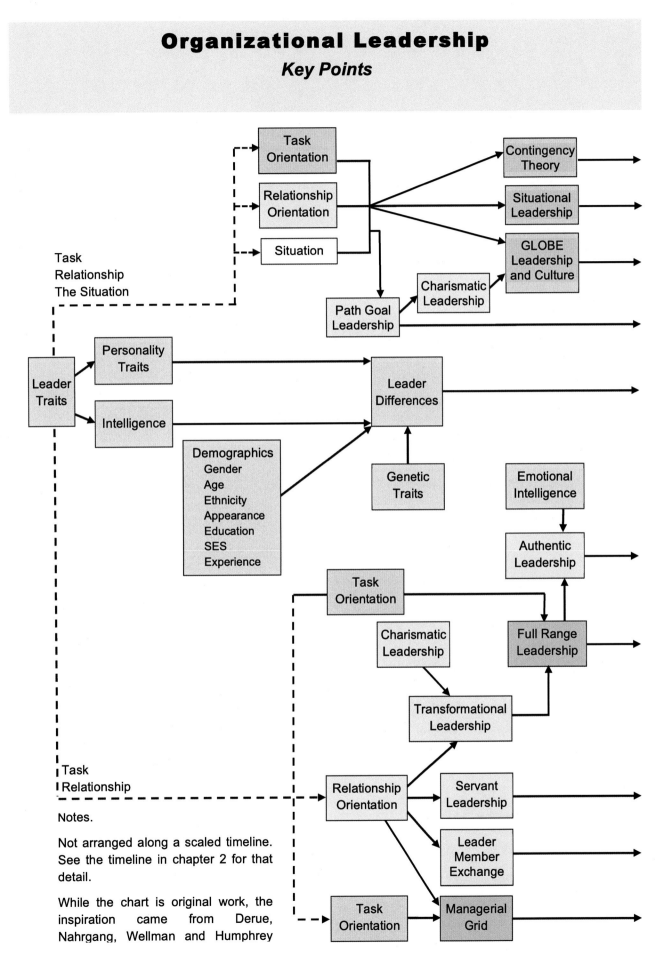

Notes.

Not arranged along a scaled timeline. See the timeline in chapter 2 for that detail.

While the chart is original work, the inspiration came from Derue, Nahrgang, Wellman and Humphrey

Subject Index

Ability, 11, 54, 60, 75, 83, 105, 109, 114, 147, 148
Age, 44, 60, 61, 91, 114, 122, 150, 153, 164, 175
Agreeableness, 40, 145, 150, 156, 173
American Leadership, 38, 108, 125, 170
Assembly Line, 53, 73
Authentic, 41, 153, 155, 164, 174, 175
Authentic Leadership, 41, 112, 134, 144, 149, 155, 157, 160, 173
Authentic Leadership Questionnaire, 41, 149, 174
Authority, 54, 55, 58, 166
Autocratic, 29, 80, 81, 82, 83–90, 107, 108, 109, 110, 112, 113, 114, 115, 116, 117

Benevolent, Authoritative, 36, 93, 167
Big-Five Personality, 134, 144
Bivariate Relationships, 41, 150
Bureaucracy, 45, 46
Business, 56, 87, 97, 142

Subject Index

Business Revolution, 44

Capacity, 14, 138, 146
Change, 13, 14, 27, 44, 45, 54, 76, 77, 84, 93, 97, 117, 137, 140, 141
Charismatic, 38, 41, 122, 124, 148, 153, 155, 157, 159, 164, 174, 175
Charismatic Leader, 116, 130
Charismatic Leadership, 102, 116, 123, 124, 126, 130, 171
  Study of, 126, 171
Charismatic Leadership Theory, 46, 130
Closed Systems, 37, 78, 92, 93, 167
Commitment, 90
Competence, 90, 145
Competitive Strategy, 43, 44
Compliance, 12, 145, 146
Computer, 4, 73, 105, 136, 137, 156, 173
  Personal, 32, 104, 105, 170
Concern For People, 36, 87, 95, 99, 169
Conduct, 6, 121, 127, 172
  Ethical, 114
Conflict, 11, 28, 42, 43, 59, 75, 77, 107
Conscientiousness, 40, 145, 150, 173
Consultative Type, 107
Contingency, 36, 91, 92, 123, 124, 155
Contingency Theory, 45, 46, 70, 79, 88, 91, 122, 153, 164, 175
Continuum, 16, 19, 24, 29, 86, 119, 127, 172
Corporation, 44, 140
Crowds, 25, 26, 42
Culture, 11, 12, 122, 153, 155, 159, 164, 175
  Organizational, 46, 123

Decisions, 27, 34, 40, 58, 77, 107, 108, 148, 149
Definitions of Leadership, 10, 11, 12, 13
Demographics, 61, 91, 122, 150, 153, 164, 175
Differentiation, 46, 89
Direction, 4, 11, 12, 14, 59
Dissatisfiers, 35, 84, 92, 94, 124, 154, 168
Dissertations, 56, 81, 82, 83, 88, 97, 98, 113, 115, 116, 118, 140, 141, 147
Dizygotic, 151
Domains of Organizational Leadership, 25, 26, 27, 28, 29
Dominance, 39, 60, 114, 121, 172

Effective Leader, 82, 143
Effectiveness, 11, 12, 76, 134, 144, 150, 155
Effectiveness and Success, 11, 12
Efficiency, 53, 54, 59, 63, 76, 165
Emotional Intelligence, 40, 44, 61, 80, 134, 144, 147, 150, 159, 173
  Five-Dimension Model of, 157, 174
  Four-Dimension Model of, 40, 174
Emotional Stability, 150
Empirical Studies, 83, 84, 85
Employees, 16, 24, 59, 75, 77, 81, 89, 94, 168

Subject Index

Excellence, 38, 113, 129
  Search of, 44, 102, 106, 110, 125, 129, 170
Expectancy Theory, 45
Experience, 61, 75, 76, 91, 109, 114, 122, 150, 153, 164, 175
Experiment, 6, 7, 8, 54, 118
Extraversion, 39–40, 145, 150, 156, 173

Facilitation, 36, 89, 169
Failure Mode, 118
FFM (Five-Factor Model), 145
Fifth Discipline, 44, 146, 159
Five Bases of Social Power, 70, 79, 83
Five-Factor Model (FFM), 145
Follower Feelings, 7
Follower Job Satisfaction, 39, 41, 150
Follower Motivation, 39
Follower Outcomes, 35
Follower Performance, 166
Follower Relationship, 123
Follower Results, 113
Followers, 7–8, 10, 12, 35, 38, 83, 85, 90, 94, 107, 116, 117, 126, 168, 169–72
  Influence, 64
  Interviewing, 82
  Surveying, 8
Follower Satisfaction, 4, 7, 39, 41, 77, 93, 150, 167
Followership, 56
Four-Factor Theory, 70, 79, 89, 99
Functions of Management, 58

Gender, 61, 91, 122, 150, 153, 164, 175
Genetic Factors, 41, 151, 157, 174
Genetic Studies, 134, 144, 151
Global Leadership, 134, 144
GLOBE Project (Global Leadership and Organizational Behavior Effectiveness), 41, 122, 123, 134,
    144, 148, 153, 157, 164, 174-175
Goal Emphasis, 89
Goals, 12, 16, 24, 26, 28, 36, 37, 58, 73, 77, 89, 113, 116, 117, 118
  Common, 11, 12, 59
  Organizational, 58
Grid, 36, 87, 91, 95, 122, 153, 164, 169, 175
  Two-Dimensional, 90, 95, 169

Hawthorne Studies, 34, 45, 50, 55, 64, 166
Holistic Concern, 108
Hygiene Factors, 35, 84, 168

Implicit Leadership Theories, 46
Industrial Management Formulations, 45
Industrial Organization, 43, 98
Industries, 40, 41, 110, 141, 156, 173
Informal Control, 108

Initiating Structure, 45, 86, 87, 89, 99, 150
Integrated Model of Leader Traits, 150
Intelligence, 39, 40, 41, 50, 60, 61, 63, 114, 121, 122, 150, 153, 164, 165, 175
  Leader Traits of, 127, 172

Knowledge, 55, 60, 76, 83, 109, 114, 143, 146

Leader Behavior Description Questionnaire, 82, 98
Leader Behaviors, 41, 82, 89, 94, 113, 116, 123, 126, 150, 168, 169, 171, 174
  Similar Dimensions of, 87, 95, 169
  Supportive, 113, 126, 171
  Participative, 126
Leader Centricity, 10, 19
Leader Decision, 37
Leader Effectiveness, 39, 41, 45, 150, 160
Leader Emergence, 155
Leader Follower Interaction, 10
Leader-Follower Relationships, 36, 95, 126, 169, 171
Leader Intelligence, 121
Leader Member Exchange Theory, 38, 45, 88, 102, 111, 115, 124, 126, 130, 171
Leader Performance, 121
Leader Personality, 41, 126, 150, 171
Leader Power, 35
Leaders, 7–8, 10, 12, 19, 26, 28, 61–63, 83, 90, 92, 107, 121–24, 126, 153–55, 165
  Authentic, 149, 157, 174
  Good, 13, 17, 18
  Poor, 13, 18
Leadership, 3, 7–20, 24–31, 42, 45, 46, 55–56, 109, 122, 123–25, 129–30, 148, 153, 164, 174–75
  Considerate, 148
  Effective, 32, 40, 134, 145, 156, 173
  Ineffective, 18, 40, 145, 156, 173
  Intellectual, 25, 42
  Military, 25, 42
  Participative, 41, 148, 157, 174
  Passive-Avoidant, 119, 127, 172
  Political, 25, 42
  Transactional, 117, 119, 123, 126, 172
Leadership Behaviors, 27, 30, 35, 36, 42, 69, 70, 75, 78, 82, 167, 168, 169, 170, 174
Leadership Effectiveness, 99, 114
Leadership Eras, 32
Leadership Grid, 99
Leadership Outcomes, 61, 160
  Predicting, 41, 150
Leadership Pattern Choice Theory, 45
Leadership Perceptions, 127, 172
Leadership Role Occupancy, 160
Leadership Self-Efficacy, 150
Leadership Skills, 37, 114, 127, 172
Leadership Style, 4, 61, 88, 160

Subject Index

Leadership Theories
  History of Organizational, 23, 30
  Situational, 45, 91, 95, 169
Leadership Traits, 30, 34, 37, 42, 49, 50, 60, 61, 91, 114, 121, 165, 166
Leader Traits, 34, 50, 60, 62, 121, 150, 165, 167
Learning, 19, 40, 97, 142, 146
Learning Organizations, 44, 134, 144, 146, 154, 159
  Leaders of, 157, 174
LMX, 124, 155
Long-Range Perspective, 14, 15
Loyalty, 76

Management, 14, 15–17, 19, 20, 24, 31, 32, 33, 34–43, 50, 58, 64, 81, 119, 166
  Scientific, 34, 43, 50, 54, 62, 63, 66, 165
Management Activities, 15, 19
Management Books, 32
Management By Objectives, 35, 70, 79, 81, 94, 98, 168
Management Practices, 125, 170
Management Sources, 31
Management Theories, 31, 32, 50, 70, 92, 102, 124, 125, 154, 170
Managerial Grid, 45, 70, 79, 87, 92, 99, 124, 155
Managers, 54, 55, 59, 64, 78, 81, 85, 92, 94, 139, 140, 142, 143, 166, 168
  Middle, 41, 148, 157, 159, 174
Maslow's Hierarchy, 70, 79, 80, 92, 94, 124, 154, 168
Mass Production Techniques, 53, 54
Measure Performance, 118, 125, 170
Mechanistic Organizations, 36, 54, 55, 63, 76, 78, 92, 165
Mechanistic and Organic Systems, 46, 70, 74, 76
Mechanistic Structures, 54, 63, 93, 165, 167
Meta-Analyses, 35, 39, 102, 121, 127, 145, 150, 156, 172, 173
Michigan Studies, 35, 70, 79, 86, 90, 95, 99, 169
Military, 26, 57, 73, 97
Monozygotic, 151
Motivation, 35, 43, 45, 46, 84, 94, 99, 168
Motivation Hygiene Theory, 45, 70, 79, 84
Motivators, 84
Motives, 11, 117
MSCEIT (Mayer-Salovey-Caruso Emotional Intelligence Test), 40, 147, 157, 159, 174
Multifactor Leadership Questionnaire, 119, 127, 130, 172

Neoinstitutional Theory, 46
Neuroticism, 40, 145, 156, 173
Non-Experimental Approaches, 6, 7, 8
Non-Leaders, 60, 70
Normative Theory, 102, 106–7

Obedience, 59, 76
Objectives, 35, 55, 70, 79, 81, 94, 168
Ohio State Studies, 70, 79, 82, 86
Open Systems, 78, 92, 124, 154
Organic Organizations, 76

Organic Structures, 54
Organic Systems, 46, 70, 74, 76
Organizational Analysis, 46
Organizational Behavior, 31, 129, 134, 144
Organizational Decision Making, 46, 77, 93, 167
Organizational Design, 78
Organizational Ecology, 46
Organizational Forms, 36, 76
Organizational Leadership, 3, 18, 25–29, 42, 74, 106, 165
Organizational Learning, 46
Organizational Learning Concepts, 46
Organizational Objectives, 16, 24, 35, 75, 93, 94, 167, 168
Organizational Policies, 77, 93, 167
Organizations, 11, 28, 30, 40, 43, 45–46, 54, 55, 58, 59, 64, 74–78, 129, 166, 167
  Mechanistic, 54, 76

Pareto Charts, 118
Participative Leaders, 148
Path-Goal Theory, 37, 45, 89, 91-92, 102, 111, 113, 122-123, 126, 153, 164, 171, 175
Peer-Reviewed Articles, 8-9, 80, 82, 83, 84, 85, 87, 88, 94, 97, 108, 113, 115, 116, 118, 141, 143, 146, 147
Perceptions, 40, 46, 82, 83, 121
Performance, 39, 44, 45, 54, 55, 58, 64, 113, 114, 118, 170
Personal Humility, 143
Personal Integrity, 60, 114
Personality, 40, 41, 43, 60, 61, 74, 75, 145, 151, 155, 156, 157, 160, 164, 173, 174–75
Personal Mastery, 40, 146, 157, 174
Personnel, 16, 24, 27
Philosophies, 18, 36, 76, 125, 170
Planning, 14, 16, 24, 89
Position Power, 36, 88
Power, 59, 83, 92, 95, 124, 137, 154, 169
Pride, 120
Problemistic, 77, 167
Problem Solving, 14, 36, 77, 93, 167
Processes, 11, 12, 53, 77, 97, 118, 134, 140
Production, 36, 53, 78, 86, 87, 89, 95, 99, 120, 169
Production Orientation, 86, 87, 89
Productivity, 7, 34, 77, 93, 110, 120, 167
Project GLOBE, see GLOBE Project

Qualitative Research, 4–5, 19
Quality, 27, 38, 107, 118, 120, 125, 170
Quality Tools, 118
Quantitative Research, 4, 5, 19, 33

Range Model, 39, 85, 102, 117, 119, 123–24, 155
Reengineering, 40, 44, 134, 139, 140, 156, 159, 173
Regression, Multiple, 118, 150, 160
Relationship, 4, 8, 28–29, 37–38, 88, 89, 91, 102, 114, 115, 122, 123, 153, 164, 175
Relationship Orientation, 42, 88, 95, 123, 169

Subject Index

Research
  Empirical, 6, 18, 20, 80
  Experimental, 6, 7
  Non-Experimental, 6, 7, 8
  Structured, 9
Responsibility, 27, 35, 58, 60, 75, 77, 84, 85, 93, 94, 108, 114, 117, 167, 168
Reward, Contingent, 41, 119, 150
Rewards, 77, 109, 113
Roles, 35, 54, 63, 73, 75, 82, 86, 93, 94, 165, 167, 168

Satisficing, 34, 58, 62, 77, 92, 124, 154
Satisfiers, 84, 92
Self-Actualization, 35, 80, 94, 168
Servant, 37, 112, 122, 124, 126, 153, 155, 164, 171, 175
Servant-Leader, 112, 126, 171
Servant Leadership, 102, 111, 112, 123, 124
Servant Leadership Constructs, 112
Shared Aspirations, 11, 12
Shared Goal, 11, 12
Short-Range View, 14, 15
Situation, 25, 60, 63, 91, 122, 123, 153, 164, 165, 175
Situational, 37, 91, 92, 123, 124, 155
Situational Element, 91, 123
Situational Leadership, 90, 91, 92, 99, 122, 153, 164, 175
Six Sigma, 38, 102, 111, 118, 124, 125, 154, 170
Skills, 27, 54, 59, 76, 89, 143
Social Background, 50, 60, 63, 114, 165
Social Power, 35, 70, 79, 83, 92, 94, 99, 168
Societies, 41, 51, 52, 72, 148, 157, 159, 174
Strategy, 16, 24, 28, 42, 43, 78, 142
Stress, 114, 116, 157
Stress-Management, 147, 174
Structure, 14, 15, 26, 36, 43, 76, 78, 82, 86, 94, 95, 112, 168, 169
  Organizational, 78
Styles, 7, 18, 37, 87, 90, 95, 155, 169
  Consistent Leadership, 95, 169
  Participative Leadership, 93, 167
Subordinates, 109, 113
Substitutes, 38, 46, 102, 106, 109, 125, 129, 170
Successful Habits of Visionary Companies, 44

Task, 27, 28–29, 36, 37, 54, 63, 90, 91, 95, 122–23, 153, 164, 165, 169, 175
  Dimensions of, 95, 169
Task Orientation, 42, 60, 88, 114
Task Performance, 39, 113
Task-Related, 60, 114
Taxonomies, 26, 27
Teams, 16, 24, 40, 58, 116, 146
Technological Determinism, 36, 46, 70, 74, 78
Technology, 36, 46, 73, 78, 105, 137, 138
Theory Y, 99

Subject Index

Total Quality Management, 39, 102, 111, 120, 124, 125, 170
Traits, 37, 50, 60, 61, 62–63, 91, 102, 111, 114, 121, 122, 150, 153, 164, 175
  List of, 60, 165
Trait Studies, 60, 114, 127, 172
Transactional Leadership, 46, 76, 119, 127, 172
Transformational, 102, 111, 112, 119, 122, 124, 127, 150, 151, 153, 155, 164, 172, 174, 175
  Envisioned, 117, 119, 126–27, 172
Transformational Leadership, 35, 38, 40, 41, 42, 97, 117, 119, 124, 126, 130, 133–61, 172, 173, 174
Trends, Societal, 32, 56, 57
Twins, 151

University of Michigan Studies, 70, 79, 86, 95, 169

Visionary, 141, 148
Visionary Companies, 44, 141

Women, 51, 52, 57, 65, 71, 72, 96, 103, 104, 125, 135, 156, 158, 170, 173
Workforce, 51, 57, 62, 71, 73, 93, 103, 105, 125, 135, 137, 167, 170

Author Index

Acar, 110
Agricola, 97
Alderfer, 45
Alliger, 39, 102, 111, 121, 127, 172
Alters, 117
Amitai ,46
Argyris, 35, 43, 4670, 74, 75, 93, 98, 167
Arvey, 41, 134, 144, 151, 160
Ashkanasy, 41
Aupperle, 110
Avolio, 39, 41, 102, 111, 119, 134, 144, 149, 157, 160, 174

Barnard, 34, 43, 45, 50, 55, 64, 66, 166
Bar-On, 40, 134, 144, 147, 157, 159, 174
Bass, 10, 14, 19, 25, 26, 28, 31, 35, 39, 80, 102, 111, 119, 127, 172
Batch, 78
Bedian, 32, 43
Behling, 11, 12
Bennis, 14, 15, 44, 46
Blake, 36, 45, 46, 70, 79, 87, 90, 95, 169
Blanchard, 37, 44, 45, 70, 79, 90, 95, 169
Blau, 46
Brattin, 34
Brenk, 159

Author Index

Burns, 10, 11, 12, 31, 35, 36, 38, 43, 46,70, 74, 76, 117, 119, 126–27, 130, 172
Burtt, 35, 70, 79, 82, 94, 168

Carlyle, 34
Carnegie, 44
Carroll, 46
Cartwright, 35, 70, 79, 86, 89, 99, 169
Caruso, 40, 134, 144, 147, 157, 159, 174
Cavanagh, 44
Ceruzzi, 32
Champy, 40, 44, 134, 139, 140
Chandler, 32, 44
Chaturvedi, 41, 134, 144, 151, 160
Chemers, 36, 70, 79
Christensen, 44
Christoforou, 41, 134, 144, 160
Coffman, 44
Cogliser, 160
Collins, 40, 44, 134, 139, 143, 156, 173
Coons, 11, 12, 35, 70, 79, 82, 89, 94, 168
Costa, 40, 41, 134, 144–45, 160
Covey, 44
Cul, 159
Cyert, 43, 46, 98
Cyert and March, 36, 70, 74, 77, 93, 167

Daft, 129
Dansereau, 38, 102, 111, 115
Davis, 160
Deci, 45
Deming, 39, 102, 111, 120, 125, 170
Derue, 41, 91, 122, 134, 144, 150, 153, 164, 175
Dickens, 160
Dickson, 43, 45
Donaldson, 46
Dorfman, 41, 134, 144, 159
Drucker, 35, 44, 70, 79, 81, 94, 168
Dunod, 66

Einstein, 80
Emery, 45
Engel, 34
Engle, 11, 12
Evans, 37, 45, 102, 111, 113

Falkus, 41, 134, 144
Fayol, 34, 43, 45, 50, 58, 62, 64, 66, 166
Fiedler, 36, 45, 70, 79, 88, 99
Fleishman, 26, 28, 35, 70, 79, 82, 94, 168
Fodor, 116
Forbes, 44, 110
Ford, 53
Freeman, 46

185

Author Index

French, 35, 66, 70, 79, 83, 99
French and Raven, 35, 70, 79, 83, 94, 168
Fuente, 97

Garcia, 36, 70, 79
Garcia, 45
Geher, 159
George, 41
Gerber, 44
Goethals, 31
Goldberg, 34, 144
Goldman, 41
Goleman, 40, 44, 134, 144, 147
Gordon, 27, 47
Graen, 45,102, 111, 115, 129
Graen and Uhl-Bien, 38, 102, 111, 115, 126, 171

Hackman, 15, 45
Haga, 38, 102, 111, 115
Halpin, 89
Hamel, 44, 159
Hamel and Prahalad, 40, 134, 139, 142, 156, 159, 173
Hammer, 40, 44, 134, 139, 140
Hamner, 45
Handy, 44
Hanges, 41, 134, 144, 159
Hannan, 46
Harris, 35, 70, 79, 82, 94, 160, 168
Hartog, 41, 134, 144
Hauppauge, 159
Hawthorne, 34
Hein, 26
Heller, 45
Hemphill, 11, 12, 35, 45, 70, 79, 82, 89, 94, 168
Herman, 31
Hersey, 45, 95, 169
Hertzberg, 35, 43, 45, 70, 79, 84, 94, 168
Hickson, 46
Hiebert, 31
Hill, 99
Hinings, 46
Homans, 43
House, 11, 12, 37, 38, 41, 45, 46, 102, 111, 113, 116, 123, 126, 129–30, 134, 144, 171
Howell, 116, 130
Humphrey, 41, 91, 122, 134, 144, 150, 153, 164, 175

Ilgen, 46

Jacobs, 11, 12
Jaeger, 38, 102, 106, 108
Jago, 37, 45, 102, 106–7, 125, 170
Jang, 160
Jaques, 11, 12

Author Index

Jefferson, 80
Jermier, 38, 102, 106, 109, 125, 129, 170
John, 41, 134, 144, 160
Johnson, 15, 44, 151, 160
Jung, 39, 102, 111, 119

Kahn, 11, 12, 35, 37, 43, 45, 70, 74, 78, 79, 86, 89, 93, 95, 167, 169
Katz, 12, 43, 45, 89
Katz and Kahn, 11, 35, 37, 70, 74, 78, 79, 86, 89, 93, 95, 167, 169
Kernis, 41
Kerr, 46, 129
Kerr and Jermier, 38, 102, 106, 109, 125, 170
Klatt, 31
Konrad, 159
Kopelman, 85
Korotkin, 26
Kotter, 14, 15, 20
Kotter, John P., 44
Kouzes, 11, 12, 15
Kreitner, 45

Larson, 130
Latham, 45
Lawler, 45
Levin, 26
Levinson, 45
Lewin, 45
Li, 41, 134, 144, 151, 160
Likert, 35–36, 70, 74, 77, 79, 86, 89, 93, 95, 98, 167, 169
Lincoln, 80, 160
Locke, 45
Loehlin, 41, 134, 144, 151, 160
Lord, 39, 46, 102, 111, 121, 127, 172
Lorsch, 43, 46
Luthans, 45

Maggio, 46
Mahar, 36, 46, 70, 79
Mann, 89
March, 43, 46
Mausner, 43
Mayer, 40, 134, 144, 147, 157, 159, 174
Mayo, 34, 43, 45, 50, 55, 64, 166
McCarthy, 160
McClelland, 43, 45
McCrae, 40, 41, 134, 144–45, 160
McGregor, 35, 70, 79, 85, 94, 168
McGue, 160
Meindl, 46
Meyer, 46
Michael, 44
Miner, 31, 32, 45

Author Index

Miner, 45
Mitchell, 46
Modu, 147
Molso, 160
Moore, 44
Moosa, 130
Morgan, 11, 12
Mouton, 36, 45, 46, 70, 79, 87, 90, 95, 169
Mumford, 26

Nahrgang, 41, 91, 134, 144, 150, 153, 164, 175
Nanus, 14, 15
Naylor,46
Negocios, 97
Neider, 113
Neuman, 44
Nohria, 31
Norton, 66

Oldham, 45
Olsen, 46
Ouchi, 38, 102, 106, 108, 125, 129, 170

Pande, 44
Paris, 66
Perrow, 46
Peters, 129
Peters, 44
Peters and Waterman, 38, 102, 106, 110, 129
Peterson, 41, 134, 144, 149, 160
Pfeffer, 46
Pinat, 66
Pitman, 66
Por, 44
Porras, 40, 134, 139, 141, 156, 173
Porter, 43-5
Posner, 11, 12, 15
Powell, 46
Prahalad, 40, 44, 134, 139, 142, 156, 159, 173
Pritchard, 46
Pugh, 46

Quintanilla, 41

Rauch, 11, 12
Raven, 35, 70, 79, 83, 94, 99, 168
Richards, 11, 12
Roethlisberger, 43, 45
Ryan, 45

Sabadin, 159
Sajid, 130
Salancik, 46
Salovey, 40, 134, 144, 147, 159

Salovey and Caruso, 40, 134, 147, 157, 174
Schein, 11, 12
Schein, 46
Schmidt-Hunter 121, 127, 172
Schriesheim, 113
Scott, 46
Seashore, 36, 70, 79, 89, 95, 99, 169
Senge, 40, 134, 144, 146, 154, 157, 159, 174
Shamir, 116, 130
Shartle, 45
Simon, 34, 43, 46, 50, 58, 77
Sloan, 44
Smircich, 11, 12
Snyder, 66
Stalker, 36, 46, 54, 70, 74, 76, 93, 98, 167
Stogdill, 34, 35, 37, 45, 60, 63, 66, 70, 79, 82, 111, 114, 127, 129, 165, 168
Synderman, 43

Taber, 27, 47
Tannenbaum, 45
Taylor, 34, 43, 45, 50, 54, 63, 66, 165
Thompson, 43, 45-6
Tuning, 129, 159

Uhl-Bien, 38, 102, 111, 115, 126, 129, 171

Vader, 39, 102, 111, 121, 127, 172
Van Seters, 31
Vroom, 37, 45, 102, 106–7, 125, 170

Walumbwa, 41, 134, 144, 149, 157, 160, 174
Waterman, 38, 44, 102, 106, 110, 129
Weber, 43, 45
Weick, 46
Wellman, 41, 91, 122, 134, 144, 150, 153, 164, 175
Wernsing, 41, 134, 144, 149, 160
Wiley, 99
Winer, 89
Witzel, 31
Woodward, 36, 43, 46, 70, 74, 78, 98
Woycke, 116
Wren, 31, 32, 43
Wright, 43

Yetton, 37, 45, 102, 106–7, 125, 170
York, 98
Yukl, 15, 27, 28, 31, 47

Zaccaro, 26
Zander, 35, 70, 79, 86, 89, 95, 169
Zhang, 41, 134, 144, 160
Zhangmand, 41, 134, 144
Zucker, 46

Graduate Leadership
Credits

Front Cover
Business Team - Licensed from East West Images through Bigstock.com
Table of Contents
Business Team with Woman Leading - Licensed from Andrey Kuzmin through Bigstock.com
Preface
Praying Woman - Licensed from Subbotina Anna through Bigstock.com
Team Meeting In Creative Office - Licensed from Cathy Yeulet through Bigstock.com
Explanation - Licensed from Dmitriy Shironosov through Bigstock.com
Woman sitting at study desks - Licensed from Wavebreak Media Ltd through Bigstock.com
Student In Library - Licensed from Jean-Marie Guyon through Bigstock.com
College Student Studying In The Library - Licensed from Arekmalang through Bigstock.com
Books - Licensed from Ghenadii Boico through Bigstock.com
Hands on Computer - Licensed from Ratchanida Thippayos through Bigstock.com
Man Doing Homework - Licensed from Diego Cervo through Bigstock.com
Paperwork - Licensed from Erol Berberovic through Bigstock.com
Mature students sitting at the library - Licensed by Wavebreak Media Ltd through Bigstock.com
In the library- pretty female student with laptop and books- Licensed by Lightpoet through Bigstock.com
Chapter 1
Bachelors Students - Licensed from Viktor Cap through Bigstock.com
Graduate Students - Licensed from Lisa F. Young through Bigstock.com
Doctoral Students - Licensed from Zsolt Nyulaszi through Bigstock.com
Books on Sale - Licensed from Rafal Olkis through Bigstock.com
Close-Up of businessman pointing with pen – Licensed from Dmitriy Shironosov through Bigstock.com
Portrait of a Businessman – Licensed from Minerva Studio through Bigstock.com
Businesswoman Talking to Her Team - Licensed from Wavebreak Media Ltd through Bigstock.com
Business Women Talking - - Licensed from MonkeyBusiness Images through Bigstock.com
Over the Shoulder Notebook Computer – Licensed from Sean Nel through Bigstock.com
Work on desk - Licensed from Sergey Nivens through Bigstock.com
Magazines – Licensed from Raga Irusta through Bigstock.com
Pills - Licensed from Steve Van Horn through Bigstock.com
Businessman Workplace with Papers - Licensed from Sergey Nivens through Bigstock.com
Finger Touching Slime - Licensed from Sergey Likov through Bigstock.com

Graduate Leadership
Credits

Successful Woman - Licensed from Dmitriy Shironosov through Bigstock.com
Man standing in front of flat panels - Licensed from Photosani through Bigstock.com
Secrets – Licensed from Edyta Linek through Bigstock.com
Asian Woman in library - Licensed from Sung Kuk Kim through Bigstock.com
Senior woman reading - Licensed from Wong Szefei through Bigstock.com
Man Holding Tablet in Library - Licensed from Wavebreak Media Ltd through Bigstock.com
Afro-American Young Woman Reading - Licensed from Pablo Calvog through Bigstock.com
Young woman writing– Licensed from Artemis Gordon through Bigstock.com
Angry Boss– Licensed from Core Pics through Bigstock.com
Chapter 2
Sprinter – Licensed from Gabriel Moisa through Bigstock.com
Loudspeaker – Licensed from Rahul Sengupta through Bigstock.com
Three Women – Licensed from Auremar through Bigstock.com
Children at the Computer Terminals - Licensed from Cathy Yeulet through Bigstock.com
Salad – Licensed from Olga Yastremska through Bigstock.com
Assembly – Licensed from Maros Markovic through Bigstock.com
Arabic Woman with colleagues – Licensed from Greg Crawford through Bigstock.com
Man in motion – Licensed from Serguei Vlassov through Bigstock.com
Crowd of people – Licensed from Rafael Ramirez Lee through Bigstock.com
Open books – Licensed from Ivan Mikhaylov through Bigstock.com
Over the Shoulder Notebook Computer – Licensed from Sean Nel through Bigstock.com
Close-Up of businessman pointing with pen – Licensed from Dmitriy Shironosov through Bigstock.com
Business woman handshake – Licensed from Andres Rodriguez through Bigstock.com
Young man with carrying box – Licensed from Franck Boston through Bigstock.com
Senior woman reading - Licensed from Wong Szefei through Bigstock.com
Man Holding Tablet in Library - Licensed from Wavebreak Media Ltd through Bigstock.com
Afro-American Young Woman Reading - Licensed from Pablo Calvog through Bigstock.com
Young woman writing– Licensed from Artemis Gordon through Bigstock.com
Mixed Group – Licensed from Cathy Yeulet through Bigstock.com
Woman raising hand in class – Licensed from Robert Kneschke through Bigstock.com
Handsome Businessman – Licensed from Gabriel Moisa through Bigstock.com
United Team of Doctors Embracing – Licensed from Blaj Gabriel through Bigstock.com
Black Executive Leather Chair – Licensed from Sergei Platonov through Bigstock.com
Empty Desk– Licensed from RTimages through Bigstock.com
Portrait of a Businessman next to Chair – Licensed from Alexandre Zveiger through Bigstock.com
Office worker sleeping on her desk– Licensed from Michal Kowalski through Bigstock.com
Frowning Business Man with Glasses– Licensed from Sarah Cheriton-Jones through Bigstock.com
Businesswoman Multitasking– Licensed from Core Pics through Bigstock.com
Blank Business Diagram – Licensed from Steve VanHorn through Bigstock.com
Happy Young Business Woman in front of Team– Licensed from Edhar Yuualaits through Bigstock.com
Business men discussing– Licensed from Edhar Yuualaits through Bigstock.com
Business Partners Deal – Licensed from Andres Rodriguez through Bigstock.com
Woman texting – Licensed from PhotosIndia LLC through Bigstock.com
Doing Calculations – Licensed from Alberto Zornetta through Bigstock.com
Woman carrying books – Licensed from Diego Cervo through Bigstock.com
College students in class – Licensed from Viktor Cap through Bigstock.com
Female student working on computer– Licensed from Arekmalang through Bigstock.com
Young Businessman Planning and Solving – Licensed from Benis Arapovic through Bigstock.com
Confident Leader with three partners in back– Licensed from Dmitriy Shironosov through Bigstock.com
Student looking for a book – Licensed from Andres Rodriguez through Bigstock.com
Woman in Library – Licensed from Cristovao Oliveira through Bigstock.com
Chapter 3
Business woman looking at camera – Licensed from Dmitriy Shironosov through Bigstock.com
Cheerful Indian woman – Licensed from Snowwhiteimages through Bigstock.com
Business woman with coffee – Licensed from Zsolt Nyulaszi through Bigstock.com
Business team cheering – Licensed from Andres Rodriguez through Bigstock.com

Graduate Leadership
Credits

Manager on factory floor – Licensed from Adrian Brockwell through Bigstock.com
Boss talking to factory worker – Licensed from Endomotion the Photographer through Bigstock.com
Brainstorming – Licensed from Dmitriy Shironosov through Bigstock.com
Clock works– Licensed from Yuri Samsonov through Bigstock.com
Group of business people Negotiating – Licensed from Endomotion the Photographer through Bigstock.com
Businesswoman writing with partner– Licensed from Rob Marmion through Bigstock.com
Taking a Test – Licensed from Kostyantine Pankin through Bigstock.com
A step Back in Time- Licensed from Debra Brissette through Bisgstock.com
Assembling– Licensed from Danis Derics through Bigstock.com
Horse and Buggy– Licensed from Kenneth Keith Stilger through Bigstock.com
Shoemaker– Licensed from Rafael Rossy through Bigstock.com
Business Interview– Licensed from Radu Razvan through Bigstock.com
Smiling Businessman in suit– Licensed from Ken Hurst through Bigstock.com
Boss Talking to Worker– Licensed Endomotion the Photographer through Bigstock.com
Manger on Factory Floor– Licensed from Adrian Brockwell through Bigstock.com
Businessman standing in front of blackboard– Licensed from Sergey Nivens through Bigstock.com
Board Room– Licensed from James Stedidl through Bigstock.com
Serious Pointing businessman– Licensed from Steve Cukrov through Bigstock.com
Empty Desk– Licensed from RTimages through Bigstock.com
Frowning Business Man with Glasses– Licensed from Sarah Cheriton-Jones through Bigstock.com
Businesswoman Multitasking– Licensed from Core Pics through Bigstock.com
Happy Young Business Woman in front of Team– Licensed from Edhar Yuualaits through Bigstock.com
Boss Yelling at Employee- Licensed from Auremar through Bigstock.com
Happy Multiracial Businesswoman with Hands Crossed– Licensed from M Sorensen through Bigstock.com
Mature Asian woman in library– Licensed from Hywit Dimyadi through Bigstock.com
Young woman learning– Licensed from Pablo Calvog through Bigstock.com
Man with tablet in library– Licensed from Wavebreak Media Ltd through Bigstock.com
Young woman writing– Licensed from Artemis Gordon through Bigstock.com
Woman in library - Licensed from Lichtmeister through Bigstock.com
Senior woman reading - Licensed from Wong Szefei through Bigstock.com
Man working - Licensed from Lichtmeister through Bigstock.com
Working Group- Licensed from Cathy Yeulet through Bigstock.com
Woman in Library - Licensed from Candybox Images through Bigstock.com
Chapter 4
Business Woman with Portfolio – Licensed from Andres Rodriguez through Bigstock.com
Business Man with his Team – Licensed from Edhar Yuualaits through Bigstock.com
Business meeting– Licensed from Dmitry Shironosov through Bigstock.com
Salesman in store - Licensed from Dimitry Kalinovsky through Bigstock.com
Girl using a laptop – Licensed from Andres Rodriguez through Bigstock.com
Clock - Licensed from Francesco Ridolfi through Bigstock.com
Woman on Cordless Phonek - Licensed from Jaimie Duplass through Bigstock.com
Female doctor smiling– Licensed from Andres Rodriguez through Bigstock.com
Salad – Licensed from Olga Yastremska through Bigstock.com
Salt, Pepper, Vinager – Licensed from Sally Scott through Bigstock.com
Man Giving Lecture to Three People- Licensed from Cathy Yeulet through Bigstock.com
Serious boss interacting– Licensed from Dmitry Shironosov through Bigstock.com
Clock works– Licensed from Yuri Samsonov through Bigstock.com
Senior Team Leader with Green File - Licensed from Arne Trautmann through Bigstock.com
Houseplant - Licensed from Elena Butinova through Bigstock.com
Gas Compressor Station - Licensed from Sergey Bobok through Bigstock.com
Vegetables in a Basket - Licensed from Wacpan through Bigstock.com
Yoga pose– Licensed from Phil Date through Bigstock.com
United Team of Doctors Embracing – Licensed from Blaj Gabriel through Bigstock.com
Empty Desk– Licensed from RTimages through Bigstock.com
Blank Business Diagram – Licensed from Steve VanHorn through Bigstock.com
Happy Young Business Woman in front of Team– Licensed from Edhar Yuualaits through Bigstock.com

Graduate Leadership
Credits

Business man– Licensed from Kurhan through Bigstock.com
Frowning business man holding glasses– Licensed from Sarah Cheriton-Jones through Bigstock.com
Multitasking– Licensed from Core Pics through Bigstock.com
Asian woman in the library– Licensed from SUNG KUK KIM through Bigstock.com
Adult Ed students– Licensed from Lisa F. Young through Bigstock.com
Group of young business people– Licensed from Zsolt Nyulaszi through Bigstock.com
Business team clapping– Licensed from Andres Rodriguez through Bigstock.com
Business women at work– Licensed from Endomotion the Photographer through Bigstock.com
Team meetings– Licensed from Cathy Yeulet through Bigstock.com
Empty desk– Licensed from RTimages the Photographer through Bigstock.com
Medical student studying– Licensed from Kai Chiang through Bigstock.com
Woman surrounded with piles of books– Licensed from Dzmitry Stankevich through Bigstock.com
Groups of adults studying– Licensed from Cathy Yeulet through Bigstock.com
Satisfied confident business team– Licensed from Francesco Ridolfi through Bigstock.com
Afro-American woman learning– Licensed from Pablocalvog through Bigstock.com
Asian senior woman– Licensed from Wong Szefei through Bigstock.com
Young confident student– Licensed from Lichtmeister through Bigstock.com
Business man in suit sitting at desk– Licensed from Lichtmeister through Bigstock.com
Man holding a tablet pc– Licensed from Wavebreak Media Ltd. through Bigstock.com
Confident business woman presentation– Licensed from Dmitriy Shironosov through Bigstock.com
Young woman writing in journal– Licensed from Todd Kuhns through Bigstock.com
Business meeting– Licensed from Dmitriy Shironosov through Bigstock.com
Charismatic chairman– Licensed from Wavebreak Media Ltd. through Bigstock.com
Black leather executive chair– Licensed from Sergei Platonov through Bigstock.com
Young man carrying box– Licensed from Franck Boston through Bigstock.com
Beautiful Hispanic woman writing at desk– Licensed from Artemis Gordon through Bigstock.com
Mature asian woman reading– Licensed from Hywit Dimyadi through Bigstock.com
Young business people arriving to office– Licensed from Zsolt Nyulaszi through Bigstock.com
Serious boss– Licensed from Andres Rodriguez through Bigstock.com
Job applicant at interview– Licensed from Goodluz through Bigstock.com
Magazines– Licensed from Rafa Irusta through Bigstock.com
Man giving lecture to three people – Licensed from Cathy Yeulet through Bigstock.com
Man in Library – Licensed from Wavebreak Media Ltd through Bigstock.com

Chapter 6

Woman praying– Licensed from Blend Images LLC through Bigstock.com
Pretty business woman– Licensed from Dmitriy Shironosov through Bigstock.com
Twin sisters– Licensed from Nataliya Litova through Bigstock.com
Two twin girls– Licensed from Andrey Arkusha through Bigstock.com
Isolated group of family members– Licensed from Franck Boston through Bigstock.com
Salt, pepper, vinergar– Licensed from Sally Scottthrough Bigstock.com
Female police officer– Licensed from John Roman through Bigstock.com
Portrait of business man– Licensed from Alexandre Zveiger through Bigstock.com
Empty desk– Licensed from RTimages the Photographer through Bigstock.com
Juicy vegetables– Licensed from Wacpan through Bigstock.com
Crazy inventor– Licensed from Andrey Burmakin through Bigstock.com
Scientist chemist– Licensed from Leah-Anne Thompson through Bigstock.com
Father holding daughter– Licensed from Artemis Gordon through Bigstock.com
Dump truck– Licensed from Andrey Bannov through Bigstock.com
Blank business diagram– Licensed from Steve VanHorn through Bigstock.com
Smiling teenage girl– Licensed from Steve Cukrov through Bigstock.com
Female medical professional– Licensed from Steve Cukrov through Bigstock.com
Young traditional woman– Licensed from Snow White Images through Bigstock.com
Father holding daughter– Licensed from Artemis Gordon through Bigstock.com
Multitasking– Licensed from Core Pics through Bigstock.com
United team of doctors– Licensed from Blaj Gabriel through Bigstock.com
Tired and overworked office worker– Licensed from Michal Kowalski through Bigstock.com

Graduate Leadership
Credits

Young business man praying– Licensed from Luca Bertolli through Bigstock.com
Business woman over white– Licensed from M Sørensen through Bigstock.com
Two men using tablet computer– Licensed from Cathy Yeulet through Bigstock.com
Happy young business woman– Licensed from Edhar Yuualaits through Bigstock.com
Business people discussing– Licensed from Edhar Yuualaits through Bigstock.com
Mature asian woman reading– Licensed from Wong Szefei through Bigstock.com
Asian woman in the library– Licensed from SUNG KUK KIM through Bigstock.com
Mid age business woman– Licensed from Cathy Yeulet through Bigstock.com
Medical student studying– Licensed from Kai Chiang through Bigstock.com
Adult Ed students in class– Licensed from Lisa F. Young through Bigstock.com
Business partners – Licensed from Andres Rodriguez through Bigstock.com
Woman surrounded by piles of books– Licensed from Dzmitry Stankevich through Bigstock.com
Frowning business man– Licensed from Sarah Cheriton-Jones through Bigstock.com
Group of adults studying– Licensed from Cathy Yeulet through Bigstock.com
Business man sitting at desk– Licensed from Lichtmeister through Bigstock.com
Young confident student– Licensed from Lichtmeister through Bigstock.com
Business woman applauding– Licensed from Andres Rodriguez through Bigstock.com
Writing on a white laptop– Licensed from Alberto Zornetta through Bigstock.com
Tasty greek salad– Licensed from Olga Yastremska through Bigstock.com
Business man in black suit– Licensed from Ken Hurst through Bigstock.com
Annoyed woman– Licensed from Selecstock through Bigstock.com
Planet earth model– Licensed from Johan Swanepoel through Bigstock.com
Woman in Library - Licensed from Wavebreak Media Ltd through Bigstock.com

Graduate Leadership
References

Alarcon, G., Eschleman, K., & Bowling, N. (2009). Relationships between personality variables and burnout: a meta-analysis. *Work & Stress*, 23(3), 244-263.

Antonakis, J., Avolio, B. J., & Sivasubramaniam, N. (2003). Context and leadership: an examination of the nine-factor full-range leadership theory using the Multifactor Leadership Questionnaire. *The Leadership Quarterly, 14,* 3, 261.

Argyris, C. (1957). *Personality and organization*. New York: Harper.

Argyris, C. (1962). *Interpersonal competence and organizational effectiveness*. Homewood, IL: Irwin-Dorsey.

Argyris, C. (1964). *Integrating the individual and the organization*. New York: Wiley.

Argyris, C. (1973). Personality and Organization Theory Revisited. *Administrative Science Quarterly, 18,* 2, 141-167.

Argyris, C. (1983). Action science and intervention. *Journal of Applied Behavioral Science*, 19, 115– 140.

Arvey, R. D., Rotundo, M., Johnson, W., Zhang, Z., & McGue, M. (2006). The determinants of leadership role occupancy: Genetic and personality factors. *The Leadership Quarterly*, 17, 1–20.

Atinc, G., Darrat, M., Fuller, B., & Parker, B. W. (2010). Perceptions of organizational politics: a meta-analysis of theoretical antecedents. *Journal of Managerial Issues : Jmi, 22,* 4, 494-512.

Aupperle, K. E., Acar, W., & Booth, D. E. (1986). An empirical critique of 'in search of excellence': how excellent are the excellent companies?. *Journal of Management*, 12(4), 499.

Avolio, B. J. (1990). Transactional leadership: Viewed as an organizational development process. In C. N. Jactions & M. R. Manning (Eds.), Organizational Development Annual, 3. Arlington, VA: American Society for Training and Development.

Avolio, B. J. (1995). Integrating transformational leadership and afro-centric management. Human Resource Management Journal, 11(6), 17-21.

Avolio, B. J. & Bass, B.M. (1995). Individual consideration viewed at multiple levels of analysis: A multi-level framework for examining the diffusion of transformational leadership. *Leadership Quarterly*, 6, 199-218.

Avolio, B. J., & Bass, B. M. (1988). An alternative strategy for reducing biases in leadership ratings. Paper, Academy of Management, Anaheim, CA.

Avolio, B. J., & Bass, B. M. (1991). *The full range leadership development programs: basic and advanced manuals.* Binghamton, NY: Bass, Avolio & Associates.

Avolio, B. J., & Bass, B. M. (1994). Evaluate the impact of transformational leadership training at individual, group, organizational, and community levels. Final report to W. K. Kellogg Foundation. Binghamton: State University of New York, Center for Leadership Studies.

Avolio, B. J., & Bass, B. M. (1996). You can drag a horse to water, but you can't make it drink: Evaluating a full range leadership model for training and development (CLS Report 96-4). Binghamton: State University of New York, Center for Leadership Studies.

Avolio, B. J., & Bass, B.M. (1998). You can drag a horse to water, but you can't make it drink except when it's thirsty. *Journal of Leadership Studies, 5,* 1-17

Avolio, B. J., & Gardner, W. L. (2005). Authentic leadership development: Getting to the root of positive forms of leadership. *Leadership Quarterly*, 16, 3, 315-338.

Avolio, B. J., & Gibbons, T. C. (1988). Developing transformational leaders: A lifespan approach. In J. A. Conger & R. N. Kanungo (Eds.), Charismatic leadership: The elusive factor in organizational effectiveness (pp. 276–308). San Francisco: Jossey-Bass.

Avolio, B. J., & Howell, J. M. (1990). The effects of leader-follower personality congruence: Predicting follower satisfaction and business unit performance. Paper, International Association of Applied Psychology, Kyoto, Japan.

Avolio, B. J., & Howell, J. M. (1992). The impact of leader behavior and leader-follower personality match on satisfaction and unit performance. In K. E. Clark, M. B. Clark, & D. R. Campbell (Eds.), Impact of leadership. Greensboro, NC: The Center for Creative Leadership.

Avolio, B. J., & Yammarino, F. J. (1997). Leadership and organizational culture in TQM. In S. B. Krause (Ed.), Human resource management issues in total quality management. Washington, D. C.: ASQC Press.

Avolio, B. J., Bass, B. M., & Jung, D. (1996). Construct validation of the multifactor leadership questionnaire MLQ-Form 5X (CLS Report 96-1). Binghamton: State University of New York, Center for Leadership Studies.

Avolio, B. J., Bass, B. M., & Jung, D. I. (1995). *MLQ multifactor leadership questionnaire: technical report.* Redwood City, CA: Mindgarden.

Avolio, B. J., Bass, B. M., & Jung, D. I. (1999). Re-examining the components of transformational and transactional leadership using the Multifactor Leadership Questionnaire. *Journal of Occupational and Organizational Psychology*, 72, 441–462.

Avolio, B. J., Gardner, W. L and Walumbwa, F. O. (2007). *The Authentic Leadership Questionnaire*. Mindgarden.com

Avolio, B. J., Waldman, D. W., & Yammarino, F. L. (1991). Leading in the 1990's: towards understanding the four I's of transformational leadership. *Journal of European Industrial Training*, 15(4), 9–16.

Avolio, B.J. (1994). The "natural" leader: Some antecedents to transformational leadership. *International Journal of Public Administration, 17*, 1559-1581.

Avolio, B.J. (1999) *Full Leadership Development: Building the Vital Forces in Organizations*. Thousand Oaks, CA: Sage.

Avolio, B.J. (2004). *Leadership Development in Balance: Made/Born*. NJ: Erlbaum.

Avolio, B.J. & Bass, B.M. (1988) Transformational leadership, charisma and beyond. In J.G. Hunt, B.R. Baloga, H.P. Dachler, & C. Schriesheim (Eds.). *Emerging leadership vistas* (pp. 29-50). Emsford, NY: Pergamon Press.

Avolio, B.J., & Bass, B.M. (1991). *The full-range of leadership development*. Center for Leadership Studies, Binghamton, NY.

Avolio, B.J., & Yammarino, F.J. (2003). Transformational and charismatic leadership: The road ahead. Oxford: Elsevier Press.

Avolio, B.J., Jung, D.I., Murry, W., Sivasubramaniam, N., & Garger, J. (2003). Assessing shared leadership: Development of a Team Multifactor Leadership Questionnaire. In C.L. Pearce & Jay A. Conger (Eds.), Shared leadership: Reframing the hows and whys of leadership. (pp. 143-172). Thousand Oaks: Sage.

Babakus, E., Yavas, U., & Ashill, N. J. (2011). Service worker burnout and turnover intentions: Roles of person-job fit, servant leadership, and customer orientation. *Services Marketing Quarterly*, 32(1), 17–31.

Bar-On, R. (1997). *The Emotional Quotient Inventory (EQ-i): A test of emotional intelligence*. Toronto, Canada: Multi-Health Systems, Inc.

Bar-On, R. (2000). *The Emotional Quotient Inventory (EQ-i): Technical manual*. Toronto, Canada: Multi-Health Systems, Inc.

Bar-On, R. (2004). The Bar-On Emotional Quotient Inventory (EQ-i): Rationale, description, and summary of psychometric properties. In Glenn Geher (Ed.), *Measuring emotional intelligence: common ground and controversy*. Hauppauge, NY: Nova Science Publishers, pp. 111-142.

Bar-On, R. (2006). The Bar-On model of emotional-social intelligence (ESI). *Psicothema, 18*, 13-25.

Barbuto Jr., J. E., & Wheeler, D. W. (2006). Scale development and construct clarification of servant leadership. *Group & Organization Management*, 31(3), 300-326.

Barnard, C. I. (1938) *The functions of the executive*. Cambridge, Mass: Harvard University Press.

Barrick, M. R., Mount, M. K., & Judge, T. A. (2001). The FFM personality dimensions and Job performance: meta-analysis of meta-analyses. *International Journal of Selection and Assessment, 9*, 9-30.

Bass, B. M. (1985). *Leadership and performance beyond expectations*. New York: Free Press.

Bass, B. M. (1985). Leadership: Good, better, best. *Organizational Dynamics,* 13(3), 26-40.

Bass, B. M. (1985). *The multifactor leadership questionnaire: Form 5.* Binghamton: State University of New York.

Bass, B. M. (1987). Charismatic and inspirational leadership: what's the difference? *Symposium, Charismatic Leadership in Management.* Faculty of Management, McGill University, Montreal, QU.

Bass, B. M. (1988). Transformational leadership and coping with crisis and stress conditions. *International Congress of Psychology*, Sydney, Australia.

Bass, B. M. (1989). The inspirational processes of leadership. Journal of Management Development, 7(5), 21–31.

Bass, B. M. (1989). The two faces of charismatic leadership. *Leaders Magazine,* 12 (4), 44–45.

Bass, B. M. (1990). *Bass and Stogdill's handbook of leadership.* New York: Free Press.

Bass, B. M. (1990). From transactional to transformational leadership: Learning to share the vision. *Organization Dynamics*, 18(3), 19–36.

Bass, B. M. (1995). The universality of transformational leadership. Distinguished Scientific Contributors Award Address, Society for Industrial/Organizational Psychology, Orlando, FL.

Bass, B. M. (1995). Transformational leadership redux. Leadership Quarterly, 6, 463–477.

Bass, B. M. (1996). *The ethics of transformational leadership.* College Park: University of Maryland, Leadership Studies Group, Center for Politics and Participation.

Bass, B. M. (1997) Does the transactional/transformational leadership paradigm transcend organizational and national boundaries? *American Psychologist, 52,* 130-139.

Bass, B. M. (1998). The ethics of transformational leadership. In J. B. Ciulla (Ed), *Ethics, the heart of leadership.* Westport, CT: Praeger.

Bass, B. M. (1998). *Transformational leadership: Industrial, military, and educational impact.* Mahwah, NJ: Lawrence Erlbaum & Associates.

Bass, B. M. (1999) Two decades of research and development in transformational leadership. European Journal of Work and Organizational Psychology, 8(1), 9-32.

Bass, B. M. (1999). Current developments in transformational leadership: Research and applications. *Psychologist-Manager Journal*, 3, 5– 21.

Bass, B. M. (2000). The future of leadership in the learning organization. *Journal of Leadership Studies*, 7(3), 18–38.

Bass, B. M. & Bass, R. (2009). *The Bass handbook of leadership: Theory, research, and managerial applications.* New York: Simon & Schuster, Inc.. Kindle Edition.

Bass, B. M., & Avolio, B. J. (1989). Potential biases in leadership measures: How prototypes, leniency, and general satisfaction relate to ratings and rankings of transformational and transactional leadership constructs. Educational Tests and Measurement, 49, 509–527.

Bass, B. M., & Avolio, B. J. (1995) *Manual for the Multifactor Leadership Questionnaire.* Redwood City, CA: Mind Garden.

Bass, B. M., & Avolio, B. J. (1996). *Multifactor leadership questionnaire feedback report.* Palo Alto, CA: Consulting Psychologists Press.

Bass, B. M., & Avolio, B. J. (1996). *Transformational leadership development: manual for the multifactor leadership questionnaire.* Palo Alto, CA: Consulting Psychologists Press.

Graduate Leadership
References

Bass, B. M., & Avolio, B. J. (1997). *Full range of leadership: Manual for the Multifactor Leadership Questionnaire.* Redwood City, CA: Mind Garden.

Bass, B. M., & Avolio, B. J. (2004). *Multifactor leadership questionnaire: Manual leader form, rater, and scoring key for MLQ (Form 5x-Short).* Redwood City, CA: Mind Garden.

Bass, B. M., & Avolio, B. J. (Eds.) (1994). *Improving organizational effectiveness through transformational leadership.* Thousand Oaks, CA: Sage Publications.

Bass, B. M., & Avolio, B. J. (undated). Intuitive-empirical approach to biodata analysis. Binghamton: State University of New York, Center for Leadership Studies.

Bass, B. M., & Bass, R. (2008). *The Bass handbook of leadership: Theory, research, and managerial applications.* New York: Free Press.

Bass, B. M., & Seltzer, J. (1990). Transformational leadership: Beyond initiation and consideration. Journal of Management, 16, 693–703.

Bass, B. M., & Steidlmeier, P.A. (1999) Ethics,character, authenticity, and transformational leadership. Leadership Quarterly, 10, 181-217.

Bass, B. M., & Yammarino, F. (1989). Transformational leaders know themselves better (Tech Rep. No. ONR-Tr-5). Alexandria, VA: Office of Naval Research.

Bass, B. M., & Yammarino, F. J. (1991). Congruence of self and others' leadership ratings of naval officers for understanding successful performance. Applied Psychology: An International Review, 40, 437–454.

Bass, B. M., & Yokochi, N. (1991). Charisma among senior executives and the special case of Japanese CEO's. Consulting Psychology Bulletin, Winter/Spring, 1, 31–38.

Bass, B. M., Avolio, B. J., & Atwater, L. (1996). The transformational and transactional leadership of men and women. International Review of Applied Psychology, 45, 5-34.

Bass, B. M., Avolio, B. J., Jung, D. I., & Berson, Y. (2003). Predicting unit performance by assessing transformational and transactional leadership. *Journal of Applied Psychology,* 88 (2), 207– 218.

Bass, B. M., Avolio, B.J., & Atwater, L. (1996). The transformational and transactional leadership of men and women. *Applied Psychology: An International Review,* 45,5-34.

Bass, B. M., Avolio, B.J., Jung, D.I., & Berson, Y. (2003). Predicting unit performance by assessing transformational and transactional leadership. *Journal of Applied Psychology,* 88, 207-218.

Bass. B. M., Avolio, B. J., & Jung, D. I. (1999). Reexamining the components of transformational and transactional leadership using the Multifactor Leadership Questionnaire (Form 5X). *Journal of Organizational and Occupational Psychology,* 72, 441– 462.

Bennis, W. G., & Nanus, B. (1985). *Leaders: The strategies for taking charge.* New York: Harper & Row.

Bernard, L. L. (1926). *An introduction to social psychology.* New York: Holt.

Bingham, W. V. (1927). Leadership. In H. C. Metcalf, *The psychological foundations of management.* New York: Shaw.

Bird, C. (1940). *Social psychology.* New York: Appleton-Century.

Bird, J., Wang, C., & Murray, L. (2009). Building budgets and trust through superintendent leadership. *Journal of Education Finance* 35 (2), 140-156.

Blake, R. R., & McCanse, A. A. (1991). *Leadership dilemmas--grid solutions*. Houston: Gulf Pub. Co.

Blake, R. R., & Mouton, J. S. (1964). *The managerial grid*. Houston, TX: Gulf.

Blake, R. R., & Mouton, J. S. (1965). A 9, 9 approach for increasing organizational productivity. In E. H. Schein & W. G. Bennis (eds.), *Personal and organizational change through group methods*. New York: Wiley.

Blake, R. R., & Mouton, J. S. (1972). The managerial grid: Key orientations for achieving production through people. Houston, TX: Gulf.

Blake, R. R., & Mouton, J. S. (1978). *The new managerial grid*. Houston, TX: Gulf.

Bono, J. E., & Judge, T. A. (2003). Self-concordance at work: Toward understanding the motivational effects of transformational leaders. *Academy of Management Journal, 46: 554-571.*

Bono, J. E., & Judge, T. A. (2004). Personality and transformational and transactional leadership: a meta-analysis. *The Journal of Applied Psychology, 89,* 5, 901-10.

Bowden, A.O. (1927), A study on the personality of student leadership in the united states, *Journal of Abnormal Social Psychology,* Vol. 21, pp. 149-60.

Bowers, D. G., & Seashore, S. E. (1966). Predicting organizational effectiveness with a four-factor theory of leadership. *Administrative Science Quarterly*, 11, 238– 263.

Bowling, N. (2010). A meta-analysis of the predictors and consequences of organization-based self-esteem. *Journal Of Occupational & Organizational Psychology, 83*(3), 601. doi:10.1348/096317909X454382

Brackett, M., & Mayer, J. (2003). Convergent, discriminant, and incremental validity of competing measures of emotional intelligence. *Personality & Social Psychology Bulletin*, 9(9), 1147-1158.

Brayfield, A. H., & Rothe, H. F. (1951). An index of job satisfaction. *Journal of Applied Psychology, 35: 307-311.*

Brown, M. E., Trevino, L. K., & Harrison, D. A. (2005). Ethical leadership: A social learning perspective for construct development and testing. *Organizational Behavior and Human Decision Processes*, 97, 117–134.

Burke, C. S., Stagl, K. C., Klein, C., Goodwin, G. F., Salas, E., & Halpin, S. M. (2006). What type of leadership behaviors are functional in teams? A meta-analysis. *The Leadership Quarterly, 17,* 3, 288.

Burns, J. M. (1978). *Leadership*. New York: Harper & Row.

Burns, T., & Stalker, G. M. (1961). *The management of innovation*. Chicago: Quadrangle Books.

Bycio, P., Hackett, R. D., & Allen, J. S. (1995). Further assessments of Bass's (1985) conceptualization of transactional and transformational leadership. *Journal of Applied Psychology*, 80, 468–478.

Cameron, K. S., Bright, D., & Caza, A. (2004). Exploring the relationships between organizational virtuousness and performance. *American Behavioral Scientist*, 47(6), 1– 24.

Campion, M. A., Medsker, G., & Higgs, C. (1993). Relations between work group characteristics and effectiveness: Implications for designing effective work groups. *Personnel Psychology*, 46, 823–850.

Graduate Leadership
References

Caplow, T., Hicks, L., & Wattenberg, B. J. (2001). *The first measured century: An illustrated guide to trends in America, 1900-2000.* Washington, D.C: AEI Press.

Carless, S. A., Wearing, A. J., & Mann, L. (2000). A short mesure of transformation leadership. *Journal of Business and Psychology,* 14(3), 389-406.

Carlyle, T., Goldberg, M. K., Brattin, J. J., & Engel, M. (1888; Republished in1993). *On heroes, hero-worship, & the heroic in history.* Fredrick A. Stokes & Brother, New York, 1888; Berkeley: University of California Press., 1993.

Carson, P., Carson, K. D., & Roe, C. (1993). Social power bases: A meta-analytic examination of interrelationships and outcomes. *Journal of Applied Social Psychology,* 23(14), 1150-1169.

Cartwright, D., Zander, A. F., & Harold D. Lasswell Collection (Yale Law Library). (1960).*Group dynamics: Research and theory. Ed. by Dorwin Cartwright [and] Alvin Zander.* New York: Harper & Row.

Caruso, D. (Date Unknown) *All About the Mayer-Salovey-Caruso Emotional Intelligence Test* (MSCEIT) downloaded from http://www.calcasa.org/sites/default/files/msceit_white_paper.pdf

Cattell, H. B. (1989). *The 16PF: Personality In Depth.* Champaign, IL: Institute for Personality and Ability Testing, Inc.

Cattell, R. B. (1946). *Description and measurement of personality.* Yonkers-on-Hudson, N. Y: World book company.

Cerit, Y. (2009). The effects of servant leadership behaviors of school principals on teachers' job satisfaction. *Educational Management Administration & Leadership,* 37(5), 600–623.

Ceruzzi, P. E. (2012). *Computing: A concise history.* Cambridge, Mass: MIT Press.

Chandler, A. D., Hikino, T., & Von, N. A. (2008). *Inventing the electronic century: The epic story of the consumer electronics and computer industries.* New York: Free Press.

Chaturvedi, S., Arvey, R., Zhang, Z., & Christoforou, P. (2011). Genetic underpinnings of transformational leadership: the mediating role of dispositional hope. *Journal of Leadership & Organizational Studies, 18,* 4, 469-479.

Chiaburu, D., Oh, I., Berry, C., Li, N., & Gardner, R. (2011). The five-factor model of personality traits and organizational citizenship behaviors: A meta-analysis. *Journal Of Applied Psychology,* 96(6), 1140-1166.

Cialdini, R. B., Trost, M. R., & Newsom, J. T. (1995). Preference for consistency: The development of a valid measure and the discovery of surprising behavioral implications. *Journal of Personality and Social Psychology,* 69(2), 318–328.

Clapp-Smith, R., Vogelgesang, G. R., & Avey, J. B. (2009). Authentic leadership and positive psychological capital: The mediating role of trust at the group level of analysis. *Journal of Leadership and Organizational Studies,* 15, 227–240.

Collins, J. C. (2001). *Good to great: Why some companies make the leap--and others don't.* New York, NY: HarperBusiness.

Collins, J. C., & Porras, J. I. (1994). *Built to last: Successful habits of visionary companies.* New York, NY: HarperCollins.

Collins, J. C., & Porras, J. I. (1996). Building your company's vision. *Harvard Business Review, 74,* 5, 65-78.

Collins, M. D. (2007). Understanding the relationship between leader-member exchange (LMX), psychological empowerment, job satisfaction, and turnover intent in a limited-service restaurant environment. *Unpublished doctoral dissertation, The Ohio State University.*

Colquitt, J. A., Scott, B. A., Rodell, J. B., Long, D. M., Zapata, C. P., Conlon, D. E., & Wesson, M. J. (January 01, 2013). Justice at the millennium, a decade later: A meta-analytic test of social exchange and affect-based perspectives. *The Journal of Applied Psychology, 98,* 2, 199-236.

Conger, J. A., & Kanungo, R. N. (1997). Measuring charisma: Dimensionality and validity of the Conger-Kanungo scale of charismatic Leadership. *Canadian Journal Of Administrative Sciences (Canadian Journal Of Administrative Sciences), 14* (3), 290.

Costa, P. T., McCrae, R. R., & Dye, D. A. (January 01, 1991). Facet scales for agreeableness and conscientiousness: A revision of the NEO personality inventory. *Personality and Individual Differences, 12,* 9, 887-898.

Costa, P. T., McCrae, R. R., & Psychological Assessment Resources, Inc. (1992). *Revised NEO Personality Inventory (NEO PI-R) and NEO Five-Factor Inventory (NEO-FFI).* Odessa, Fla. Psychological Assessment Resources.

Cyert, R. M., & March, J. G. *A behavioral theory of the firm.* Englewood Cliffs, N. J.: Prentice Hall, 1963.

Daft, R. L. (2004). Theory Z: Opening the corporate door for participative management. *The Academy of Management Executive, 18,* 4, 117.

Dansereau, F., Graen, G. B., & Haga, W. J. (1975). *A vertical dyad linkage approach to leadership within formal organizations: A longitudinal investigation of the role making process.* Champaign, Ill: Institute of Labor and Industrial Relations, University of Illinois at Urbana-Champaign.

Dansereau, F., Graen, G., & Haga, W. (1975). A vertical dyad approach to leadership within formal organizations. *Organizational Behavior and Human Performance,* 13, 46– 78.

Dawda, D., & Hart, S. D. (2000). Assessing emotional intelligence: reliability and validity of the Bar-On Emotional Quotient Inventory (EQ-i) in university students. *Personality and Individual Differences, 28,* 4, 797-812.

De Jong, A., de Ruyter, K.,&Wetzels, M. (2005). Antecedents and consequences of group potency: A study of self-managing service teams. *Management Science,* 1(11), 1610– 1625.

DeGroot, T., Kiker, D. S., and Cross, T. C. (2009). A Meta-Analysis to Review Organizational Outcomes Related to Charismatic Leadership. *Canadian Journal of Administrative Sciences / Revue Canadienne Des Sciences De L'administration,* 17, 4, 356-372.

Deming, W. E. (1986). *Out of the crisis.* Cambridge, Mass: Massachusetts Institute of Technology, Center for Advanced Engineering Study.

Deming, W. E. (1994). *The new economics for industry, government, education.* Cambridge, Mass: M.I.T. Press.

Den Hartog, D. N., Van Muijen, J. J., & Koopman, P. L. (1997). Transactional versus transformational leadership: an analysis of the MLQ. *Journal of Occupational and Organizational Psychology,* 70, 19–34.

Den Hartog. D. N., House, R. J., Hanges, P. J., Ruiz-Quintanilla, S. A., Dorfman, P. W., Brenk,

K. M., Konrad, E., Sabadin, A. (1999). Culture specific and cross culturally generalizable implicit leadership theories: Are attributes of charismatic/transformational leadership universally endorsed?. *The Leadership Quarterly, 10,* 2, 219-256.

Derue, D. S., Nahrgang, J. D., Wellman, N., & Humphrey, S. E. (2011). Trait and behavioral theories of leadership: An integration and meta-analytic test of their relative validity. *Personnel Psychology, 64,* 1, 7-52.

Digman, J. M. (1997). Higher-order factors of the Big Five. *Journal of Personality and Social Psychology*, 73, 1246–1256.

Dorfman, P., Javidan, M., Hanges, P., Dastmalchian, A., House, R. (2012). GLOBE: A twenty year journey into the intriguing world of culture and leadership. *Journal of World Business, 47,*4, 504-518.

Downton, J. V. (1973). *Rebel leadership: Commitment and charisma in the revolutionary process.* New York: Free Press.

Drucker, P. F. (1946). *Concept of the corporation.* New York: John Day.

Drucker, P. F. (1954). *The practice of management.* New York: Harper & Row.

Druskat, V. U. (1994). Gender and leadership style: transformational and transactional leadership in the Roman Catholic Church. The Leadership Quarterly, 5, 99–119.

Dulewicz, V., Higgs, M., & Slaski, M. (2003). Measuring emotional intelligence: content, construct and criterion-related validity. *Journal of Managerial Psychology*, 18(5), 405.

Eagly, A. H. (2005). Achieving relational authenticity in leadership: Does gender matter? *Leadership Quarterly,* 16, 459– 474.

Eagly, A. H., Johannesen-Schmidt, M. C., & van Engen, M. L, (2004). Transformational, transactional, and laissez-faire leadership styles: A meta-analysis comparing women and men. *Psychological Bulletin, 129,* 4, 569-91.

Edú Valsania, S., Moriano León, J., Molero Alonso, F., & Topa Cantisano, G. (2012). Authentic leadership and its effect on employees' organizational citizenship behaviours. *Psicothema, 24*(4), 561-566.

Ehrhart, M. G. (2004). Leadership and procedural justice climate as antecedents of unit level organizational citizenship behavior. *Personnel Psychology*, 57(1), 61–94.

Eisenberger, R., Armeli, S., Rexwinkel, B., Lynch, P. D., & Rhoades, L. (2001). Reciprocation of perceived organizational support. *Journal of Applied Psychology*, 86, 42–51.

Eisenberger, R., Karagonlar, G., Stinglhamber, F., Neves, P., Becker, T. E., Gonzalez-Morales, M. G., & Steiger-Mueller, M. (2010). Leader–member exchange and affective organizational commitment: The contribution of supervisor's organizational embodiment. *Journal of Applied Psychology*, 95, 1085–1103.

Epstein, D. (2001). *20th century pop culture.* Philadelphia: Chelsea House.

Evans, M. G. (1970). The effects of supervisory behavior on the path-goal relationship. *Organizational Behavior and Human Performance*, 5, 277– 298.

Eysenck, H. J. (1997). Personality and experimental psychology: The unification of psychology and the possibility of a paradigm. *Journal of Personality and Social Psychology, 73,* 1224–1237.

Fayol, H, (1916), *Administration industrielle et générale; prévoyance, organisation, commandement, coordination, controle* (in French), Paris, H. Dunod et E. Pinat

Fayol, H. (1949). *General and industrial management.* London: Pitman.

Fend, H., Helmke, A., & Richter, P. (1984). *Inventar zu Selbstkonzept und Selbstvertrauen.* Konstanz: Univ. Konstanz.

Ferres, N., & Travaglione, T. (2003). The development and validation of the workplace trust survey: Combining qualitative and quantitative methodologies. Paper presented at the 9th Asia Pacific Researchers in Organization Studies Conference, Oaxaca, Mexico.

Fiedler, F. E. (1964). A contingency model of leadership effectiveness. In L. Berkowitz (ed.), *Advances in experimental social psychology,* vol. 1. New York: Academic Press.

Fiedler, F. E. (1966). The effect of leadership and cultural heterogeneity on group performance: A test of the contingency model. *Journal of Experimental Social Psychology,* 2, 237– 264.

Fiedler, F. E. (1967). *A theory of leadership effectiveness.* New York: McGraw–Hill.

Fiedler, F. E. (1971). *Leadership.* New York: General Learning Press.

Fiedler, F. E. & Garcia, J. E. (1987). *New approaches to effective leadership: Cognitive resources and organizational performance.* New York: Wiley.

Fiedler, F. E., & Chemers, M. M. (1974). *Leadership and effective management.* Glenview, IL: Scott, Foresman.

Fiedler, F. E., & Mahar, L. (1979). A field experiment validating contingency model leadership training. *Journal of Applied Psychology,* 64, 247– 254.

Fiedler, F. E., & Mahar, L. (1979). The effectiveness of contingency model training: Validation of leader match. *Personnel Psychology,* 32, 45– 62.

Fiedler, F. E., Chemers, M. M., & Mahar, L. (1976). *Improving leadership effectiveness: The leader match concept.* New York: Wiley.

Fisher, B. M., & Edwards, J. E. (1988). Consideration and initiating structure and their relationships with leader effectiveness: A meta-analysis. *Academy of Management Best Papers Proceedings, 8,* 1, 201-205.

Fleishman, E. A. (1989). *Leadership Opinion Questionnaire (LOQ) examiner's manual.* Park Ridge, IL: Science Research Associates.

Fleishman, E. A. (1989). *Supervisory Behavior Description Questionnaire (SBD) examiner's manual.* Park Ridge, IL: Science Research Associates.

Fleishman, E. A., Harris, E. F., & Burtt, H. E. (1955). *Leadership and supervision in industry.* Columbus: Ohio State University, Bureau of Educational Research.

Fleishman, E. A., Mumford, M. D., Zaccaro, S. J., Levin, K. Y., Korotkin, A. L., & Hein, M. B. (1991). Taxonomic efforts in the description of leader behavior: A synthesis and functional interpretation. *The Leadership Quarterly, 2,* 4, 245-287.

Fleishman, E.A. (1953). The description of supervisory behavior. *Personnel Psychology, 37,* 1-6.

French, J. R. P. (1950). Field experiments: Changing group productivity. In J. C. Miller (ed.), Experiments in social process. New York: McGraw-Hill.

French, J. R. P. (1956). A formal theory of social power. *Psychological Review,* 63, 181– 194.

French, J. R. P. and Raven, B.H. (1959), "The Bases of Social Power", in Cartwright, D. (Ed.),*Studies of Social Power,* Institute for Social Research, Ann Arbor, Michigan.

Gardner, W. L., Avolio, B. J., & Walumbwa, F. O. (2005). Authentic Leadership Theory and Practice: Origins, Effects and Development. *Monographs in Leadership and Management, Volume 3.* Emerald Group Publishing.

George, B. (2003). *Authentic leadership: Rediscovering the secrets to creating lasting value.* San Francisco: Jossey-Bass.

George, B., & Sims, P. (2007). *True north: Discover your authentic leadership.* San Francisco, Calif: Jossey-Bass/John Wiley & Sons.

Georgesen, J. C., & Harris, M. (1998). Why's my boss always holding me down? A meta-analysis of power effects on performance evaluations. *Personality & Social Psychology Review* (Lawrence Erlbaum Associates), 2(3), 184

Gerstner, C. R., & Day, D. V. (January 01, 1997). Meta-Analytic review of leader-member exchange theory: correlates and construct issues. *Journal of Applied Psychology, 82,* 6, 827.

Geyer, A. L. J., & Steyrer, J. M. (1998). Transformational leadership and objective performance in banks. *Applied Psychology: An International Review, 47,* 397–420.

Giallonardo, L. M., Wong, C. A., & Iwasiw, C. L. (2010). Authentic leadership of preceptors: Predictor of new graduate nurses' work engagement and job satisfaction. *Journal of Nursing Management,* 18, 993–1003.

Gilbreth, L. M., & Witzel, M. (2001). *The psychology of management.* Bristol: Thoemmes.

Goethals, G. R., Sorenson, G. J., & Burns, J. M. G. (2004). *Encyclopedia of leadership.* Thousand Oaks, Calif: Sage Publications.

Goldberg, L. R. (January 01, 1990). An alternative "description of personality": the big-five factor structure. *Journal of Personality and Social Psychology, 59,* 6, 1216-29.

Goleman, D. (1995). *Emotional intelligence.* New York: Bantam Books.

Goleman, D. (1998). What makes a leader. *Harvard Business Review, 76*(6), 92-102.

Gowing, M. K. (2001). Measurement of individual emotional competence. In C. Cherniss, & D. Goleman (Eds.), *The emotionally intelligent workplace: How to select for, measure, and improve emotional intelligence in individuals, groups, and organizations* (pp. 83–131). San Francisco, CA: Jossey-Bass.

Graeff, C. L. (1997). Evolution of situational leadership theory: A critical review. *Leadership Quarterly,* 8(2), 153-170.

Graen, G. B. (1976). Role-making processes within complex organizations. In M. D. Dunnette (Ed.), *Handbook of industrial and organizational psychology* (pp. 1202– 1245). Chicago: Rand McNally.

Graen, G. B., & Cashman, J. (1975). A role-making model of leadership in formal organizations: A developmental approach. In J. G. Hunt & L. L. Larson (Eds.), *Leadership frontiers* (pp. 143– 166). Kent, OH: Kent State University Press.

Graen, G. B., & Scandura, T. A. (1987). Toward a psychology of dyadic organizing. In B. Staw & L. L. Cumming (Eds.), *Research in organizational behavior* (Vol. 9, pp. 175– 208). Greenwich, CT: JAI.

Graen, G. B., & Uhl-Bien, M. (1991). The transformation of professionals into self-managing and partially self-designing contributions: Toward a theory of leadership making. *Journal of Management Systems, 3 ,* 33– 48.

Graen, G. B., & Uhl-Bien, M. (1995). Relationship-based approach to leadership: Development of leader– member exchange (LMX) theory of leadership over 25 years: Applying a multi-level, multi-domain perspective. *Leadership Quarterly*, 6(2), 219– 247.

Graen, G.B., Novak, M., and Sommerkamp, P. (1982). The effects of leader-member exchange and job design on productivity and satisfaction: Testing a dual attachment model. *Organizational Behavior and Human Performance*, 30, 109-131.

Graham, J. (1991). Servant-leadership in organizations: Inspirational and moral. *Leadership Quarterly*, 2(2), 105–119.

Green, M. (2012). *Visualizing Transformational Leadership*. North Charleston, SC.

Greenleaf, R. K. (1970). *The servant as leader*. Cambridge, Mass: Center for Applied Studies.

Greenleaf, R. K. (1972). *The institution as servant*. Cambridge, Mass: Center for Applied Studies.

Greenleaf, R. K. (1974). *Trustees as servants*. Cambridge, Mass: Center for Applied Studies.

Greenleaf, R. K. (1977). *Servant leadership*. Essay, Robert K. Greenleaf Center, Indianapolis, IN.

Greenleaf, R. K. (1979). *Servant leadership: A journey into the nature of legitimate power and greatness*. New York: Paulist Press.

Griffin, M., Neal, A., & Parker, S. (2007). A new model of work role performance: Positive behaviors in uncertain and interdependent contexts. *Academy of Management Journal*, 50, 327–347.

Hackman, J. & Oldham, G. (1975). Development of the Job Diagnostic Survey. *Journal of Applied Psychology*, 60, 1975, 159-170.

Hackman, M. & Johnson, C. (2009). *Leadership: A communication perspective*. Long Grove, IL: Waveland Press, Inc.

Hale, J. R., & Fields, D. L. (2007). Exploring servant leadership across cultures: A study of followers in Ghana and the USA. *Leadership*, 3(4), 397–417.

Halpin, A. W. (1957). *Manual for the Leader Behavior Description Questionnaire*. Columbus, OH: Bureau of Business Research, Ohio State University.

Halpin, A.W. & Winer, B.J. (1957). A factorial study of the leader behavior descriptions. In R.M. Stogdill and A.E. Coons (eds), *Leader behavior: Its description and measurement*. Columbus, OH: Bureau of Business Research, Ohio State University.

Hamel, G., & Prahalad, C. K. (1994). Competing for the Future. *Harvard Business Review*, 72(4), 122.

Hamel, G., & Prahalad, C. K. (1996). *Competing for the future*. Boston, Mass: Harvard Business School Press.

Hammer, M., & Champy, J. (1993). *Reengineering the corporation: A manifesto for business revolution*. New York, NY: Harper Business.

Hannah S.T., Walumbwa F.O., & Fry L.W. (2011). Leadership in action teams: Team leader and members' authenticity, authenticity strength, and team outcomes. *Personnel Psychology*. 64, 771-802.

Hannah, S. T., Avolio, B. J., & Walumbwa, F. O. (2011). Relationships between Authentic Leadership, Moral Courage, and Ethical and Pro-Social Behaviors. *Business Ethics Quarterly*, 21(4), 555-578.

Hannah, S., Avolio, B. and Walumbwa, F. (2011). Relationships between Authentic Leadership, Moral Courage, and Ethical and Pro-Social Behaviors. *Business Ethics Quarterly, 21*(4), 555-578

Harms, P. D., & Credé, M. (2010). Emotional Intelligence and Transformational and Transactional Leadership: A Meta-Analysis. *Journal of Leadership & Organizational Studies* (Sage Publications Inc.), 17(1), 5-17.

Hassan, A., & Ahmed, F. (August 01, 2011). Authentic leadership, trust and work engagement. *Proceedings of World Academy of Science, Engineering and Technology,80,* 750-756.

Hater, J. J., & Bass, B. M. (1988). Superiors' evaluations and subordinates' perceptions of transformational and transactional leadership. *Journal of Applied Psychology*, 73, 695–702.

Helms, M. M. (2000). *Encyclopedia of management*. Detroit, [Mich.: Gale Group

Hemphill, J. K., & Coons, A. E. (1957). Development of the Leader Behavior Description Questionnaire. In R. M. Stogdill & A. E. Coons (eds.), *Leader behavior: Its description and measurement*. Columbus: Ohio State University, Bureau of Business Research.

Herman, R. D. (1994). *The Jossey-Bass handbook of nonprofit leadership and management*. San Francisco: Jossey-Bass.

Hersey, P., & Blanchard, K. H. (1969). Life cycle theory of leadership. *Training & Development Journal*, 23, 26– 34.

Hersey, P., & Blanchard, K. H. (1969). *Management of organizational behavior*. Englewood Cliffs, NJ: Prentice-Hall.

Hersey, P., & Blanchard, K. H. (1973). *Leader effectiveness and adaptability description– self*. Escondido, CA: Center for Leadership Studies.

Hersey, P., & Blanchard, K. H. (1977). *Management of organizational behavior: Utilizing human resources*. Englewood Cliffs, NJ: Prentice-Hall.

Herzberg, F. (1959). *The motivation to work*. New York: Wiley.

Herzberg, F. (1966). *Work and the nature of man*. Cleveland: World Pub. Co.

Herzberg, F. (1976). *The managerial choice: To be efficient and to be human*. Homewood, Ill: Dow Jones-Irwin.

Hiebert, M., & Klatt, B. (2001). *The encyclopedia of leadership: A practical guide to popular leadership theories and techniques*. New York: McGraw-Hill.

Hinkin, T. R., & Schriesheim, C. A. (2008). A theoretical and empirical examination of the transactional and non-leadership dimensions of the Multifactor Leadership Questionnaire (MLQ). *Leadership Quarterly, 19,* 5, 501-513.

Hinkin, T. R., Tracey, J. B., & Enz, C. A. (1997). Scale construction: developing reliable and valid measurement instruments. *Journal of Hospitality and Tourism Research,* 21, 100–120.

Hmieleski, Cole and Baron. (2012). Shared authentic leadership and new venture performance. *Journal of Management*, 38(5), 1476-1499

Hofstede, G. (1980). *Culture's consequences: International differences in work-related values*. London: Sage.

Hofstede, G. (2001). *Culture's consequences: Comparing values, behaviors, institutions and organizations across nations,* (2nd edition). Thousand Oaks, CA: Sage.

Graduate Leadership

References

Hollander, E. P. (1958). Conformity, status, and idiosyncrasy credit. *Psychological Review*, 65, 2, 117-27.

Hollander, E. P. (1961). Emergent leadership and social influence. In L. Petrullo & B. M. Bass (Eds.), *Leadership and interpersonal behavior* (pp. 30 – 47). New York: Holt, Rinehart, and Winston.

Hollander, E. P. (1964). *Leaders, groups, and influence.* New York: Oxford University Press.

Hollander, E. P., & Kelly, D. R. (1990). *Rewards from leaders as perceived by followers.* Paper presented at the meeting of the Eastern Psychological Association, Philadelphia, PA.

House, R. J. (1971). A path goal theory of leader effectiveness. *Administrative Science Quarterly*, 16, 321– 338.

House, R. J. (1977) A 1976 theory of charismatic leadership. In J. G. Hunt & L. L. Larson (eds.), *Leadership: The cutting edge.* Carbondale, IL: Southern Illinois University Press.

House, R. J. (1996). Path-goal theory of leadership: Lessons, legacy, and a reformulated theory. *Leadership Quarterly.* p. 323 - 340.

House, R. J., & Global Leadership and Organizational Behavior Effectiveness Research Program. (2004). *Culture, leadership, and organizations: The GLOBE study of 62 societies.* Thousand Oaks, Calif: Sage Publications.

House, R. J., & Shamir, B. (1993). Towards the integration of transformational, charismatic, and visionary theories. In M. M. Chemers & R. Ayman (eds.), *Leadership theory and research: Perspective and directions. New* York: Academic Press.

House, R. J., Howell, J. M., Shamir, B., et al. (1992). Charismatic leadership: A 1992 theory and five empirical tests. Unpublished manuscript.

House, R. J., Woycke, J., & Fodor, E. M. (1988). Charismatic and non-charismatic leaders: Differences in behavior and effectiveness. In J. A. Conger & R. N. Kanungo (eds.), *Charismatic leadership: The elusive factor in organizational effectiveness.* San Francisco: Jossey-Bass.

Howell, J. M., & Avolio, B. J. (1992). Charismatic leadership: Submission or liberation? Academy of Management Executive, 6(2), 43-53.

Howell, J. M., & Avolio, B. J. (1993). Transformational leadership, transactional leadership, locus of control, and support for innovation: Key predictors of consolidated business business-unit performance. *Journal of Applied Psychology*, 78, 891–902.

Hsiung, H. (2012). Authentic leadership and employee voice behavior: A multi-level psychological process. *Journal Of Business Ethics, 107*(3), 349-361.

Hu, J., & Liden, R. C. (2011). Antecedents of team potency and team effectiveness: An examination of goal and process clarity and servant leadership. *Journal of Applied Psychology* 1–12.

Ilies, R., Nahrgang, J. D., & Morgeson, F. P. (January 01, 2007). Leader-member exchange and citizenship behaviors: a meta-analysis. *The Journal of Applied Psychology, 92, 1,* 269-77.

Indvik, J. (1986a). Path-goal theory of leadership: A meta-analysis. *Proceedings, Academy of Management*, Chicago, 189– 192.

Institute for Public Health Sciences. (2002). *11 questions to help you make sense of descriptive/cross-sectional studies.* New York: Yeshiva University.

Irving, J. A., & Longbotham, G. J. (2007). Team effectiveness and six essential servant leadership themes: A regression model based on items in the organizational leadership assessment. *International Journal of Leadership Studies*, 2(2), 98–113.

Jackson, T. A., Meyer, J. P., & Wang, X. (2013). Leadership, commitment, and culture: A meta-analysis. *Journal of Leadership & Organizational Studies, 20*(1), 84-106.

Jacobs, T. O., & Jaques, E. (1990). Military executive leadership. In K. E. Clark and M. B. Clark (Eds.), *Measures of leadership.* West Orange, New Jersey: Leadership Library of America, pp 281-295.

Jaramillo, F., Grisaffe, D. B., Chonko, L. B., & Roberts, J. A. (2009). Examining the impact of servant leadership on sales force performance. *Journal of Personal Selling & Sales Management,* 29(3), 257–275.

Jenkins, M., & Stewart, A. C. (2010). The importance of a servant leader orientation. *Health Care Management Review,* 35(1), 46–54.

Jensen, J. L., Olberding, J. C., & Rodgers, R. (1997). The quality of leader-member exchange (LMX) and member performance: A meta-analytic review. *Academy of Management Best Papers Proceedings, 8,* 1, 320-324.

Jensen, S. M., & Luthans, F. (2006). Relationship between Entrepreneurs' Psychological Capital and Their Authentic Leadership.*Journal Of Managerial Issues*, 18(2), 254-273.

Johnson, A. M., Vernon, P. A., McCarthy, J. M., Molso, M., Harris, J. A., & Jang, K. J. (1998). Nature vs nurture: Are leaders born or made? A behavior genetic investigation of leadership style. *Twin Research*, 1, 216– 223.

Joseph, D., Newman & D. A., (2010). Emotional Intelligence: An Integrative Meta-Analysis and Cascading Model. *Journal of Applied Psychology*, 95(1), 54-78.

Joseph, D., Newman, D. A., & Sin, H. (2011), Leader–Member exchange (LMX) measurement: evidence for consensus, construct breadth, and discriminant validity, in Donald D. Bergh, David J. Ketchen (ed.) *Building Methodological Bridges (Research Methodology in Strategy and Management, Volume 6)*, Emerald Group Publishing Limited, pp.89-135

Joseph, E. E., & Winston, B. E. (2005). A correlation of servant leadership, leader trust, and organizational trust. *Leadership & Organization Development Journal*, 26(1), 6–22.

Judge, T. A., & Ilies, R. (2002). Relationship of personality to performance motivation: A meta-analytic review. *Journal Of Applied Psychology*, 87(4), 797-807.

Judge, T. A., & Piccolo, R. F. (2004). Transformational and transactional leadership: A meta-analytic test of their relative validity. *The Journal of Applied Psychology, 89,* 5, 755-68.

Judge, T. A., Heller, D., & Mount, M. K. (2002). Five-factor model of personality and job satisfaction: A meta-analysis. *The Journal of Applied Psychology, 87,*3, 530-41

Judge, T. A., Piccolo, R. F., & Ilies, R. (2004). The forgotten ones? The validity of consideration and initiating structure in leadership research. *The Journal of Applied Psychology, 89,* 1, 36-51.

Kanste, O., Miettunen, J., & Kyngäs, H. (2007). Psychometric properties of the Multifactor Leadership Questionnaire among nurses. *Journal of Advanced Nursing, 57,* 2, 201-212.

Kanungo, R. B. & Conger, J. (1989) Dimensions of executive charisma, *Perspectives*, Vol.14, No 4, 1-8.

Kaptein, M. (2008). Developing and testing a measure for the ethical culture of organizations: The corporate ethical virtues model. *Journal of Organizational Behavior*, 29, 23–947.

Kark, R., Shamir, B., & Chen, G. (2003). The two faces of transformational leadership: empowerment and dependency. *The Journal of Applied Psychology, 88,* 2, 246-55.

Katz, D. & Kahn, R.L. (1952). Some recent findings in human relations research, In E. Swanson, T. Newcombe and E. Hartley (eds), *Readings in social psychology,* NY: Holt, Reinhart and Winston.

Katz, D., & Kahn, R. L. (1966). *The social psychology of organizations.* New York: Wiley.

Katz, D., & Kahn, R. L. (1978). *The social psychology of organizations.* New York: Wiley.

Kernis, M. H. (2003). Toward a conceptualization of optimal self-esteem. *Psychological Inquiry,* 14, 1–26.

Kernis, M. H. and Goldman, B. M. (2005) Authenticity: a multicomponent perspective, in Tesser, A., Wood, J. and Stapel, D. (eds) O*n Building, Defending, and Regulating the Self: A Psychological Perspective*, Psychology Press, New York, pp. 31–52.

Kernis, M. H. and Goldman, B .M. (2006) A multicomponent conceptualization of authenticity: research and theory. Advances in Experimental Social Psychology, 38, 284–357.

Kerr, S., & Jermier, J. (1978). Substitutes for leadership: Their meaning and measurement. *Organizational Behavior and Human Performance,* 22, 374– 403.

Kilbourne, C. E. (1935). The elements of leadership. *Journal of Coast Artillery,* 78, 437– 439.

Kinicki, A. J., McKee-Ryan, F. M., Schriesheim, C. A., & Carson, K. P. (2002). Assessing the construct validity of the Job Descriptive Index: A review and meta-analysis. *Journal of Applied Psychology, 87*(1), 14-32

Koh, W. L., Steers, R. M., & Terborg, J. R. (1995). The effects of transformational leadership on teacher attitudes and student performance in Singapore. *Journal of Organizational Behavior,* 16, 319–333.

Kopelman, R. L. (2008). Douglas McGregor's Theory X and Y: Toward a Construct-valid Measure. *Journal of Managerial Issues,* 20(2), 255-271.

Kopp, T., & Schuler, H. (2003). Vertrauen gegenüber Vorgesetzten und Akzeptanz von Entgeltsystemen. *Zeitschrift für Personalpsychologie,* 2(4), 182–192.

Kotter, J. P. (1990). What leaders really do. *Harvard Business Review, 68,*3.

Kotter, J. P. (1996). *Leading change.* Boston, Mass: Harvard Business School Press.

Kotter, J. P. (1999). *John P. Kotter on what leaders really do.* Boston: Harvard Business School Press.

Kouzes, J. M., & Posner, B. Z. (2002). *The leadership challenge.* San Francisco: Jossey-Bass.

Kouzes, J. M., & Posner, B. Z. (2007). *Leadership Is everyone's business.* San Francisco, Calif: Jossey-Bass.

Kurtz, J. E., & Parrish, C. L. (2001). Semantic response consistency and protocol validity in structured personality assessment: the case of the NEO-PI-R. *Journal of Personality Assessment, 76,* 2, 315-32.

Lapierre, L. M., & Hackett, R. D. (2007). Trait conscientiousness, leader-member exchange, job satisfaction and organizational citizenship behaviour: A test of an integrative model. *Journal of Occupational and Organizational Psychology, 80,* 3, 539-554.

Laub, J. A. (1999), *Assessing the servant organization: development of the Servant Organizational Leadership Assessment (SOLA) instrument*, Dissertation Abstracts International, UMI No. 9921922.

Lee, K., & Allen, N. J. (2002). Organizational citizenship behavior and workplace deviance: The role of affect and cognitions. *Journal of Applied Psychology*, 87, 131–142.

Leister, A., Borden, D., & Fiedler, F. E. (1977), Validation of Contingency Model Leadership Training: Leader Match, *Academy of Management Journal,* Vol. 20, No. 3, pp. 464-470.

Leroy, H., Palanski, M., & Simons, T. (2012). Authentic Leadership and Behavioral Integrity as Drivers of Follower Commitment and Performance. *Journal Of Business Ethics*, *107*(3), 255-264.

Letts, L., Wilkins, S., Law, M., Stewart, D., Bosch, J., & Westmorland, M. (2007). Critical review form: Qualitative studies (version 2.0).

Li, W. D., Arvey, R. D., Zhang, Z., & Song, Z. (2011). Do leadership role occupancy and transformational leadership share the same genetic and environmental influences?. *The Leadership Quarterly.*

Liden, R. C., & Graen, G. B. (1980). Generalizability of the vertical dyad linkage model of leadership. *Academy of Management Journal,* 23, 451–465.

Liden, R. C., & Maslyn, J. M. (1998). Multi-dimensionality of leader–member exchange: An empirical assessment through scale development. *Journal of Management*, 24, 43–72.

Liden, R. C., Wayne, S., Zhao. H. & Henderson, D. (2008). Servant leadership: Development of a multidimensional measure and multi-level assessment. *Leadership Quarterly*, 19(2), 161.

Lievens, F., Van Geit, P., & Coetsier, P. (1997). Identification of transformational leadership qualities: an examination of potential biases. *European Journal of Work and Organizational Psychology,* 6, 415–530.

Likert, R. (1961). *New patterns of management*. New York: McGraw-Hill.

Likert, R. (1967). *The human organization: Its management and value*. New York: McGraw-Hill.

Likert, R., & Likert, J. G. (1976). *New ways of managing conflict*. New York: McGraw-Hill.

Loehlin, J. C., McCrae, R. R., Costa, P. T., & John, O. P. (1998). Heritabilities of common and measure-specific components of the big five personality factors. *Journal of Research in Personality*, 32, 431– 453.

Lord, R. G., de Vader, C. L., & Alliger, G. M. (1986). A meta-analysis of the relation between personality traits and leadership perceptions: An application of validity generalization procedures. *Journal of Applied Psychology, 71,* 3, 402-410.

Lowe, K. B., Kroeck, K. G., & Sivasubramaniam, N. (1996). Effectiveness correlates of transformational and transactional leadership: A meta-analytic review of the MLQ literature. *The Leadership Quarterly*, 7(3), 385-415.

Luthans, F. and Avolio, B., (2003). Authentic Leadership Development, in Cameron, K. S., Dutton, J. E., & Quinn, R. E. (2003). *Positive organizational scholarship: Foundations of a new discipline*. San Francisco, CA: Berrett-Koehler.

Luthans, F., Avolio, B., Avey, J., & Norman, S. (2007). Psychological capital: Measurement and relationship with performance and satisfaction. *Personnel Psychology*, 60, 541–572.

Lytle, R. S., Hom, P. W., & Mokwa, M. P. (1998). SERV_OR: A managerial measure of organizational service-orientation. *Journal of Retailing*, 74, 455–489.

March, J. G., & Simon, H. A. (1958). *Organizations*. New York: Wiley

Martins, A., Ramalho, N., & Morin, E. (2010). A comprehensive meta-analysis of the relationship between emotional intelligence and health. *Personality & Individual Differences, 49*(6), 554-564.

Maslow, A. H. (1954). *Motivation and personality.* New York: Harper.

Maslow, A. H. (1965). *Eupsychian management: A journal.* Homewood, IL: Dorsey.

Maslow, A. H. *Toward a psychology of being.* Princeton, N. J.: Van Nostrand, 1962.

May, D. R., Chan, A. Y. L., Hodges, T. D., & Avolio, B. J. (2003). Developing the moral component of authentic leadership. *Organizational Dynamics, 32,* 247–260.

Mayer, D. M., Bardes, M., & Piccolo, R. F. (2008). Do servant leaders help satisfy follower needs? An organizational justice perspective. *European Journal of Work and Organizational Psychology, 17*(2), 180–197.

Mayer, J. D., Caruso, D., & Salovey, P. (2000). Selecting a measure of emotional intelligence: the case for ability scales. In R. Bar-On, & J. D. Parker (Eds.), *Handbook of emotional intelligence* (pp. 320–342).New York: Jossey-Bass.

Mayer, J. D., Roberts, R. D. and Barsade, S. G. (2008). Human abilities: Emotional intelligence. *Annual Review of Psychology, 59,* 507–536. p. 511.

Mayer, J. D., Salovey, P., & Caruso, D. R. (2004). Emotional Intelligence: Theory, Findings, and Implications. *Psychological Inquiry, 15,* 3, 197-215.

Mayer, J. D., Salovey, P., Caruso, D. R., & Sitarenios, G. (2003). Measuring emotional intelligence with the MSCEIT V2.0. *Emotion, 3,* 97–105.

Mayer, R.C., Davis, J.H., and Schoorman, F.D. (1995), "An Integration Model of Organizational Trust," *Academy of Management Review,* Vol. 20, 709-729.

Mayo, E. (1933). *The human problems of an industrial civilization.* New York: Macmillan.

Mayo, E. (1945). *The social problems of an industrial civilization.* Boston, MA: Harvard University, Graduate School of Business Administration.

McCrae, R. R., & Costa, P. T. J. (1987). Validation of the five-factor model of personality across instruments and observers. *Journal of Personality and Social Psychology, 52,* 1, 81-90.

McCrae, R. R., & Costa, P. T., Jr. (1997). Personality trait structure as a human universal. *American Psychologist, 52,* 509– 516.

McCrae, R. R., & Costa, P. T., Jr., (1990). *Personality in adulthood.* New York: Guilford.

McCrae, R. R., & Costa, P. T., Jr., (1992). Discriminant validity of NEO-PIR facet scales. *Educational & Psychological Measurement, 52* (1), 229.

McCrae, R. R., & Costa, P. T., Psychological Assessment Resources, Inc. (2010). *NEO inventories for the NEO Personality Inventory-3 (NEO-PI-3), NEO Five-Factor Inventory-3 (NEO-FFI-3), NEO Personality Inventory-Revised (NEO PI-R): Professional manual.* Lutz, FL: PAR.

McCrae, R., Zonderman, A. B., Costa, P. T. Jr., Bond, M. H., & Paunone, S. V. (1996). Evaluating replicability of factors in the revised NEO personality: Confirmatory factor analysis versus Procrustes rotation. *Journal of Personality & Social Psychology, 70* (3), 552– 566.

McGregor, D. (1960). *The human side of enterprise.* New York: McGraw-Hill.

McGregor, D. (1966). *Leadership and motivation.* MIT Press.

Meyer, J. P., Allen, N. J., & Gellatly, I. R. (1990). Affective and continuance commitment to the organization: Evaluation of measures and analysis of concurrent and time-lagged relations. *Journal of Applied Psychology, 75*, 710–720.

Meyer, J. P., Allen, N. J., & Smith, C. A. (1993). Commitment to organizations and occupations: Extension and test of a three-component conceptualization. *Journal of Applied Psychology, 78*(4), 538–551.

Miner, J. B. (2006). *Organizational Behavior 3: Historical origins, theoretical foundations, and the future.* Armonk, NY: Sharpe.

Miner, J. B., (2003). The rated importance, scientific validity, and practical usefulness of organizational behavior theories: a quantitative review. *Academy of Management Learning and Education, 2,* 3, 250-268.

Mitchell T, Biglan A and Fiedler F (1970), The contingency model: criticism and suggestions, *Academy of Management Journal*, Vol. 13, No. 3, pp. 253-267.

Moosa, K., & Sajid, A. (2010). Critical analysis of six sigma implementation. *Total Quality Management & Business Excellence*, 21(7), 745-759

Mowday, R. T., Steers, R. M., & Porter, L. W. (1979). The measurement of organizational commitment. *Journal of Vocational Behavior, 14:* 224-247.

Neider, L. A. (2011). The Authentic Leadership Inventory (ALI): Development and empirical tests. *Leadership Quarterly*, 22(6), 1146.

Neubert, M. J., Kacmar, K. M., Carlson, D. S., Chonko, L. B., & Roberts, J. A. (2008). Regulatory focus as a mediator of the influence of initiating structure and servant leadership on employee behavior. *Journal of Applied Psychology,* 93(6), 1220–1233.

Newsome, S., Day, A. L., & Catano, V. M. (2000). Assessing the predictive validity of emotional intelligence. *Personality and Individual Differences*, 29(6), 1005–1016.

Ng, T. H., Eby, L. T., Sorensen, K. L., & Feldman, D. C. (2005). Predictors of objective and subjective career success. A meta-analysis. *Personnel Psychology,* 58(2), 367-408.

Nielson, L. (2011). *Computing: a business history.* New York. New Street Communication.

Noel, C., John, U. F., James, M. H., & David, L. (1991). In search of excellence ten years later: strategy and organization do matter. *Management Decision, 29,* 4

Nohria, N., & Khurana, R. (2010). *Handbook of leadership theory and practice: An HBS centennial colloquium on advancing leadership.* Boston, Mass: Harvard Business Press.

Northouse, P. (1999). *Leadership : theory and practice.* Sage Publications.

Northouse, P. (2013). *Leadership : theory and practice.* Sage Publications.

Nwogu, O. G. (2004). Servant leadership model: The role of follower self-esteem, emotional intelligence, and attributions on organizational effectiveness. Paper presented at the *Servant Leadership Roundtable*, Regent University.

Nyhan R. (2000). Changing the paradigm: Trust and its role in public sector organizations. *American Public Review of Administration,* 30, 87–109.

Ouchi, W. (1981). Going from A to Z: Thirteen steps to a Theory Z organization. Management Review, 70(5), 8.

Ouchi, W. G. (1981). *Theory Z: How American business can meet the Japanese challenge.* Reading, Mass: Addison-Wesley.

Ouchi, W. G. (1984). *The M-form society: How American teamwork can recapture the competitive edge.* Reading, Mass: Addison-Wesley.

Ouchi, W. G., & Jaeger, A. M. (1978). *Type z organization: A better match for a mobile society.* Stanford, Calif.: Graduate School of Business, Stanford University.

Ouchi, W. G., & Jaeger, A. M. (1978). Type z organization: stability in the midst of mobility. *Academy Of Management Review,* 3(2), 305-314. doi:10.5465/AMR.1978.4294895

Page, D. P. (1935). Measurement and prediction of leadership. *American Journal of Sociology,* 41, 31– 43.

Page, D., & Wong, T. P. (2000). A philosophy conceptual framework for measuring servant leadership. In S. Adjibolosoo (Ed.), *The Human factor in shaping the course of history and development.* Lanham, MD: University Press of America.

Parris, D. L., & Peachey, J. W. (2013). A systematic literature review of servant leadership theory in organizational contexts. *Journal of Business Ethics, 113,*3, 377-393.

Patterson, K. (2003). *Servant leadership: A theoretical model.* Dissertation Abstracts International, 64(2), 570 (UMI No. 3082719).

Peters, T. J., & Waterman, R. H. (1982). *In search of excellence: Lessons from America's best-run companies.* New York: Harper & Row.

Peterson, K., Malouff, J., & Thorsteinsson, E. B. (2011). A meta-analytic investigation of emotional intelligence and alcohol involvement. *Substance Use & Misuse, 46*(14), 1726-1733.

Podsakoff, P. M., Bommer, W. H., Podsakoff, N. P., & MacKenzie, S. B. (2006). Relationships between leader reward and punishment behavior and subordinate attitudes, perceptions, and behaviors: A meta-analytic review of existing and new research. *Organizational Behavior and Human Decision Processes, 99,* 2, 113-142

Rafferty, A. E., & Griffin, M. A. (2004). Dimensions of transformational leadership: Conceptual and empirical extensions. *The Leadership Quarterly,* 15, 329–354.

Randolph-Seng, B., & Gardner, W. L. (2013). Validating Measures of Leader Authenticity: Relationships Between Implicit/Explicit Self-Esteem, Situational Cues, and Leader Authenticity. *Journal Of Leadership & Organizational Studies* (Sage Publications Inc.), 20(2), 214-231.

Rauch, C. F., & Behling, O. (1984). Functionalism: Basis for an alternate approach to the study of leadership. In J. G. Hunt, D. M. Hosking, C. A. Schriesheim, and R. Stewart (Eds.), *Leaders and managers: International perspectives on managerial behavior and leadership.* New York: Pergamon Press, pp. 45-62.

Rego, A. (2013). Are authentic leaders associated with more virtuous, committed and potent teams?. *Leadership Quarterly, 24*(1), 61-79.

Rego, A., Sousa, F., Marques, C., & Cunha, M. (2012). Authentic leadership promoting employees' psychological capital and creativity. *Journal Of Business Research, 65*(3), 429-437

Richards, D. & Engle, S. (1986). After the vision. In *Transforming leadership,* J.D. Adams (Ed), Alexandria, VA. Miles River Press.

Rieke, M., Hammermeister, J., & Chase, M. (2008). Servant leadership in sport: A new paradigm for effective coach behavior. *International Journal of Sports Science & Coaching,* 3(2), 227–239.

Graduate Leadership
References

Rost, J. C. (1991). *Leadership for the twenty-first century*. New York: Praeger.

Rousseau, D. M., Sitkin, S. B., Burt, R. S., & Camerer, C. (1998). Not so different after all: A cross-discipline view of trust. *Academy of Management Review*, 23, 393–404.

Russell, R., & Stone, A. G. (2002). A review of servant leadership attributes: Developing a practical model. *Leadership and Organizational Development Journal*, 23(3), 145–157.

Salovey, P. & Mayer, J. D. (1990). Emotional intelligence. *Imagination, Cognition, and Personality, 9*, 185-211.

Scandura, T. A., & Graen, G. B. (1984). Moderating effects of initial leader-member exchange status on the effects of a leadership intervention. *Journal of Applied Psychology*, 69, 428–436.

Schaubroeck, J., Lam, S. S. K., & Peng, A. C. (2011). Cognition based and affect-based trust as mediators of leader behavior influences on team performance. *Journal of Applied Psychology*, 96(4), 863–871.

Schaufeli W.B. & Bakker A.B. (2003) *Utrecht Work Engagement Scale (UWES) Preliminary Manual*. Occupational Health Psychology Unit, Utrecht University, ND.

Schein, E. H. (1992). *Organizational culture and leadership*. San Francisco: Jossey-Bass.

Schlaerth, A., Ensari, N., & Christian, J. (2013). A meta-analytical review of the relationship between emotional intelligence and leaders' constructive conflict management. *Group Processes & Intergroup Relations, 16*(1), 126-136.

Schriesheim, C. A., & Cogliser, C. C. (2009). Construct validation in leadership research: Explication and illustration. *The Leadership Quarterly*, 20, 725–736.

Schriesheim, C. A., Castro, S. L., & Cogliser, C. C. (1999). Leader-member exchange (LMX) research: A comprehensive review of theory, measurement, and data-analytic practices. *The Leadership Quarterly, 10,* 1, 63-113

Schriesheim, C. A., Tepper, B. J., & Tetrault, L. A. (1994). Least Preferred Co-Worker Score, situational control, and leadership effectiveness: A meta-analysis of contingency model performance predictions. *Journal Of Applied Psychology,*79(4), 561-573.

Schutte, N. S., Malouff, J. M., Hall, L. E., Haggerty, D. J., Cooper, J. T., Golden, C. J., & Dornheim, L. (1998). Development and validation of a measure of emotional intelligence. *Personality and Individual Differences*, 25(2), 167-177.

Schutte, N. S., Malouff, J. M., Thorsteinsson, E. B., Bhullar, N., & Rooke, S. E. (2007). A meta-analytic investigation of the relationship between emotional intelligence and health. *Personality & Individual Differences, 42*(6), 921-933.

Seligman, M. E. P. (1998). *Learned optimism*. New York: Pocket Books.

Sendjaya, S., & Pekerti, A. (2010). Servant leadership as antecedent of trust in organizations. *Leadership & Organization Development Journal*, 31(7), 643–663.

Sendjaya, S., Sarros, J., & Santora, J. (2008). Defining and measuring servant leadership behavior in organizations. *Journal of Management Studies*, 45(2), 402–424.

Senge, P. M. (1990). *The fifth discipline: The art and practice of the learning organization*. New York: Doubleday/Currency.

Simon, H. A. (1947). *Administrative behavior: A study of decision-making processes in administrative organization*. New York: Macmillan Co.

Simons, T. L., & McLean-Parks, J. (2000). The sequential impact of behavior integrity on trust, commitment, discretionary service behavior, customer satisfaction and profitability. Paper presented at the annual *Academy of Management Conference*, Toronto, ON.

Smircich, L., & Morgan, G. (1982). Leadership: The management of meaning. *Journal of Applied Behavioral Science*, 18, 257–273.

Smith, C. A., Organ, D. W., & Near, J. P. (1983). Organizational citizenship behavior: Its nature and antecedents. *Journal of Applied Psychology*, 68(4), 653-663.

Smith, P. C., Kendall, L. M., & Hulin, C. L. (1969). *The measurement of satisfaction in work and retirement.* Chicago: Rand-McNally.

Snyder, C. R., Irving, L., & Anderson, J. R. (1991). Hope and health: Measuring the will and the ways. In C. R. Snyder, & D. R. Forsyth (Eds.), *Handbook of social and clinical psychology* (pp. 285–305). Elmsford, NY, Pergamon.

Snyder, T. D., & National Center for Education Statistics. (1993). *120 years of American education: A statistical portrait.* Washington, D.C: U.S. Dept. of Education, Office of Educational Research and Improvement, National Center for Education Statistics.

Spears, L.C. (1994). Servant leadership: Quest for caring leadership. *Inner Quest*, 2, 1-4.

Spears, L.C. (1995). (Ed.). *Reflections on leadership: How Robert K. Greenleaf's theory of servant-leadership influenced today's top management thinkers.* New York: John Wiley & Sons, Inc.

Spears, L.C. (Ed.). (1998). *Insights on leadership: Service, stewardship, spirit and servant-leadership.* New York, NY: John Wiley & Sons.

Stamps P.L. (1997) *Nurses and Work Satisfaction: An Index for Measurement, 2nd ed.* Health Administration Press, Chicago, IL.

Stewart, G. L., Carson, K. P., & Cardy, R. L. 1996. The joint effects of conscientiousness and self-leadership training on employee self-directed behavior in a service setting. *Personnel Psychology*, 49: 143-164.

Stodgill, R.M., Goode, O.S. and Day, D.R. (1962). New leader behavior description subscales. *Journal of Psychology, 54*, 259-269.

Stogdill, R. M. (1948). Personal factors associated with leadership: A survey of the literature. *Journal of Psychology*, 25, 35– 71.

Stogdill, R. M. (1963). *Manual for the Leader Behavior Description Questionnaire Form XII.* Columbus: Ohio State University, Bureau of Business Research.

Stogdill, R. M. (1963). *Team achievement under high motivation.* Columbus, Ohio: Ohio State University, Bureau of Business Research, College of Commerce and Administration.

Stogdill, R. M. (1974). *Handbook of leadership: A survey of theory and research.* New York: Free Press.

Stoltz, P., Ude´n, G., & Willman, A. (2004). Support for family careers who care for an elderly person at home - A systematic literature review. *Scandinavian Journal of Caring Sciences*, 18, 111–118.

Taylor, F. W. (1911). *The principles of scientific management.* New York: Norton.

Tead, O. (1935). *The art of leadership.* New York: McGraw-Hill.

Tepper, B. J., & Percy, P. M. (1994). Structural validity of the multifactor leadership questionnaire. *Educational and Psychological Measurement, 54*, 734–744.

Toor, S., & Ofori, G. (2009). Authenticity and its influence on psychological well-being and contingent self-esteem of leaders in Singapore construction sector. Construction Management and Economics, 27, 299–313

Tracey, J. B., & Hinkin, T. R. (1998). Transformational leadership or effective managerial practices? *Group and Organization Management*, 23, 220–236.

Trice, H. M., & Beyer, J. M. (1986). Charisma and its routinization in two social movement organizations. *Research in Organizational Behavior,* 8, 113– 164.

United States, & U.S. Census Bureau. (1878). *Statistical abstract of the United States.* Washington: U.S. G.P.O.

Van Dierendonck, D. (2011). Servant leadership: A review and syntheses. *Journal of Management*, 27(4), 1228–1261.

van Dierendonck, D., & Nuijten, I. (2011). The Servant Leadership Survey: Development and Validation of a Multidimensional Measure. *Journal Of Business And Psychology, 26*(3), 249-267.

van Dyne, L. V., Graham, J. W., & Dienesch, R. M. (1994). Organizational citizenship behavior: Construct redefinition, measurement, and validation. *Academy of Management Journal,* 37, 765–802.

Van Rooy, D. L., & Viswesvaran, C. (2004). Emotional intelligence: A meta-analytic investigation of predictive validity and nomological net. *Journal Of Vocational Behavior,* 65 (1), 71-95.

Van Seters, D. & Field, R. (1990). The evolution of leadership theory. *Journal of Organizational Change Management, 3,* 3, 29-45.

von Collani, G., & Blank, H. (2003). Perso¨nlichkeitsmerkmale, soziale U¨ berzeugungen und politische Parteienpra¨ferenzen: Eine Internetbefragung zur Bundestagswahl 2002. Zeitschrift fuer Politische Psychologie, 11(4), 307–324.

Vroom, V. H., & Jago, A. G. (1978). On the validity of the Vroom-Yetton model. *Journal of Applied Psychology*, 63, 151– 162.

Vroom, V. H., & Jago, A. G. (1988). *The new leadership: Managing participation in organizations.* Englewood Cliffs, NJ: Prentice-Hall.

Vroom, V. H., & Yetton, P. W. (1973). *Leadership and decision-making.* Pittsburgh: University of Pittsburgh Press. New York: Wiley.

Walumbwa, F. Luthans, F. Avey, J. and Oke, A. (2011) Authentically leading groups: The mediating role of collective psychological capital and trust Journal of Organizational Behavior 32, 4–24

Walumbwa, F. O., & Lawler, J.J. (2003). Building effective organizations. Transformational leadership, collectivist orientation, work-related attitudes, and withdrawal behaviors in three emerging economies. *International Journal of Human Resource Manage*ment, 14, 1083-1101.

Walumbwa, F. O., Avolio, B. J., Gardner, W. L., Wernsing, T. S., & Peterson, S. J. (2008). Authentic leadership: Development and validation of a theory-based measure. Journal of Management, 34, 89–126.

Walumbwa, F. O., Avolio, B., Gardner, W., Wernsing, T., & Peterson, S. (2008). Authentic Leadership: Development and Validation of a Theory-Based Measure. *DigitalCommons@University of Nebraska - Lincoln.*

Walumbwa, F. O., Hartnell, C. A., & Oke, A. (2010). Servant leadership, procedural justice climate, service climate, employee attitudes and organizational citizenship behavior: A cross-level investigation. *Journal of Applied Psychology,* 95(3), 517–529.

Walumbwa, F. O., Lawler, J.J., Avolio, B.J., & Wang, P. (2003). *Relationship between transformational leadership and work-related attitudes: The Moderating effects of collective and self-efficacy across cultures.* Working paper, University of Nebraska, Lincoln.

Walumbwa, F. O., Wang, P., Lawler, J. J., & Shi, K. (2004). The role of collective efficacy in the relations between transformational leadership and work outcomes. *Journal of Occupational and Organizational Psychology, 77,* 4, 515-530.

Walumbwa, F. O., Wang, P., Wang, H., Schaubroeck, J., & Avolio, B. J. (2010). Psychological processes linking authentic leadership to follower behaviors. *The Leadership Quarterly, 21*(5), 901-914.

Walumbwa, F. O., Wu, C., & Ojode, L. (2004). Gender and instructional outcomes: The mediating effects of leadership styles. *Journal of Management Development*, 23, 2.

Wang, C & Bird, J. (2011). Multi-level modeling of principal authenticity and teachers' trust and engagement Academy of Educational Leadership Journal, Volume 15, Number 4, 2011

Wang, D., & Hsieh, C. (2013). The effect of authentic leadership on employee trust and employee engagement. *Social Behavior And Personality,* 41(4), 613-624.

Wang, G., Courtright, S. H., Colbert, A. E., & Oh, I. (2011). Transformational leadership and performance across criteria and levels: A meta-analytic review of 25 years of research. *Group and Organization Management, 36,* 2, 223-270.

Washington, R. R., Sutton, C. D., & Feild, H. S. (2006). Individual differences in servant leadership: The roles of values and personality. *Leadership & Organization Development Journal*, 27(8), 700–716.

Wayne, S. J., Shore, L. M., & Liden, R. C. (1997). Perceived organizational support and leader-member exchange: A social exchange perspective. *Academy of Management Journal,* 40: 82-111.

Weber, M. (1924/1947). *The theory of social and economic organization* (Trans. T. Parsons). New York: Free Press.

Welbourne Theresa, M., E. Johnson Diane, Erez Amir, 1998. The Role-based Performance Scale: Validity Analysis of a Theory-based Measure. *Academy of Management Journal*, 415: 540-555.

Welbourne, T. M., Johnson, D. E., & Erez, A. 1998. The role-based performance scale: Validity analysis of a theory-based measure. *Academy of Management Journal*, 41: 540-555.

Williams, L. J., & Anderson, S. E. (1991). Job satisfaction and organizational commitment as predictors of organizational citizenship and in-role behaviors. *Journal of Management*, 17, 601–617.

Witzel, M. (2011). *A history of management thought.* Milton Park, Abingdon, Oxon: Routledge.

Wofford, J., Liska, L. (1993). Path-goal theories of leadership: A meta-analysis. *Journal of Management, 19,* 4, 857-87

Wong and Giallonardo, (2013). Authentic leadership and nurse-assessed adverse patient outcomes. *Journal of Nursing Management*, 21, 740-752.

Wong, C. A., & Cummings, G. G. (2009). The influence of authentic leadership behaviors on trust and work outcomes of health care staff. Journal of Leadership Studies, 3(2), 6–23

Wong, C. A., & Laschinger, H. S. (2013). Authentic leadership, performance, and job satisfaction: the mediating role of empowerment. Journal Of Advanced Nursing, 69(4), 947-959.

Woodward, J. (1965). *Industrial organization: theory and practice.* London: Oxford University Press.

Woodward, J. (1970). *Industrial organization: behavior and control.* London: Oxford University Press.

Woolley, C. and Levy, F. (2011). Authentic leadership and follower development: Psychological capital, positive work climate, and gender. *Journal of Leadership & Organizational Studies.* 10 (5), 1-11.

Wren, D. A (2005). *The history of management thought.* Hoboken, N.J: Wiley.

Wren, J. T. (1995). *The leader's companion: Insights on leadership through the ages.* New York: Free Press.

Yammarino, F. J., Spangler, W. D., & Bass, B. M. (1993). Transformational leadership and performance: a longitudinal investigation. *The Leadership Quarterly*, 4, 81–108.

Yukl, G. A. (2012). *Leadership in organizations.* Boston: Pearson.

Yukl, G., Gordon, A., & Taber, T. (2002). A Hierarchical Taxonomy of Leadership Behavior: Integrating a Half Century of Behavior Research. *Journal of Leadership & Organizational Studies*, 9, 1, 15-32.

Zamahani, M., Ghorbani, V., & Rezaei, F. (2011). Impact of Authentic Leadership and Psychological Capital on Followers' Trust and Performance. *Australian Journal Of Basic & Applied Sciences*, 5(12), 658-667.

Zhao, H., & Seibert, S. E. (2006). The Big Five Personality Dimensions and Entrepreneurial Status: A Meta-Analytical Review. Journal of Applied Psychology, 91(2), 259-271.

Zimmerman, R. D. (2008). Understanding the impact of personality traits on individuals' turnover decisions: a meta-analytic path model. *Personnel Psychology*, 61(2), 309-348.

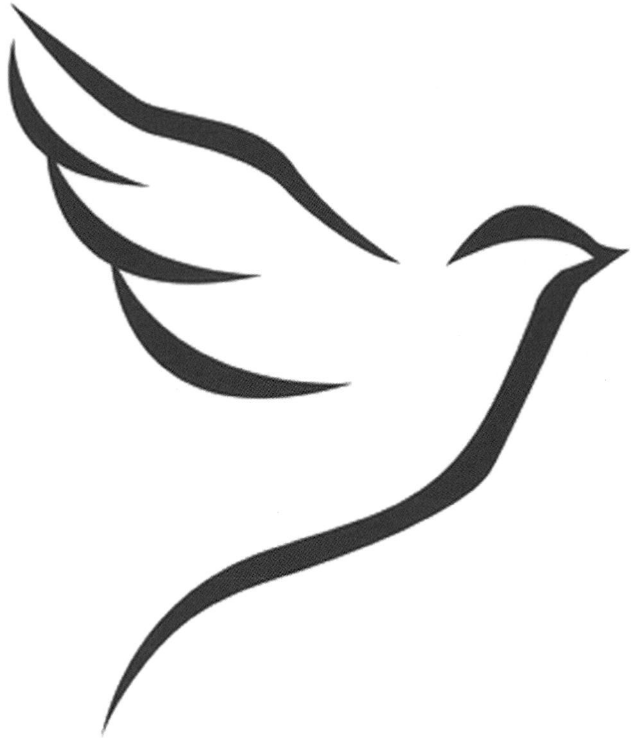